Justice and Politics in People's China:

Legal Order or Continuing Revolution?

LAW, STATE AND SOCIETY SERIES

Editors

Z. BANKOWSKI, *Department of Public Law, University of Edinburgh, U.K.*
M. CAIN, *Department of Law, London School of Economics and Political Science, U.K.*
W. CHAMBLISS, *Department of Sociology and Anthropology, University of Delaware, Newark, U.S.A.*
M. MCINTOSH, *Department of Sociology, University of Essex, Colchester, U.K.*
P. FITZPATRICK, *Darwin College, University of Kent at Canterbury, U.K.*

1. Marx and Engels on Law *by* M. Cain and A. Hunt
2. Reading Ideologies: an investigation into the Marxist theory of ideology and law *by* C. Sumner
3. Pashukanis: Selected Writings on Marxism and Law *by* P. Beirne and R. Sharlet
4. Law and State in Papua New Guinea *by* P. Fitzpatrick
5. Law, Society and Political Action: towards a strategy under late capitalism *by* T. Mathiesen
6. Housing Action in an Industrial Suburb *by* A. Stewart
7. The Police: Autonomy and Consent *by* M. Brogden
8. Justice and Politics in People's China: legal order or continuing revolution? *by* J. Brady

Forthcoming Titles
Law and Economy: the legal regulation of corporate capital *by* K. Jones
The Limits of the Legal Process: a study of landlords, law and crime *by* D. Nelken

Justice and Politics in People's China:

Legal Order or Continuing Revolution?

JAMES P. BRADY

Department of Sociology, University of Massachusetts, Boston, USA

1982

ACADEMIC PRESS

A Subsidiary of Harcourt Brace Jovanovich, Publishers

London · New York

Paris · San Diego · San Francisco · São Paulo · Sydney

Tokyo · Toronto

ACADEMIC PRESS INC. (LONDON) LTD.
24/28 Oval Road
London NW1

United States Edition published by
ACADEMIC PRESS INC.
111 Fifth Avenue
New York, New York 10003

British Library Cataloguing in Publication Data

Brady, James P.
   Justice and politics in People's China. — (Law,
   state and society series)
   1. Justice, Administration of — China — History
   I. Title   II. Series
   345.107′09   KD654

   ISBN 0-12-124750-3

Phototypeset by
Dobbie Typesetting Service, Plymouth, Devon

Printed in Great Britain by
St. Edmundsbury Press, Bury St. Edmunds, Suffolk

Preface

This book did not originate from scholarly inquiry so much as from two powerful and protracted experiences: my exposure to conditions within prisons in the USA, which convinced me of the need to search widely for alternative models of justice, and the war in Vietnam, which forced Americans to confront Asian communism, and which made some better understanding of China essential.

My years spent working professionally within the American prison system left me frustrated with our penal institutions and disillusioned with the prospects for progressive reform. Whether employed as a guard or teacher at Vermont's now abandoned bastille at Windsor, or as a research co-ordinator and justice planner for "community based correctional reform" in Massachusetts, I was confronted with the same entrenched problems. Ill-conceived rehabilitation programmes and enforced idleness within the walls, coupled with inadequate post-release assistance doomed any hopes of correcting offenders.

The appalling recidivism rates make it clear that something is terribly wrong with the state of justice in the United States. My dismay is widely shared, and today virtually no one—justice planners, scholars, or public alike—expects significant improvement in crime rates or recidivism patterns in the near future. The long "War on Crime", begun under President Johnson and later politicized under President Nixon, has been acknowledged as a massive defeat, despite the expenditure of billions from the national treasury and a generation of reform and modernization at all levels of the legal system under the guidance of the now defunct Law Enforcement Assistance Administration. Today a profound cynicism sets the tone of both street conversations and judicial policies newly proposed by the Reagan administration and the various state governments. There is no longer even the promise of "eliminating the causes" of crime or of preventing its occurrence, and officials speak guardedly about "containing" crime at its present levels. The emphasis in federal and state budgets is on longer sentences, though we know that even the present upsurge in prison construction cannot relieve the overcrowding within the cell blocks and reformatories. We are now reduced to the expansion of institutions whose failure is a proven fact, with little prospect of a different outcome other than the further burdening of the taxpayers.

It is perhaps professional heresy to suggest that the present situation calls for a widening, rather than a narrowing, of our horizons on justice. The cultural isolation so characteristic of our proudly nationalistic country is costly in scholarly pursuits and downright suicidal in matters of politics and social policy. If the problems of crime and justice are so embedded in the structure of this society, then perhaps we must look further afield when reformulating our solutions. A comparative approach to criminology has become absolutely necessary, and our understanding is weakest where politics has most discouraged serious study, i.e. we know next to nothing about crime and justice in socialist countries. China was once one of the most crime-ridden societies in the world, with millions of drug addicts and organized racketeering on a mammoth scale. Given the present low level of both crime and legal expenditure there, their modern experience in remaking justice and politics under socialism would seem to warrant attention.

The Vietnam war was the second powerful impetus which ultimately pointed me toward this book. The contradictions between fact and propaganda which surfaced with the war prompted a national process of critical reflection about our own national interests and about the forces of Asian communism which were so insistently presented to us as our mortal foe. As sentiment against the war grew to explosive proportions, China was brought into a different sort of focus. Many who rejected the idealized portrayal of America as the saviour of freedom almost immediately accepted the Peking regime's idealized portrayal of itself as the champion of self-determinism in the Third World. Like those who yet embraced cold war jingoistic patriotism, many radical activists also saw the world in simplistic moral terms. The uncritical embrace of Mao Tse-tung and Maoism, along with other heroes of Third World revolutions, reflected genuine political commitments, but also revealed the degree of alienation among a generation who defined themselves almost as non-citizens in their own nations. Those who came to regard China as the heroic model society had only a slightly better understanding than those who continued to accept the cold war image of the "yellow peril".

Neither caricature of China prepared the beholder for the dramatic turn of events and relations that followed "ping-pong diplomacy" and the Nixon visit to Peking in 1973. Suddenly two decades of hostile containment policy gave way to "most favoured nation" trade status and an unofficial military alliance with the West. There is no critical analysis inherent in the substitution of one Chinese stereotype for another, however. The bridge of transition from one image to another is little stronger than the opaque walls of a ping-pong ball. The size and strategic importance of the country, and the painful collisions of the Korean and

Vietnam wars, have forced us to take China into account, but the current idea that we can play China as a "card" in geopolitics is dangerously naïve and born of even more dangerous arrogance. We must come to grips with China in terms of its own culture and history.

This book aims to describe the development of judicial policies and institutions in modern China. Part of the problem in writing it over the last seven years has been the furious pace of change within China; a pattern of political and social upheaval which makes a broadly conceived historical perspective on their legal system essential. The book will offer no easy solutions readily applicable to the problems of our own American justice institutions, but some general principles may be discerned which inform us about major issues of socialist transformation, community organization, the relations between legal professionalism and citizen activism, and the impact of egalitarian social change on criminality. There is much in this history which offers hope and encouragement, but there is also failure, repression and bitter conflict over the course of legal and social development in People's China. My intent here is neither to praise nor condemn, but rather to understand the contradictions and tensions that have made the revolution in China the most volatile of modern revolutions.

July 1982   James Brady
                                                                      Boston

Acknowledgements

I owe thanks to a great many individuals, groups and institutions for their help in the preparation of this book. The Center for Chinese Studies at the University of California, Berkeley, the Hoover Institution at Stanford and the Harvard Law School Center for East Asian Legal Studies have provided a great store of materials, and their respective staffs and directors have given me considerable attention. Chief among my mentors have been Victor Li at Stanford Law School and Paul Takagi at the University of California, Berkeley, both of whom read much of this manuscript and offered many useful suggestions. Paul Takagi is not only a sensitive and astute scholar, but he stands out as the most committed and courageous intellectual activist I have yet encountered. I will always consider myself his student. My activist comrades in the North East Prison Association and a dozen other anti-crime or prison reform organizations have helped make criminology more than an academic career. Bill Chambliss (Delaware) has been a wonderful friend who has sharpened my critical analysis and healed more than a few moments of despair with laughter and wise counsel. Hal Pepinsky (Indiana) and Brian Hipkin (London Polytechnic) have lent insight drawn from their own considerable studies of Chinese justice. I have been fortunate to work with two vigorous radical criminology collectives in Boston where we regularly criticize and discuss one another's work. These have included: John Baumann, Nicki Hahn, Erika Kates, Alex Liazos, Gary Marx, Stephen Pfohl, Richard Quinney, Richard Speigelman and Steve Spitzer. The editors of the Law, State and Society Series at Academic Press have been patient, helpful and energetic in bringing the book to final completion.

Two beagle hounds of unusual virtue, the renowned "Ginger" and "Bandit", have each helped to maintain my spirits during the long process of research and composition. Among all of these friends and colleagues there is also one particular renaissance art historian in Rome who has shared countless evenings with me amidst our respective scribblings, and whom I have come to love over a thousand cups of cappucino and talks of China and Caravaggio. Finally, I must thank my parents, Bonner and Marguerite Brady, for their steady affection and faith in a son whose rebel ways and ideas at bottom share more with their own ethics than they can know. To them I dedicate this my first book.

James Brady
Boston

Contents

xi

Part I

Historical Background and Current Issues in the Development of Chinese Justice and Society

1 Problems of Understanding Socialist Legality: Dialectic Themes in Chinese Development and the Trial of the Gang of Four

Few of capitalism's brute facts so mock its proclaimed "social progress" as the persistence of crime and corruption despite technological and material improvements. Few of socialism's promises are so appealing as the ideals of a just government and an egalitarian community secure from violence and predation. Yet, though radical scholars in the West have developed a systematic critique of the bourgeois state, its contradictory legal system and crimino-genic economy, little effort has been made toward an understanding of how crime and justice might be transformed under socialism.

The Waiting Obligation of Radical Criminology

There are a number of reasons for this failure to consider socialist justice, apart from anti-communism and nationalistic chauvinism typical of Western education and social science. An earlier generation of Marxists writing hopefully about the young revolution in the Soviet Union were bitterly disappointed by the secret trials, assassinations and mass imprisonment of the Stalin era and by the continuing dominance of a privileged bureaucratic elite in Eastern European states (Djilas, 1957; Buchholz, 1977). This negative appraisal of Soviet-style justice has not infrequently led to a cynical rejection of socialist legality in other quite different societies (Solomon, 1978). In contrast, the more recent generation of radical justice scholars have, like Marx himself (Marx, 1970; Hirst, 1972), devoted little thought to the problems of socialist transformation and have assumed rather naively that the resolution of crime and problems of justice would follow almost "naturally" from the overthrow of capitalism (Platt, 1974; Marzotto et al., 1975; Brady, 1975; Quinney, 1977, pp.150-8).

The Marxists' silence, for whatever reasons, leaves a serious gap in the intellectual and political appeal of radical criminology. Even if their criticisms of capitalist society and its legal order are accepted by a British or American public grown increasingly cynical of the existing arrangements under the "free enterprise" system (Miller, 1974; Caplan, 1976), the looming question remains: "What is the alternative?".[1] The working population is neither so desperate nor so unsophisticated as to make a "leap of faith" and embrace socialism on the strength of its Utopian communist vision (Klockars, 1979). Those radical scholars who venture from their libraries into the work of organizing the masses in the workplace or the community will find no lack of issues or unrest (Brady, 1981a, b), but the healthy scepticism that makes bourgeois politicians and corporate executives increasingly uneasy, also makes more challenging the tasks of agitation and political education (Crozier et al., 1977, pp.74-85).

In the 1960s there was a tendency to describe the bourgeois state as being merely an emanation of capitalist class interests and the legal order as a blunt instrument of working class control (CRCJ, 1977, pp.7-9; Quinney, 1977, p.3). This viewpoint reflected the early partisan experience of many radical intellectuals in struggles for prisoners' rights and in the anti-war, minority and women's movements. The dramatic clashes with police, courts and prison authorities contributed to our general conceptual rigidity in those stormy times. Too often we wrongly labelled all police and justice workers "the enemy" and romanticized street criminals and prisoners. Such vulgar distortion of justice and society contributed to the isolation of radicals in the last decade and to the public's rejection of such leftist proposals as the Berkeley and Chicago "community control of police" initiatives (Brady, 1974, 1981; CRCJ, 1977) and the various prisoners unions' demands (Martin, 1976). Fortunately, in more recent years that type of crudely "instrumental" view of the state has been replaced by a more mature and dialectical perspective on capitalism, its judicial system and the various alternative reform strategies (Bierne, 1979; Platt, 1978; Balkan et al., 1980).

Radical criminology has developed tremendously in the last 15 years, but the tasks left undone are not only enormous, but seemingly contradictory. We must critically assess the bourgeois legal order, identifying its hidden ideological and economic functions, but recognizing also those progressive reforms and internal bureaucratic dynamics that defy any simple-minded economic determinism (Spitzer, 1975). The repressive functions of the state are real, but so also are at least the principles of civil liberties. These principles of due process and individual rights must be insisted upon as part of the defence of working class interests, especially in times of political repression and social unrest. Indeed, as citizens become more socially alienated from and distrustful of government, we may expect them to cling even more tightly to the shelter of individual rights (Brady, 1982).

A Marxist analysis must point to the limitations of these "protections" even as it makes visible the reasons for the prolonged crisis and decline of the bourgeois state and society. In going beyond liberalism, Marxism must advance an alternative notion of freedom and community under a new system of justice and society. The socialist ideal must be considered against the hard experience of the various socialist states. These nations and their respective legal systems allow few easy generalizations and must each be approached in a critical and dialectical way, with attention to historic development and the strengths and weaknesses of legal philosophy and practice. To date, there is little here beyond the bare bones promise of socialist transformation, and virtually no literature on socialist legal systems which rests on the solid methods of historical and material analysis. The interpretation of socialist legality has unfortunately been left to others whose ideological bias and training has rendered them poor guides indeed.

Misunderstanding China: Five Generations of Scholarly Inquiry

The study of China and its legal system shows the mark of five generations of scholars, whom I will call the "collaborators", "cold warriors", "legalists", "functionalists" and "Marxists". While the Western press and academy have generally denigrated all socialist states, the portrayal of China (even before socialism) has been particularly distorted and often in ways that fit the foreign policy objectives.

Western lawyers and academics writing as advisers and collaborators for the pre-communist Kuomintang dictatorship (1922-49) helped to legitimize that government, particularly overseas. Influential scholars such as Roscoe Pound of Harvard Law School worked closely with justice officials of the Chiang Kai Shek regime and published glowing reports of new constitutional guarantees for individual rights, legal modernization and social progress, while denying outright or ignoring the vast patterns of political corruption, brutal exploitation, repression and rebellion in China at that time (*see* Chapter 3). These intellectual contributions to our misunderstanding of China made more credible the cruder propaganda efforts of the "China Lobby" in the United States (comprising Chinese government agents and US corporate investors). The mythology of "growing democracy" in China was insistently projected by the US State Department and adopted by the mass media. Consequently, few citizens in the

West had any sort of realistic conception of pre-communist China under the tutelage of the Kuomintang, and most were unprepared for the post-World War II explosion of renewed rebellion and the eventual Communist victory in 1949 (Greene, 1964). The handful of more objective observers known as "China Hands" disputed the collaborators' apologia during the Roosevelt era; but the Hands were largely purged in the hysterical scapegoating which followed the "loss" of China in 1949. The official policy of "containment" precluded any serious understanding of Chinese society in its first formative decades.

A new "cold warrior" scholarship emerged after the "loss" of China and contributed decisively to the containment policy. It helped to explain "Red China" without admitting that the Chinese might have freely and rationally *chosen* socialism over the pro-Western Kuomintang. It is to the credit of American intellectuals that the McCarthy era of witchhunting and intimidation was considered necessary to stifle anyone dissenting from these views within the government and universities, and so assure the unchallenged hegemony of cold war politics and scholarship. That hegemony was established, and 20 years of half-truths and distortions were to follow as the mainstream of academy inquiry into things legal and Chinese (Kahn, 1975).

Few intellectual pursuits have been so politically captive as the early studies of Chinese socialism and its system of justice. The close connection between US foreign policy and cold warrior writing is apparent not only in the distorted content of most early works, but also in the fact that much of this research was directly sponsored and controlled by the US government. The prominent HRRI series compiled by Chinese nationalists at Maxwell Air Force Base, for example, were for decades prominently cited treatises on courts, the law and police in mainland China (Wei, 1955; Yu, 1955; Ong, 1955; Chen, W. C., 1955).

There were some variations in the major works of the period, but typically the thrust of their argument was that the Communists' victory in the Civil War was due to their leaders' superior organizational abilities, rather than the unravelling of basic social tensions or the conscious action of the Chinese masses (Vogel, 1971, pp.10-11).

The trials of former landlords, capitalists and Kuomintang officials were dismissed as mere propaganda techniques for further terrorizing the general population. The influential works of Walker and Barnett, for example, deny that class conflict or ideology served as anything more than a propaganda device, arguing:

> All of these [revolutionary] achievements are a testimonial to the amazing organizing energy of Mao, Chou and their colleagues. They have accomplished what they successfully prevented the Nationalist government from doing (Walker, 1955, pp.51-2)

> In practical operational terms, the deliberate manipulation of class conflict

has been and continues to be of a very great significance in the functioning of the political system in Communist China . . . The [old ruling classes] are regarded as social pariahs and provide concrete targets for class hostility and abuse (Barnett, 1964, pp.404-405)

Our experts were unwilling to consider seriously the popular appeal or ideology which lay behind the seeping Communist victory of 1949 (Barnett, 1964, pp.399-406; Pye, 1968, pp.8-9, 235-40; Sharan, 1968, pp.13-16). Instead they advanced frightening images of "mass persuasion" and "brainwashing" as pseudo-scientific explanations for the revolution. The undeniable success of the new socialist government in bringing order to historically crime-ridden cities like Shanghai and Canton was attributed to the ominous powers of "thought control" (Vogel, 1971, pp.47-49, 64-68; Barnett, 1964, pp.385-94). The Chinese legal system was simply dismissed as a "blunt instrument of terror", and Maoist theoreticians and legal officials were tarred as demagogues or manipulators of mass hatred (Barnett, 1964, pp.18-24; Pye, 1968, pp.67-77).

It is noteworthy that the most careful study of "thought reform", compiled by Robert Lifton (1963) from a study of US prisoners of war in Korea, did not support such lurid imagery. Lifton found that American POWs defected in Korea for much the same reasons that US troops later mutinied and murdered their officers in Vietnam, as will be discussed later in this chapter.

Nevertheless, most scholars continued to portray Chinese government and particularly their political-legal system as essentially demonic. (The works of Walker (1955), Pye (1968), Barnett (1964) and Vogel (1967a, b, 1969) are examples.) A flavour of these cold warrior scholars' views may be sensed in the following excerpts:

> . . . the degree to which the Chinese Communists have extended their apparatus of mass persuasion and ideological control to the villages is remarkable . . . They have created in fact as well as theory, a system of control which effectively meshes the mass of the population . . .

> The testimony of numerous emigrés indicates that there is a fairly pervasive sense of anxiety, and on the part of many it is active fear-about punishment that may result from any action or words that can be interpreted by the Party members as opposition to their will. This anxiety which reinforces the tendency to be submissive and responsive to the authority of the cadres is a very important element which helps explain the political system as it operates (Barnett, 1964, pp.341-2)

> At the level of creating cadres (party members) the communists have created a new system of conversion and changing of thought patterns which in many ways constitutes a new dimension of power in the world today . . . For creating cadres the communists approach humans with a manipulative attitude. The trainees constitute just so many bodies to be transformed into parts of the organization which will function

automatically yet with enthusiasm and with almost fanatical devotion to the party.

Much of the power of the communist regime is based on terror which is designed to paralyze the will of all its subjects to resist (Walker, 1955, pp.151-2)

The cracking of the "Communist Monolith" along Sino-Soviet lines and the entry of China into the UN prompted a revision of Western views. A new sort of "legalist" scholarship led by such anti-communist liberals as Jerome Cohen at Harvard Law School's Roscoe Pound Center still describes China as a "totalitarian" state, but looks forward to that nation's "progress" toward a more Westernized system of justice and legal scholarship. The legalists have devoted most of their attention (and sympathies) to the growth of legal professionalism, codified law and specialized research institutes in China (Cohen, 1968a, 1970; Ginsbergs and Stahnke, 1964a, b, 1965; Chen Shih hsiang, 1973). These elements of Chinese justice and scholarship have been fairly well described. On the other hand, the more informal aspects of volunteer community crime control are considered anachronisms (Cohen, 1966), and the "arbitrary interference" of non-specialists from government or the Communist Party is most emphatically deplored (Cohen, 1968a, b; Chin, 1977; Leng, 1967). The legalists' chauvinism and their refusal to take seriously anything but a Westernized model of legal professionalism is represented in the following remarks by Cohen, Berman and Leng:

. . . the Chinese communists have successfully developed in judicial administration some remarkable techniques of mass persuasion and "brainwashing" . . . the Peking regime has shown little effort to channel the Chinese legal development in the direction of codification and stability . . . As the revolution becomes settled down, and as a mature socialist society emerges, one can expect a more stable legal order and a respect for judicial procedures and restraints . . . (Leng, 1967, pp.175, 177)

It has been apparent that pressures to increase (legal) specialization, professionalism, and functional autonomy are being suppressed by an aging but still zealous first generation of revolutionary leaders who are obsessed with maintaining Party domination of all aspects of life (Cohen, 1968b, p.53)

In studying the legal system of Communist China, we may be aided by viewing it from the perspective of Soviet law, since Soviet law is closely related to both Chinese law and to Western law. To draw a metaphor from kinship relations, one might say that Soviet law is the illegitimate son of Western law, now grown to maturity; and Chinese law is a wayward daughter of Soviet law, still walking the streets (Berman, 1970, p.315)

The legalists have provided commentaries full of insight on a narrow range of formal documents and institutions, but they have ignored or distorted many of the most important aspects of socialist justice. When they complain, for example, about the "interference" of the Chinese Communist Party and socialist ideology with the "development of a legal system", they betray a complete misunderstanding of the role of the legal system in the process of socialist transformation. They resemble those who point to the demise of private law practices as the "end of legality" in socialist Cuba. The legalists, in short, tell us more about their own professional pretensions and presumptions than about the actual content of judicial policy.

The intense debates over national purpose and Asian revolution which followed the American disaster in Vietnam contributed to the emergence of a third generation of China scholarship. This more recent approach to Chinese society and its judicial system, stresses the *functional* utility of Chinese institutions as measured in terms of their effectiveness in establishing peace and security. The functionalists set aside legalistic questions about China's "progress" toward a Western due process and professionalism model and ask even whether the Chinese methods might provide insight to help us rethink our own system of justice. The functionalists' writings examine not only the legal bureaucracies and professions in China, but also the more informal mechanisms of social control, such as neighbourhood mediation committees, local "study criticism" groups, and "mass rectification" campaigns. They take China's Confucian heritage much more seriously than do the legalists or cold warriors, and have attempted to sort out the traditional and revolutionary elements of contemporary political-legal institutions and the shifting roles of political-legal scholars and officials. The functionalist school includes such writers as Bennett (1977), Edwards (1977), Lubman (1967, 1969), Greenblatt (1977), Pepinsky (1973, 1975, 1976) and especially Li (1973, 1975, 1977). Their focus and perspective are exemplified in the following excerpts:

> Emphasis on function, as distinguished from haste to stress the forms with which we are most familiar, is only a tentative beginning. From such a beginning may come additional useful speculation about the role of legal institutions in political and economic development . . . Thus, the emphasis I am suggesting may lead us to conduct not only inquiries which are natural ones for lawyers to make, such as the study of judicial independence, but more far reaching investigation into the nature of judicial and administrative decision-making . . . Moreover, the emphasis suggested here may lead us to question the assumption of some that Western-type legal institutions are essential to the stability of developing nations (Lubman, 1969, pp.535-6)

> What kinds of evaluation, then, do we make of the Chinese system for handling deviance? . . . It would appear that China's peer group sanctioning system provides considerable access to a person being criticised . . . I would

[stress] the great improvements in economic and social conditions in China . . . One might consider the Chinese approach to be the model of participatory democracy. Law should indeed be everyone's business, and not a social function that is the exclusive province of legal specialists (Li, 1979, p.231)

All three approaches to Chinese justice and society continue to appear in the literature, and the functionalist shift away from narrow legalistic chauvinism holds promise for clearer understanding in the West. The fact remains, however, that the study of Chinese justice has been largely left to Western lawyers, and they make the typical lawyer's error of not linking the study of things legal to larger political and economic forces. The functionalists, like the cruder legalists and cold warriors before them, provide an essentially static description of Chinese justice and society, and they have notably failed to explain the great sweeping reversals in judicial policy and legal professionalism. Such an understanding demands an historical and material analysis of the larger contradictions in Chinese politics and society.

This book belongs to the youngest and smallest generation—the Marxists. Like the works of Richard Pfeffer (1968, 1972, 1975) and Brian Hipkin (1981), this volume will draw on the earlier generation's research, documented Chinese sources and also the relevant literature of comparative economics and political science. It should be pointed out that the Chinese themselves use the term "cheng fa", which literally means "political-legal", to describe their criminal justice institutions, procedures and personnel. We cannot deal with justice and law as a specialized sphere but must consider things legal alongside political economics and ideology. The fact that there is more than one set of political economic strategies to be considered makes this more difficult, but no less essential.

Such an integrated sociological approach raises questions that often go unexamined in the three earlier scholarly traditions. For example, what notion of freedom is implicit in socialist legality and is it substantially different from that of capitalist nations? How do the law and legal institutions contribute to the process of economic transformation and changing property relations? How does the sense of the community and social obligation change within the context of socialist justice and society? Do justice and the law necessarily play a conservative and stabilizing role or can they be transformed to challenge, order and promote ongoing revolutionary change? How do the twin aims of socialist transformation, i.e. material-technological advance and social egalitarianism, play themselves out in the legal order? Such questions should be to the fore of an analysis of socialist legality.

The study of socialist legal systems should also make us more critically aware of the implicit political assumptions and economic interests which lie embedded in our own Western legal tradition. This great potential of comparative studies is largely unrealized within the narrow confines of the traditional literature on socialist justice. The study of Chinese justice which follows is advanced both as a description of legal development and as a window on the larger dynamics and conflicts of socialist transformation. I have not attempted to develop here a discussion of the specific implications of the Chinese experience for a re-thinking and a possible reconstruction of American or British justice along socialist lines. However, such a task is most necessary and will hopefully be taken up at some future point by one of the generation of Marxist criminologists who must ultimately come to terms with the meaning of socialist legal innovations.

Method and Perspective

This book will consider the transformation of justice in modern China, and will attempt to apply the methods of Marxist analysis to the critique of a society pledged to Marxist goals. This requires more than the usual perfunctory bows to politics and history which one finds in most comparative legal studies. Indeed, this book is almost as much a political and economic history as an examination of laws, criminal procedures and legal institutions. This emphasis on material and historical matters is not only essential to Marxism, it is also absolutely imperative when considering a country with such an immense cultural heritage and such explosive economic contradictions as China.

These great conflicts did not reach a final climax with the Civil War and the liberation victory of 1949, for China, certainly more than any other country which has experienced a modern revolution, is still unsettled and politically volatile. Indeed, over the course of ten years' research and preparation for this book, the shape and texture of the subject has changed at a dizzying rate. Writing a book on "present-day" China is sometimes like bird-watching in a hurricane, and one often wishes, like Joshua, that time and the race of events would halt long enough to finish the task at hand. Those attempting to understand Chinese justice by the traditional methods of reading statutes and diagrammatizing formal institutions have been repeatedly frustrated and caught off balance by dramatic events like the Cultural Revolution, which swept away previous legal arrangements, and by the Chinese reluctance, until very recently, to codify a complete criminal law or to finalize the roles of courts, police and other justice bureaux.

An historical imagination is vital here. Obviously what is needed is not so much an empirical image of Chinese judicial policy at any particular point in time, but rather an understanding of the forces and ideas which together and in contradiction shape that volatile legal development. We must begin with an assessment of the political, legal and economic legacy inherited by the victorious revolutionaries in 1949 in order then to appreciate the aims and methods adopted in the subsequent process of socialist transformation. The arrangements for handling crime and conflict, and indeed the very definition of crime, have change dramatically in keeping with the larger struggles over what political and economic strategies should be adopted for the modernization of the country.

The picture which emerges from this book does, I think, inspire some considerable confidence in the capacity of a people to remake their society and legal order along more fair and democratic lines; and even the most conservative scholars will today agree that the Chinese are incomparably better off than under the feudal emperors or the fascist Kuomintang government. However, a close reading of the actual process of transformation does not support either naive utopianism or economic determinism. The Chinese judicial system is neither the crude instrument of terror and brainwashing described by the cold war and legalist scholars in the West, nor a steady and consistent protector of democratic rights and egalitarian advance. There is genuine social liberation in this political-legal history, but there is also failure, factional infighting and dangerous tendencies to backslide into an almost Confucian bureaucratic rigidity, or alternatively to vulgarize Marxism by twisting justice to suit competing leadership cliques.

Today, as the Peking leadership attempts to reconstruct the legal order to fit a new post-Mao China, there is a clear and present threat of a fundamental defeat for the Revolution. Already there are warning signs that a Soviet-style elite of officials and intellectuals is assuming increased privileges and powers, and developing a new legal system as a defence against further egalitarian change (Chapter 8). There are no final conclusions in this book; the revolutionary process in justice, as in politics, is still too much in motion. There are, however, some major unifying themes which illuminate the main forces, traditions and ideas that have shaped and reshaped Chinese judicial practice in the course of socialist transformation.

Unifying Themes: The Dialectics of China's Two Judicial Traditions and Contradictions in State, Community and Economy

The central thesis here is that Chinese society has been historically regulated by not one but two judicial systems, a formal one based upon the centralized state and an informal one rooted in community associations. The study of the relations between the two systems serves as a window on the larger developments and conflicts in the political economy of feudalism, capitalism and, most importantly, Chinese socialism.

Pre-communist China was locked into underdevelopment by the combination of entrenched feudal elites, the stultifying Confucian ideology and the shattering penetration of foreign imperialist powers. The inability of a Chinese bourgeoisie to emerge and modernize the country left the feudal empire and the fascist Republic too weak to defend the national territory or cope with the economic crisis brought about by a primitive agriculture's inability to support an expanding population.

The *official* legal arrangements adopted by the Imperial and later the Republican governments, had neither the capacity to regulate the social order closely, nor the intention. Formal litigation was infrequent and strongly disapproved of under Confucian principles of compromise and submission. The state's legal system was in any case outstanding for its brutality, corruption and explicit defence of social and class hierarchies. A *private* judicial system based on kinship (clan) or occupational (guild) associations was more important in resolving conflicts through informal procedures and internal sanctions. The private judicial system also reproduced the social hierarchy, but in a gentler fashion. Since these private arrangements grouped together landlords and peasants, masters and apprentices, merchants and labourers, they were essential to the containment of class tensions and the maintenance of social cohesion (*see* Chapter 2).

The pressures of economic collapse and foreign invasion caused a violent tearing of the Chinese state, community and justice along the lines of class conflict. The Imperial Government simply evaporated in the face of rebellion and national fragmentation and the subsequent Kuomintang coalition exploded into murderous Civil War. The community associations of clan and guild divided along class lines, with peasant associations and trade unions emerging to defend the interests of peasants and workers from social elites who became increasingly detached and at odds with their former subordinates. The state judicial system, despite the massive expansion of the police and the assistance of gangster societies, proved unable to control mounting disorder and dissent. The breakdown of Confucian ethics and community associations rendered the old private judicial systems unworkable and made the formation of new legal and community institutions an essential task of the socialist revolutionaries (*see* Chapter 3).

The transformation of the Chinese state and society began in the Yenan base area during the Civil War, and was initially guided by the ideology of the "mass line" (*see* Chapter 4). This important Maoist innovation emphasizes the role of mass citizens' organizations motivated by egalitarian reforms and directed by a self-sacrificing Communist Party cadre. A radical centralization of government was designed to draw the peasantry into political education and decision-making within the context of intimate community "small groups". Economic policies gradually closed gaps in wages and social status, and cadres or intellectuals were obliged to share in the drudgeries of manual labour in order to help combat elitism.

The Maoist emphasis on the mass line as a modernization strategy has been repeatedly confirmed, most dramatically in the Great Leap Forward of 1958-61 and the Great Proletarian Cultural Revolution of 1966-70. The problems of continuing inequalities and the danger of bureaucratic elitism has prompted new ideological doctrines, such as the "continuous revolution", along with determined efforts to level wages, revitalize mass organizations, widen educational opportunities and collectivize agricultural and urban life. The Great Proletarian Revolution, of course, incorporated all these reforms, along with a wholesale shakedown and reorganization of the Party (*see* Chapter 7). The Maoist revolutionary policies and principles have historically drawn their greatest support from those elements of the population who stand to benefit most from continued egalitarian change, i.e. students from poorer backgrounds, unskilled labourers, the poorer peasants and women.

An alternative conservative approach to Chinese development has emerged gradually since 1949 (*see* Chapter 5) to reach its fullest expression in the policies and outlook of the Peking leadership in 1981. Partly inspired by the Soviet Union and partly by the economic failures of some radical Maoist initiatives, the conservatives have stressed the need for social stability and centralized planning by "expert" managers and administrators. At the heart of the conservatives' philosophy is the position that the Chinese Revolution is over, and that major redistribution of wealth and power is no longer wise or necessary.

Conservatives have been consistently inclined to support the granting of large material incentives to skilled workers, intellectuals and officials, in order to spur the efforts of these "most essential" members of China's largely untrained labour force. Likewise, their reliance on specialists and experts has rigidified hierarchies and diminished the effective role of the mass organizations and their populace in decision-making. The concentration of educational and industrial development in those most advanced urban districts seems most sensible to the conservatives, even if this means that rural zones will lag further behind in material and cultural terms.

The conservative approach, like the Maoist ideology, has developed in bits and pieces over the course of national experience since the Civil War. Initially, the writings of figures like Mao, Chou en Lai and Liu Shao chi contained a mixture of both radicalism and conservative pragmatism, as did the social and economic policies adopted in the first decade. However, disagreements over the Soviet Union's style of bureaucratic socialism, acrimonious conflicts following the Great Leap Forward and, of course, the violent upheavals of the Cultural Revolution effectively polarized both the ideological positions and the political elites.

The "Two Line Struggle", as it became known after 1966, has dominated Chinese politics ever since, and there has been no easy compromise between the positions and their adherents. Indeed, in the most recent years since Mao's death conflicts have deepened as the latent material interests behind the ideological contest have become increasingly apparent. The fall of the radical Gang of Four and the reversal of egalitarian policies since 1976 have in fact prepared the way for a new sort of post-revolutionary order in China. It would not be an exaggeration to speak of this as "revisionism", in that a conservative political ideology is now closely linked to the material privileges of a bureaucratic-intellectual elite and to the systematic dismantling of Maoist institutions which maximized popular influence and minimized elitism.

The judicial system developed under socialism bears both the marks of this fundamental political conflict and the legacy of the pre-Communist social and legal traditions. There are, in fact, two modern judicial systems which, despite systematic co-operation in many practical tasks and some historic periods, are nevertheless distinguished by quite different institutions, procedures, social functions and operating ideologies. There is a *bureaucratic* justice built along lines not unlike the Soviet system, and also a *popular* justice which depends not upon law and professional staff, but upon citizen volunteers applying general Maoist principles within the framework of the mass organizations (Brady, 1977a; Li, 1975).

The bureaucratic judicial system is based on statutory provisions in China's successive constitutions of 1954, 1974, and 1978, as well as a series of "organic laws", the Security Administration Punishment Act of 1957 and the new criminal and penal codes of 1980. These laws authorize a three-branch legal system (police, courts and procuracy) and formal criminal procedures relying upon checks and balances between these three branches. Crimes are defined as specific acts punishable by specific sanctions, ranging from fines to terms of confinement for "labour re-education", the more punitive "reform through labour", and finally execution. The justice bureaux have argued that laws are best understood and administered by professionals trained in "legal science" at specialized institutions and guided in their decisions by regular standardized procedures. This legal professionalism, like the criminal codes, serves a conservative function in protecting the existing distribution of property and power while tightly regulating social change and the role of the citizenry in justice as in politics.

The justice bureaux have not, however, yet fully realized the powers granted them under Chinese statutes. Their development has been frustrated by political challenges mounted by the radical Maoists and are forced to co-exist with the institutions and ideas of popular justice. Following each repeated setback (as in the 1957 Anti-Rightist Movement or the Cultural Revolution), the justice agencies have sought to recover and expand to the dimensions of the "paper shell" authorized in previous legislation. Today, for the first time, the bureaucratic system may have sufficient political force actually to fill out those shells and attain full ascendancy over the popular justice alternative. Before considering the latter, it is worthwhile noting the authorized elements of this now expanding bureaucratic justice:

1. The People's Courts: a hierarchy of three-judge panels decide cases at law and hear appeals. Legally trained professional jurists and lay judges ("assessors") serve together with theoretically equal voting rights at lower level courts; appelate bodies are entirely staffed by professionals. The judges hear evidence, determine guilt and pronounce sentences.

2. The People's Procurate: a hierarchy of offices at the city, district, province and national levels (corresponding with court and police divisions) is charged with preparing evidence for prosecution, and with the review of legal procedures in cases undertaken by the police, as well as the review of contract compliance by various other agencies of government. The Procurate has been the most professional of the justice agencies and its regular staff includes many legally trained personnel.

3. The Ministry of Public Order: serves as local and national police force, and is responsible for arrests, investigation, the operation of wall prisons and labour reform camps, as well as the official supervision of citizens placed under "mass control" (roughly analogous to probation). The police have also assumed greater powers in adjudication and sentencing under the SAPA Act of 1957. The police ranks include many ex-soldiers and former community activists, as well as a relatively high percentage of Communist Party members; but there are few legally trained professionals.

4. Ministry of Control/Party Control Commissions: an internal investigatory bureau which hears complaints and prepares charges against government or party officials who have violated the law. The staff is almost entirely comprised of party members who are sometimes also legal specialists though usually not law school graduates. The Ministry of Control was formally abolished in 1959; but the Party Control Commissions have taken on the task of official control work and the Commissions have essentially recovered from the serious challenges and retrenchments that immediately followed the Cultural Revolution.

The popular justice system can be traced back to the Civil War period and so substantially pre-dates the bureaucratic legal institutions. The early popular tribunals and mass movements were a primary means of class struggle in land reform, limited expropriation of capitalist and suppression of counter-revolutionaries and secret gangster societies in the cities (see Chapters 4 and 5). The gentler side of popular justice as a peace-keeping arrangement has included mediation, volunteer policing and ongoing criticism/self-criticism within local branches of the various mass organizations. In all of these aspects, popular justice draws its guidance and legitimacy not so much from laws as from the general ideological principles of "mass line" and "continuing revolution". Indeed, the leading Maoist theoreticians have been most reluctant to finalize law codes by enactment which might bring an end to direct popular intervention in justice and politics (as in mass movements). The continued existence of historic social inequalities, and the creation of new gaps (as between the life styles of people and cadres) also makes the radicals suspicious of codes which might finalize the distribution of property and power. Clearly, the ordinary citizens who fill out the mass organizations and their popular justice bodies have a clear material stake in the continuation of wage levelling and in the rectification of elitist tendencies among officials and intellectuals.

In defining and controlling "crime", the more informal popular process emphasizes the importance of an offender's class background and the egoistic attitudes which lie behind criminal acts but are, in themselves, a form of ideological deviance. The popular approach to conflicts, both behavioural and ideological, is insistently educational. The continuous criticism/self-criticism process within mass organizations and the more intense "struggle" sessions involving serious deviants, have been guided especially by the doctrines expounded in Mao's "On the Correct Handling of Contradictions Among the People", which emphasizes the importance of applying punitive sanctions only to those whose class position stands in "antagonistic contradiction" to that of the working people, while using informal means of persuasion and "a gentle wind and a light rain" in dealing with conflicts among the great majority. Explicit in this doctrine is the notion that conflicts between officials, intellectuals and party members, while normally "non-antagonistic", do have the potential of becoming "antagonistic" contradictions if the tendency of such elites to privilege and egoism is unchecked by education and rectification.

The Maoist theory of "handling contradictions" has, in times of radical prominence, essentially displaced a reliance on codified law. It begins with the observation that social conflict (or "contradiction") is essential to social progress and socialist democracy. Thus, it could call for future mass rectification movements even though they are disruptive and have no legal standing. The role of the political legal system then is not to prevent or contain all conflict but to distinguish between those contradictions which are rooted in class conflicts (i.e. antagonistic) from those which are rooted in differences of consciousness (non-antagonistic) among the working classes. While the essentially non-punitive means of peer pressure, mediation and criticism are appropriate to handling non-antagonistic conflict, the more severe and formal measures of the legal system are reserved for antagonistic contradictions. This theory and the related principle of "continuing revolution" hold that class conflict is a continuing phenomenon in

China, hence the origin of crime as discussed by the theorist, Ts'as Tsu Tan (1964):

> Crime and class struggle form two mutually dependent and closely related social phenomena that exist objectively in class society. The pre-requisite for the emergence of crime is the appearance and conflict of class interests.

> We must aim the sharp point of our law against the reactionary classes, the landlords, Kuomintang counter-revolutionaries and comprador capitalists.

> The exploiting class has been overthrown, but it will be impossible to consider that the exploiting class has been already eliminated. At the same time, in the protracted complex class struggle during the period of transition, there is the possibility that certain wavering elements among the people will degenerate into bourgeois elements.

The contradictions theory is the conceptual link between judicial practice and radical social policy, but the problem is that the class categories here are essentially meaningless. Former landlords and capitalists of course exist, but they have not functioned as a class now for generations. The Maoists are unwilling to describe the bureaucracy or the Communist Party or the intellectuals as a potentially exploiting *class*. Likewise, they are unwilling to designate as important those *intra-class* differences among peasants, workers or intellectuals. Rather than come to grips with the political and economic roots of modern social conflicts in China, the Maoists insist that the new contradictions arise from the "degeneration" of individuals whose socialist ethics have gone sour.

The tautology of this theory is rather obvious and sometimes ugly in practice. Since crimes are understood to be the result of class conflict, then anyone who commits a serious offence must have adopted the outlook of one of the old "exploiting classes". In practice this may mean continued classification of the children and grandchildren of gentry or capitalists as "landlords" or "capitalists". Others may be adjudged "bad elements" on the basis of their deviant ideas or misconduct, and so consigned to this third rather imprecise category of social outsiders. These class labels or "caps" may be removed after a rectification or after an offender is deemed reformed by the community and local cadres; but it may be re-imposed for some future offence or as part of the general intensification of social conflict in another rectification movement. The language and concepts of class analysis in China bear little relation to reality and this seriously weakens both the educational value and the practical relevance of the handling contradictions theory. (For a thorough discussion of these issues see especially Kraus (1977).)

The theory does contain an essential optimism, since it argues that criminals are reformable if only they can throw off their "bad class" consciousness. Thus, the Maoists make a point of "curing the disease to save the patient" and share the traditional Confucian confidence in the power of reflection and criticism to work a change of heart. However, the theory leaves them unable to account for patterns of crime and corruption which are greater than the individual deviant (even if they criticize whole agencies of government). Moreover, it may be quite easily twisted for opportunistic purposes, as in the Red Guards' practice of branding their opponents (often other students) as enemies or bad elements because they had another interpretation of Maoist thought, or, worse still, simply because they were competitors in the same campus or community. The brutal savagery of Red Guard "justice" during 1966-69 was justified as class struggle by the convenient application of this rather un-Marxist theory (Pan and de Juegher, 1968, pp.130-140).

Finally, and of most controversial importance, the popular justice tradition and the underlying Maoist principles call for periodic mass intervention, not only to correct the errors of individual cadres or intellectuals, but also to rectify elite tendencies toward "commandism, bureaucratism, subjectivism" on a national scale through the tumultuous process of the mass rectification movements. In such times especially the cadres must not be judged solely on whether they have obeyed the laws and the formal obligations of their position, but also on their performance against the measure of the mass line. Whole bureaux and departments of production, government, or education are disrupted in these periodic events, and charges of elite arrogance, corruption, or bureaucratic isolation have commonly resulted in wholesale transfers, demotions, or humiliating public criticisms. The mass movements, of course, infringe upon the "turf" of the legal bureaux in a vast way and, more to the point, the justice bureaux have themselves been frequent targets of attack. Not surprisingly, the popular and bureaucratic forces stand in sharp ideological and practical conflict on the point of proper jurisdiction and procedures.

It would be a mistake, however, to stress only the conflicting side of relations between popular and bureaucratic justice. The succeeding chapters also describe how citizen volunteers co-operate regularly and extensively with the justice professionals in preventing and controlling routine conflicts and crimes in the community. Likewise, the eradication of organized crime syndicates in 1950-51 was accomplished by popular-professional collaboration (*see* Chapter 4). The Chinese police force would probably be unable to maintain order without the assistance of local volunteer "security defence teams"; and the People's Courts regularly involve citizen volunteers as "assessor" judges and as informal consultants in specific cases. An enormous proportion of local conflicts among families and neighbours are resolved informally by local volunteer mediation teams. The regular justice officials recognize and need this auxilliary assistance, but have sought to confine popular judicial practice within the tight constraints of formal procedures and bureaucratic supervision. The professionals have not been at all comfortable with the notion that popular activism should extend to actual influence over the conduct of the judicial agencies themselves.

The historical pattern has thus emerged: in times of conservative dominance the judicial bureaucracies advance and limit the influence of the popular institutions. Conversely, in times of radical dominance and rapid social change, popular participation increases and the judicial bureaucracies come under fire from the radical activists in the party and the mobilized community. By 1981 the popular forces were clearly on the wane, and the judicial bureaucracies are steadily narrowing the popular field of action in both its peace-keeping work and, especially, in the realms of political rectification and mass campaigns. Popular justice, then, has no constant dimension, but its most important components over the last 50 years have been:

1. Systematic monitoring of those government officials in direct contact with the public (such as judges or police) is handled by *People's Supervisory Committees.* The committees keep files on local officials, and they compile and forward complaints in preparation for community hearings, accusation meetings, or action by higher authorities in government or the Communist Party.

2. Participation of public representatives within the forms of official justice agencies has been extensive. Most notable are the *People's Assessors* who sit as rotating judges alongside the professional jurists of the People's Courts.

3. The mass organizations maintain their own peace-keeping bodies for internal order and conflict resolution. These local groups include: *security defence teams* and *militia* forces (volunteer police), and also *mediation teams* which arbitrate quarrels, handle minor offences and prevent conflicts from becoming violent or criminal patterns.

4. Mobilization of the general public for national *mass rectification campaigns* has been a fundamental fact of political–legal life in China. These campaigns are concerned with social justice as defined in political terms and are more guided by political ideology than by codified law.

5. Suppression of class enemies, political corruption and bureaucratic abuse has been commonly assigned to temporary non-professional bodies known as *People's Tribunals.* Tribunal judges are elected from the mass organizations or chosen by local members of the Communist Party. Usually the tribunals are created during the mass campaigns and are not an integral part of the People's Court bureaucracy.

Thought Reform, the Confucian Heritage and Rectification

The popular justice emphasis on the "reform of incorrect thought" deserves some further introductory discussion here, since there is probably no other aspect of Chinese society that is so misunderstood or so widely feared in the West. Certainly the decades of distortion by cold war and legalist scholars have contributed to this misunderstanding, but there is also much that is genuinely exotic and in need of explanation. The lurid representation of "brainwashing" as a demonic combination of oriental cruelty and science fiction was developed by American politicians and media outlets originally to explain the defection of American prisoners captured in the Korean War. However, a closer reading of Lifton's classic work (1963) on Korean War thought reform does not support this characterization by the media and such scholars as Barnett (1964), Vogel (1969) and Walker (1955). The Chinese did not use any secret mind probes in Korea, nor were their techniques in prisoner of war camps remarkably different from those used by enemies of the Allied Forces in World War II. American soldiers defected or became depressives in Korea for essentially the same reasons that they later mutinied, assassinated ("fragged") officers or abused narcotics in Vietnam: they found themselves fighting a war without any apparent rationale against an enemy with whom some found they could even sympathize (Lubenski, 1970; Fisher, 1972; Lifton, 1973). Perhaps the experience of Vietnam may one day prompt an honest reappraisal of the first war against Asian socialism, but for our present purposes it will be sufficient just to push aside the layered propaganda for a brief sketch of thought reform as an actual Chinese practice.

The first point to be made is that thought reform is not a creation of Chinese socialism, but was an integral part of Confucian philosophy and government for thousands of years under the Chinese Empire. As Munro (1977a, pp.26-57) has so thoroughly demonstrated, Confucian cosmology regarded thought as "springs to action" and taught that social order depended not upon the control of incorrect behaviour but upon the cultivation of correct thoughts. The Neo-Confucian Wang Yang-ming paraphrased this central aspect of the Sage's teachings as follows:

> In their learning people of today separate knowledge and action into two different things. Therefore, when a thought is aroused, although it is evil, they do not stop it because it has not been translated into action. I advocate the unity of knowledge and action precisely because I want people to understand that when a thought is aroused it is already action (Chan Wing-tsit, 1953, p.201)

In imperial China, correct attitudes entailed acceptance of one's place in the hierarchy of family, state and society, and the obligation to submit to one's superiors and also to help and protect one's subordinates. The wise emperor, official, landlord or father ruled by the force of moral example rather than the force of law, and relied upon the clan, guild and family to instill in their members the proper attitudes of respect and duty. Sanctions in both official and private justice would be determined not only by the nature of the offending act, but also by the apparent motive and the subsequent repentance of the offender. Whether in the prevention or resolution crime and conflict, the deviant's thoughts as well as his behaviour were seen as fit objects for correction (Legge, 1960).

Comparative law scholars point out with consistency that the Judaeo-Christian heritage, upon which Western law is based, grants to the individual a greater degree of freedom than this. The "social contract" implicit in "natural law", as developed by writers such as Mill, sets one's thoughts outside the limits of legal or social responsibility. The principle of *Nulla peona sine lege* is held up as a measure of Western civilization. Nevertheless, the extensions of moral obligation and correction into the realm of thought, like the avoidance of litigation in resolving conflicts, is not so foreign to the Judaeo-Christian tradition as some might assert. Consider the following passage from the Sermon on the Mount:

> Think not I am come to destroy the Law or the prophets, I am not come to destroy but to fulfill.
>
> You have heard that it was said by them of old time, that whosoever shall kill shall be in danger of judgement. But I say unto you, that whosoever is angry with his brother without a cause shall be in danger of judgement.
>
> Agree with thine adversary quickly, whilst thou art in the way with him, lest at anytime the adversary deliver thee to the judge, and the judge deliver thee to the officer and thou be cast in prison.
>
> Ye have heard that it was said by them of old time, thou shalt not commit adultery. But I say unto you, that whosoever looketh on a woman to lust after her hath committed adultery with her already in his heart.
>
> And if thy right eye offend thee pluck it out and cast it from thee, for it is profitable that one of thy members should perish and not that thy whole body should be cast into hell (King James version, 1973, p.372)

The Maoists have attempted to revolutionize traditional Confucian thought reform by confronting and overturning the old feudal hierarchies. The continuous process of criticism/self-criticism and political study within the local "small groups" of mass organizations is designed to develop a shared socialist value. As Victor Li (1973, 1977) has so eloquently shown, there is in this arrangement an invasion of the private world to which most Westerners are accustomed; but at the same time the potential for preventing serious conflicts and for re-integrating offenders is greatly enhanced. The popular judicial principles of handling contradictions and mass line (with their emphasis on class and ideology) replace Confucian compromise and submission as a theoretical guide for thought reform (Lubman, 1967).

Whether in the resolution of domestic quarrels or the rectification of cadre elitism, the aim is "to cure the disease to save the patient"; i.e. to correct deviant attitudes in order to preserve collective cohesion and restore the deviant to the community. This, of course, is an ideal never perfectly realized; but it is an ideal very distinct from the bureaucratic adjudication of deviant "acts" and the formal sanctions which can only remove the deviant from the community. The concern of popular justice with attitudes and moral obligations is more flexible and penetrating, especially when applied to the problem of elitism and rectification. Not surprisingly, political conservatives and judicial bureaucrats have been especially uncomfortable with this sort of check on officials and so emphatically prefer a bureaucratic definition of crime, based on classifiable acts and professionally dominated procedures (Liu Shao chi, 1957; Teng Hsiao Peng, 1978).

While the co-operative side of the popular–bureaucratic relationship (in routine peace-keeping) must be appreciated, China's two systems of justice have also been highly visible objects and instruments of political conflict. The stormy debates over citizen participation and legal professionalism, ideology and law, the definition of crime and, above all, the function of justice in political rectification touch the very heart of the "Two Line Struggle". It is not surprising then that the Red Guards of 1966-67 should have picked the police, courts and procurate as particular targets; or that the National Police Chief, Lo Jui ching, was then singled out by the popular justice Tribunals as the "Number Two Leading Person in Authority Taking the Capitalist Road" (*see* Chapter 7). In the aftermath of the Cultural Revolution, the professional justice bureaux were the most slowly and carefully rebuilt government institutions, and the law schools were the last academic departments to reopen in China's reformed universities (Ruge, 1976; Cohen, 1973; Lamb, 1976).

The final chapter of this book describes how the new conservative Peking regime has relied upon these newly rebuilt offices of justice to suppress their radical opponents, while also resuming the stalled process of codification and legal professionalization as a means of legitimizing and arming the new post-Mao social order. Along with this has been a systematic effort to tame and control popular justice, whose auxilliary peace-keeping functions have been retained while its more ambitious and combative "rectification" capacity ended, along with many forms of individual political expression. The trial of the "Gang of Four" was also of enormous importance and this showcase event highlighted both the "Two Line Struggle" and differences in bureaucratic and popular justice, especially when compared with earlier political trials of the Cultural Revolution.

The Trial of the Gang of Four—Echoes of a Political-Legal Contest

The trial of Chiang Ching (erroneously referred to as "Mrs. Mao" by the bourgeois press), Chang Chun-chiao, Yao Wen Yuan and Wang Hung Wen, known as the Gang of Four, along with six lesser radicals from the Chinese central leadership, was clearly staged as a showcase trial for the new conservative regime in Peking. The political economic issues behind this case are treated in Chapter 8 of this book, but the trial itself also illuminates the procedural and ideological differences between bureaucratic and popular justice, particularly when compared with earlier political trials staged by the radicals. This short discussion aims to present the trial alongside the most prominent legal proceedings of the Cultural Revolution, i.e. the trial of former Communist Party Central Committee President, Liu Shao chi.

The arrest of the Gang of Four and (later) many of their supporters in Party leadership followed within weeks of Mao Tse-tung's death. A special Peking police unit, acting under direct orders from Premier Hua Kuo Feng, arrested the Four in the night and confined them to house arrest. The arrest came as a surprise to most observers since there had been no previous denunciations of the Four who were charged immediately with high treason. Their trial was delayed until 1 January 1981 when the newly enacted criminal code became law in China. The questionable constitutionality of trying persons under statutes not in effect at the time the alleged crimes had been committed might seem a moot point but for the fact that the judges at the trial were so proudly insistent of its procedural regularity (Onate, 1978).

The trial's importance as a demonstration of the new bureaucratic legal system is also obvious in the choice of professional staff. The two courts involved were headed by none other than the Vice President of the Supreme People's Court and the Deputy Chief of Staff for the People's Liberation Army (whose role is probably intended to show military support for the new regime and agreement over the fate of the accused radicals). The Chief Prosecutor for the Supreme People's Procurate presented the evidence marshalled by the Procurate and the police, whose National Minister for Public Security was also personally involved in prosecution. The appearance of virtually the entire elite of the newly re-emergent judicial bureaucracy, along with the prominence of other legally trained jurists as defence attorneys and witnesses, is clearly intended as a display of China's new legal professionalism (Wang Hsiao t'ing, 1978).

The defendants were alleged to have committed a total of 48 specific criminal *acts* in violation of four main sections of the criminal law, including:

> sedition and conspiracy to overthrow the political power of proletarian dictatorship;

> the framing and persecution of Party and state leaders and usurpation of Party leadership and state power;

> persecution and suppression of cadres and masses of the people and practice of a fascist dictatorship;

> plotting to murder Chairman Mao and engineering a counter-revolutionary armed rebellion (PR, 29th October, 1976; PR, 2nd February, 1981)

Though the formal trial procedures followed fairly closely the guidelines established under the oft cited new criminal code, much of the evidence cited against the defendants does not stand up under even a cursory examination. In several instances, defendants were accused of acts in a particular city, when previously published photographs and articles clearly establish that they were elsewhere. It is difficult to accept charges of "usurpation" when the Four in particular were appointed through much the same process that brought prosecution officials to power, and often indeed by the same officials. The accusations of an assassination plot against Mao are simply absurd. No one was more closely identified with Mao or benefited more from his support than did the radical defendants. Indeed, Mao's death precipitated the crisis that led to their fall (Gao Ji, 1981).

Almost all of the "crimes" lodged against the defendants were committed during the tumult of the Cultural Revolution. In fact, the defendants were virtually charged with personal responsibility for that cataclysmic event which involved hundreds of millions of Chinese across the country. Indeed, the lengthy trial indictment charges the gang with "34,800 persons persecuted to death and 729,511 framed and persecuted". These figures are further broken down as comprising: "142,000 cadres and teachers, 53,000 scientists, 500 medical professors and 2600 literary or art cadres" (PR, 1st December, 1980).

The ridiculousness of such charges is not the point. Most Chinese know, of course, that the Cultural Revolution was not the fabrication of ten leaders. The point is that the new regime is, by blaming the Gang, also denying that the Cultural Revolution sprang from real grievances and the genuine political expressions of the populace. Moreover, in reciting the list of "wronged people" the Peking leaders are identifying the radicals as the enemies of particular social classes — namely the intellectuals and cadres of the government and Party. This may be intended to strengthen the growing alliance between intellectuals and the conservative officials now ruling the country.

The new Peking leaders have described themselves as restorers of law and order in the country, and many of them, such as Teng Hsiao Peng and the current leaders of the judicial bureaucracy, were personally attacked, criticized, humiliated and demoted during the course of the Cultural Revolution. There is much more here than revenge, however. It should also be remembered that a large percentage of the current members of the Communist Party were recruited during the Cultural Revolution, often after active personal participation as Red Guards and Rebel Workers following the lead of Mao and the later embattled radical defendants. By apportioning all of the blame for the Cultural Revolution to the defendants, it was made easier for these younger members of the Party to renounce their own past involvement as radical activists and critics of the current leadership.

There is one thing that the radicals were *not* accused of and that is incorrect thought or ideology. Indeed the Chief Procurator and the Judges in the court room repeatedly made the point that

> The prosecution against Lin Piao (deceased), Chiang Ching and company involves only their counter-revolutionary crimes which violated the Criminal Law, and does not touch upon their errors in work, including those related to political line (PR, 2nd February, 1981)

This is extremely significant, for, as Chiang Ching screamed defiantly from the defendant's chair, this was nothing but a trial of ideology. The link between the defendants was obviously not some bizarre conspiracy with the dead Lin Piao. They shared a common point of view, and a commitment to the Maoist approach to modernization via continuing revolution.

The trial was in fact more about ideology than any alleged criminal acts. The defendants were accused of undermining the positions of leading officials and intellectuals during the Cultural Revolution. Are we now to believe that there were no ideological issues in that national confrontation? The importance of these issues is precisely why they must be denied and hidden under the new formalities of legal procedure.

The prosecution asked for the death penalty against the defiant Chiang Ching. Lesser figures among the ten were treated more leniently, especially the young Wang Hung Wen who "confessed" to all the charges against him. There is to be no subsequent rehabilitation and re-emergence of these defendants. The purpose of the trial has nothing to do with "political rectification". Its purpose is ideological eradication, the re-writing of social history and the sowing of a cultural amnesia. Only such methods can establish the sort of hegemony necessary to stabilize the new social order emerging from Peking's revisionist policies.

It is not surprising that "centrists" in the Peking leadership group (led by Premier Hua Kuo Feng) then found that the destruction of the "left" by the consolidated "right" in this trial was followed swiftly by an attack on themselves. Premier Hua is now facing removal on charges that he, as Minister of the Police Force in the 1970s did participate in the support of Gang positions and the persecution of their enemies. The former Deputy Minister, Xie Fuzhi, was among the ten defendants at the radical trial in Peking. He was appointed to that high police post, like his superior Hua Kuo Feng, as a replacement for the discredited justice leadership headed by Lo Jui ching. Hua and Xie have been regraded both inside and outside China as moderates who attempted to amalgamate some limited reforms in their rebuilding of the police organization. Now Xie is charged with treason and it is specifically alleged that he:

> Ordered the framing and persecution of leading cadres of the public security (police) organs, the procurate organs and the courts at various levels . . . Xie incited people to "smash the public security, procurate and judicial organs all over the country" (PR, 24th December, 1980)

It would not be surprising if Hua Kuo Feng were also soon targeted for trial for his "criminal acts". What is especially noteworthy in the trial of Xie, like that of Chiang Ching, is the deliberate attempt to rewrite history by denying the role of ideology and conscious mass action in the Cultural Revolution struggles over the offices of justice. By affixing all blame for the controversy on Xie, the present Peking leadership aimed to obscure any social, historical or material basis for the struggle between popular and professional justice (PR, 1st December, 1978).

The case of former head of state Liu Shao chi strikes an illuminating contrast with the radical trial of 1981. Political disagreements within the Party's Central Committee had grown increasingly bitter in 1966 between the conservatives, then led by Liu, and the Maoist radicals. Liu was determined that the Cultural Revolution, which had just begun with Peking encouragement, be strictly confined to cultural themes and limited to schools and universities. The Maoists instead voiced support for student rebels whose wide-ranging criticisms of academic elitism and curricular irrelevance had already begun to touch on issues of national social policy and political leadership. When Liu dispatched "work teams" to control and sanction student rebels, the Central Committee radicals reacted with attacks on President Liu (Lee, 1978, pp.98-114).

The first phase of the rectification process against Liu was kept within the chambers of the Central Committee where Liu was censured and ultimately wrote a "self-criticism". Lin Piao sharply criticized Liu in subsequent meetings of the Central Committee. Liu remained in power, however, and his writings continued to appear in the national press (Esmein, 1973, pp.120-121).

The conflict became increasingly public, however, when student Red Guards began to write and display "big character posters" attacking Liu. The Red Guards grew in militance, numbers and confidence, especially after Mao Tse-tung appeared alongside them in Peking. Liu was rather pointedly invited to a series of demonstrations culminating in the famous review of 26 July 1967. At that rally he was confronted and questioned relentlessly by Red Guard representatives. His answers, delivered in weakening tones, did not satisfy them. Liu remained in office, but made no further formal appearances. Press articles began to criticize his leadership with increasing frequency and invective (Ch'i Pen Yu, 1967; Lee, 1978, pp.38-40, 115-20).

Massed demonstrations were held by Red Guards calling for his removal from national leadership. Liu responded to all these attacks with a third self-criticism, submitted in the form of a letter to the faculty, students and workers of Peking Agricultural College. This was also rejected as incomplete and insincere, but the national campaign against him gradually tapered off as the Cultural Revolution ended with ideological compromise and institutional reforms (Fan, 1968, pp.269-72).

What were the charges against Liu? He was repeatedly castigated for his attempt to suppress student unrest with the work teams despatched in the summer of 1966, and for his efforts to limit the political scope of the Cultural Revolution. There were some half-hearted attempts to charge him with certain treasonable actions during the 1925-29 period of the Civil War, but the evidence was far from convincing and these charges were not insistently advanced. The central accusations pointed at Liu's *ideology*, however, and in particular at his "Six Theories" which were described as "black thought", "revisionist", "anti-socialist" and "poisonous weeds" (Lee, 1978, pp.119-24; MacFarquhar, 1974, pp.81-4; Fan, 1968, pp.268-73). The critics cited Liu's speeches and writings as evidence of his beliefs that:

1. The era of class struggle was over in China.

2. Party cadres should submit to their superiors in Confucian-like silence, even if their leadership were incorrect (i.e. Liu did not support the idea that "it is right to rebel").

3. Education should be a process of discipline and concentration on learning materials, and should not be "disrupted" by undue political activism or rebellion.

4. Large material incentives and piece work bonuses were necessary to stimulate the performance of individual workers.

5. Rural capitalism through the system of private plots and market fairs helped speed production.

6. The management of production in communes and factories was best left in the hands of "experts" and not to the local mass organizations of workers.

Liu was never brought before any formal court, nor was he accused of violations of law or subjected to formal penal sanction. The "court" which found him guilty of ideological errors was a combination of central Maoist leadership and massed students and workers who found their own interests in direct opposition to the policies of Liu. The process of examination and criticism of Liu combined both a strong measure of humiliation with the insistence that Liu could and must correct his attitudes. What infuriated his critics was that Liu in his three self-criticisms acknowledged his erring *acts* such as the despatch of the repressive work teams), but refused to foreswear his *ideological* positions. This constituted his "insincerity" (PHHP, 5th August, 1967; Snow, 1971, pp.94-5; *Hung Ch'i*, 8th May, 1967; MacFarquhar, 1974, pp.160-64).

In summary then, there are three major differences between the 1981 trial of the Gang and the 1966-68 "trial" of Liu. Firstly, the role of the masses in the more recent trial was essentially that of passive television or courtroom onlookers, the action being dominated totally by the legal professionals. The action against Liu, in contrast, involved both the central Maoist leadership and the mobilized students, workers and mass organizations in the dialectic form familiar to China and known as the "mass movement". Secondly, the charges against the Gang were made against standards of law which they had allegedly violated through criminal acts. In Liu's case, he was judged against the principles of the mass line and found to have erred in certain acts, but more especially in his conservative and elitist ideology. Thirdly, the process of sanction was formal and penal in the case of the Gang trial. We can be sure that none of the defendants will ever return to high office; and the effects of sanction are to distance them from the population and stigmatize them permanently. Liu Shao chi and the other conservatives attacked in the Cultural Revolution were dealt with in an informal style which, though certainly rough, also held out the possibility of rehabilitation through ideological rectification. Many of the purged conservatives were to return to office, and even Liu, though stripped of power, lived out his life on a quiet farming commune outside Peking. It is most unlikely that the defendants in the Peking trial of 1981 will be permitted such an end (Thornton, 1973, pp.324-7; Esmein, 1973, pp.157-9).

Hopefully the contrast in these two political trials will make more understandable the theoretical and practical divergencies of the popular and bureaucratic judicial tradition and the larger conflicts in political leadership. My narrative will now return to its starting point and trace the development of the Chinese state, community and judicial system through the long age of feudalism and the short era of Kuomintang fascism preceding the present era of socialist transformation. The chapters of the socialist era are cadenced by the momentous mass movements and the great events of Civil War and liberation, a structural division which points once more to the link between legal history and the political economy.

Note

1. Note that our critics have taken us very much to task for our silence here—see Klockars (1979), who charges: "The failure of Marxist criminology to consider the details of Maoist, Gulag, or Cuban solutions to the problems of crime [means] it is powerless to explain the criminality which exists in states where private ownership of the means of production has been abolished . . . Consequently, while they look to such states with willing hearts, they do so with empty hands.".

2 The Imperial Tradition and its Collapse

The greatest feat of Chinese Communism was not the Long March, but the transformation and fusion of the two politics that had ruled China for 25 centuries. Alongside the official government, headed successively by Tang, Sung, Ming, Ch'ing and earlier dynasties had functioned a vast network of what were in fact private governments based on kinship or occupational groupings in villages and towns. The internal rupture of these arrangements by violent class conflicts and the severing of the mutually supportive ties between the state and the private governments hastened the collapse of feudal society. The Communists successfully redirected and reconstructed both the Chinese state and the informal community arrangements, and in so doing created a critical mass of revolutionary potential.

China's Two Governments and Changing Class Relations

Western images of imperial China as a backward and corrupt society based upon the unreservedly brutal exploitation of the peasantry by parasitic landlords and degenerate officials are perhaps a fair approximation of that society from the mid-19th century onwards; but it is a gross caricature of China in the long centuries before Western intrusion. The Chinese Communists, too, tend to emphasize the final decades of imperialism when feudalism was most oppressive, in part to heighten the present class consciousness and also to keep alive revolutionary memories.

Obviously, a society so morally bankrupt and retreatist was untenable, but it is important to understand the philosophical and political strengths that made the Chinese Empire the world's longest surviving society. So let us set aside the

19th century momentarily and consider the structure of Chinese life over the earlier stretch of time. Since this is necessarily an abbreviated discussion, a great many dynastic changes will be telescoped for analysis.

The ideological bulwark of the Empire was, of course, the Confucian code, which stressed both submission to one's superiors and protection of one's subordinates. The superior was charged with continual cultivation and improvement of the self through study and reflection, so as to be more just and benevolent in the administration of office or position (Hucker, 1975, pp.68-80, 364-71). These mutual obligations applied both to the "natural" hierarchy of male over female and elder over youth, and also to the social levels of emperor, scholar-officials, gentry (landlords), merchants, artisans and peasants. The class ranking was somewhat complicated by the fact that merchants were accorded low status but enjoyed considerable wealth and power, while peasants were esteemed in theory but often miserable in reality (Wakeman, 1975).

The dominant elites of emperor, officials and gentry were not simply parasitic, though they of course lived off the surplus created by the labouring peasants. These elites did perform real services and commonly felt genuine obligation to the populace. In addition to defending the realm from barbarian invasion or internal warlord predations, the emperor, together with local officials and gentry, planned and financed roads, bridges and the vital irrigation and water conservation system upon which agriculture (especially in the South) depended. The gentry also often maintained emergency stocks of grain against times of famine (Chung li, 1955, pp.55-70). The peasants performed the actual physical labour of building roads or dams, and of course any grain given in emergency had to be later repaid with interest, but these services were nevertheless real and necessary. Likewise, the merchant and the master craftsmen protected their underlings in the cities from insecurity by guaranteeing employment, skilled training and injury compensation to those working within their trade or craft monopolies (Hucker, 1975, pp.348-51; Burgess, 1928). Major profits were siphoned off by these urban elites and rural elites, to support extended families, but even this systematic nepotism contributed to social cohesion, as will be discussed later.

The imperial state was in many ways considerably more egalitarian and flexible than the feudal states of Europe. The Chinese state was supported not by an hereditary nobility of largely ignorant warriors, but by highly educated scholars chosen in competitive examination. The Confucian classics were the heart of these three-tiered examinations and candidates devoted most of their lifetimes in studious preparation. The fact that only one in thousands could succeed meant that Confucian thought would be disseminated far beyond the actual office holders and would enjoy undisputed hegemony in the culture (Wakeman, 1975, pp.21-24). Although paternalistic and scholarly devotion was authentic, the chief incentive for sitting the examinations was the handsome salary and access to lucrative bribes that came with office. Since the emperor could afford to employ only a single multi-purpose official (a magistrate or "Yamen") for a large "hsien" area with residents in the hundreds of thousands, the state could not hope to regulate closely the lives of the population (Watt, 1972).

The lone magistrate was endowed with considerable powers, including revenue collection and the negotiation of state contracts, which allowed for a vast additional income through "fees" and favours (Ch'uan, 1968; Jiang, 1968).

Social antagonisms arising from the exploitation inherent in all of these arrangements was muted not only by the Confucian philosophy, but also by the structure of private governments—the rural clan and the urban guild. These grouped together landlords and peasants, merchants and craftsmen on the basis of common bloodline or occupation (Burgess, 1928, pp.220-234). Nor were these mere associations of sentiment, for they held real powers and provided significant benefits to their members. Wealthy landlords and merchants benefited especially from their dominance of these associations, but the local elites also contributed heavily to the purchase and upkeep of special fields, temples and halls used by all members of that particular clan or guild. Likewise, though a rich man might choose to finance his own son's study for the all important imperial exams, he might also support especially promising sons of poorer guild or clan members in the hope that they might earn higher degrees and so gain a lucrative public office. Office holders were then expected to repay their individual sponsors generously and to put money into the clan or guild treasury (Chung li, 1955, pp.349-52).

Imperial society was no crude arrangement resting on sheer brutality. It offered probably more opportunity for individual mobility than did the feudal societies of Europe (Wakeman, 1975, pp.19-25). The private government effectively regulated the local economy while minimizing social friction. The state provided centralized direction over such vast enterprises as irrigation, defence and commerce. The common training in Confucian classics provided an ideological system effectively linking the private and state government systems (Hucker, 1975, pp.155-161; Chung li, 1955, pp.197-203). As long as China was able to hold off invading barbarians from the North and continue its own conquests in the South, fertile new lands could support her growing population. As long as landlords needed labour, they would not press the peasants too hard who were, after all, commonly their clan cousins (Hinton, 1967). The 19th century, however, was to bring new enemies and unleash latent tensions which the sophisticated but static feudal order simply could not contain. However, before turning to that final moment in the long day of the Chinese Empire, let us consider the justice arrangements of the era.

Confucian Thought and the Relativity of Law

The Confucian mixture of idealism and oppression was most evident in the workings of both the official and the private system of justice. The virtuous individual closely observed the Confucian code of social obligations and deference to superiors which comprise the way of "li". Principles of li required that individuals or groups in conflict resolved their differences through discussion and compromise (Greene, 1962b, p.189; Bodde and Morris, 1968; Escarra, 1961, pp.13-19).

The social philosophy of li resisted the development of written law in old China (Van der Sprenkel, 1962, pp.20-26). The idea of a codified law defining offences and individual rights and thereby *institutionalizing conflict* was abhorrent to Confucian scholar-officials. A high ranking bureaucrat from the pre-Empire state of Cheng aroused great controversy when he ordered that a code of laws be posted for public notice. An official in another of old China's petty states reacted as follows:

> Originally, Sir, I had hopes for you but now that is all over. Anciently, the early kinds conducted their administration by deliberating on matters; they did not put their punishments and penalties [into writing], fearing this would create a contentiousness among the people that could not be checked. Therefore they used the principle of social uprightness to keep the people in bounds . . .
>
> But when the people know what the penalties are they lose their fear of authority and acquire a contentiousness which causes them to make their appeal to the written words [of the penal law] . . . As soon as the people know the grounds on which to conduct disputation, they will reject the [unwritten] accepted ways of behaviour [li] . . . Disorderly litigation and bribery will become current. By the end of your era, Cheng will be ruined (Van der Sprenkel, 1962, 16-17)

While China remained a loose array of competing petty states, each with only a small government and population, there was little reason to trade the pervasive order of li for the untried and "unnatural" mechanism of written law.

This epoch of simple small-scale societies ended with the invasion of the Ch'in forces in 221 B.C. The Ch'in consolidated fragmented China and thus established the Empire. The size and complexity of the Empire demanded a tighter organization of government; and this need for control prompted the Ch'in to enact the first national laws. The skies of the new Empire were soon smudged by the smoke from pyres of Confucian classics books, torched by the Ch'in wherever found (Van der Sprenkel, 1962, p.27; Escarra, 1961, p.47). That philosophy was unwelcome among the Ch'in and found no place in their rule by codified law.

Those first laws are yet remembered in Chinese folklore as a foreign mechanism, left behind by a barbarian invader (Bodde, 1964). The Chinese have historically viewed law as a "right of conquest" and as a political servant created by and for whatever government was in power. Each imperial dynasty raised up a (new) set of laws. The courts and laws were far more concerned with preserving order than with enforcing any abstract concept of sin or right and wrong (Greene, 1962b, p.188; Bodde, 1964). Imperial law did not guarantee liberties to citizens and the code contained no bill of rights.

The political convenience of Confucian principles can be readily seen. On the other hand li encouraged submission to authority, compromise in disputes and avoidance of courtroom battles (Cheng, 1969). At the same time the laws and courts could cite Confucian teachings as the reason for their severe punishment of rebellion against authority if it did occur and Confucianism guaranteed a special privileged legal status for landlords and government officials. Such a two-way system is rare in politics and was deservedly appreciated by imperial rulers. It should be noted, in fairness to the philosophy, that Confucianism was rather distorted by the official selection and emphasis of those ideas most helpful to the rule of the rich and powerful.

Let us now turn from legal theory to the actual practice of justice under that Confucian law tradition.

Imperial Justice: the Benign Brutality of Confucian Order

> I desire, therefore, that those who have recourse to the tribunals should be treated without pity, and in such a manner that they shall be disgusted with law, and tremble to appear before a magistrate.

This threat of judicial brutality (Jernigan, 1905, p.191), as expressed by the Emperor K'ang hsi (1662–1722) quite accurately suggests the quality of imperial justice. This official attitude had been characteristic since the Nan dynasty and was carried even beyond this 18th century declaration. The Confucian-dominated government and imperial law regarded litigation as an extreme form of self-assertion and thus defendants, witnesses and litigants alike were tortured, extorted and humiliated in a casually routine fashion throughout judicial or penal processes (Cheng, 1969).

The (sole) official government representative in a district (hsien) was an appointed scholar who served a 3-year term as magistrate and general administrator of the area. As part of the imperial policy of preventing power concentrations (though ostensibly to prevent corruption), magistrates were barred from serving in their local provinces and were rotated frequently.

Thus the current magistrate in a district was essentially a foreigner, unable to speak the local dialect and unfamiliar with local customs (Watt, 1972).

The lone magistrate typically regarded his assignment as but an interlude in his bureaucratic career-making. As a Confucian scholar he was untrained in legal matters, and this unfamiliarity with both law and the local dialect further removed him from the business of his office and made him rather dependent upon the local hirelings who staffed his court. Thus he was generally unable to prevent the hired help from following his own more sophisticated example of systematic corruption, and such generalized corruption was characteristic of imperial government at all levels (Moore, 1966, pp.172-6; Cohen, 1971, pp.1212-3).

Citizens foolish enough to ignore the "compromise and submit" principles of li found the imperial warning fulfilled in the court and offices (yamen) of the magistrate. Petitions for investigation of offences, as well as the investigation itself were handled by the office staff. Bribes and special fees were frequently necessary to prompt and continue such procedures (Cheng, 1969, pp.1-5). Later the unofficial court police (runners) were sent to arrest defendants and escort plaintiffs and witnesses to the magistrate's office and detention centre.

Since admission of guilt greatly simplified legal proceedings, and was even required for convictions under some laws, confessions were highly prized (Cohen, 1966, p.1214). The judge generally rewarded any member of his staff able to deliver a confession from either the defendant or the accuser. Typically, defendants were quickly sized-up by the runners who then demanded bribes from the unfortunate. This extortion continued along the journey to the jail. Should the defendant at any point refuse payment, the runners demonstrated their proficiency in various torture techniques. Once jailed, the guards continued the bribe-or-torture rehabilitation programme (Cohen, 1966, pp.1214-5; Cohen, 1968b, p.472).

When brought before the court the defendants were again asked to confess. If they refused, torture was applied, as provided for *by law* (Van der Sprenkel, 1962, pp.34-5), on the floor of the courtroom. Members of the court staff stood prepared with clubs and knives for this purpose. Should their efforts ultimately fail, it was not uncommon to turn the eye of justice upon plaintiffs in the hope that they would "admit" to a false accusation. If one of the witnesses refused to bribe court officials, or appeared open to persuasion, he was also beaten and tortured, also *according to law*. A confession from someone usually resulted.

It should be noted that the ruling classes were largely protected from the discomfort of these courts. Magistrates were reluctant to arrest or bring to trial any of the more prominent family members in the area, as such families often had powerful connections in the government (Schurmann, 1966b, p.368) and, in any case, the system of fees and bribery made law responsive to money. Moreover, the laws specifically exempted "persons of great merit" and the whole of the Mandarin-bureaucrat class from the common courts and established a special judiciary for cases involving them. Finally, the laws of the Ch'ing dynasty forbade the beating of convicted gentry and allowed them to pay fines instead (Van der Sprenkel, 1962, pp.34-35).

It can be stated with assurance that a great many magistrates and their hired staff profited nicely from the proceedings in and around the district courts. A survey of imperial records also shows that a large number of defendants and witnesses died from torture *en route* to or in jail, or during court proceedings. Many others committed suicide rather than go to trial (Cheng, 1969). The imperial government was on occasion presented with complaints regarding the cruelty, deceit and extortion so common in the courts, and a number of government campaigns against "litigation tricksters" were launched, but very few were brought to trial (Watt, 1972). The chief response of the government to its own judicial racket was to warn the people against litigation and to suggest that they seek an alternative solution outside the official courts. That alternative, of course, was to seek justice within the sphere of private government (Cheng, 1969).

The terror of imperial justice made a private justice alternative essential to the survival of the working people.

Their illiteracy and lack of power left them helpless in the imperial courts for they could scarcely afford the fees and bribes demanded of them under state justice. One of the chief functions of local private government was thus to keep conflicts "among the folks" and avoid official notice. Although actual crime statistics are not available, it appears that private government succeeded on this score (Vogel, 1967a, pp.2-3).

Private Justice in the Shadow of Imperial Neglect

The leadership of local private government was a valuable aide to the imperial government. The local elite shared the aspirations, education, social philosophy and (often) the career background of the imperial elite. Most clans, guilds and villages boasted a few scholars-without-portfolio (men who possessed degrees but were not yet on the payroll of the imperial bureaucracy). Other leaders were ex-bureaucrats who had retired from government careers to live on home-province estates bought with the rich rewards of corrupt service to the Emperor (Yang, 1945, pp.93-96). Open elections for clan or guild leadership were infrequent and in those instances the educated gentry with government connections presented the best choice to a membership looking for protection and government favour (Townsend, 1969, pp.16-17). Most local leaders operated informally (without office) and were chosen by their predecessors (Golas, 1968).

The co-operation of local elites spared bureaucrats the expense (in money and loss of caste) which is the cost of direct government (Hsiao, K.-C., 1961, pp.320-23, 347-60). In a vast sea of virtual illiterates, it was only natural that educated and affluent men (as both local and official elites were) would see one another as colleagues who "spoke the same language".

In this running elite conversation, crime and litigation were the least pleasant of topics. If the gentry-led private government could keep these disquieting forces subdued, the officials were delighted. The imperial encouragement of private justice is clear from the official establishment of anti-litigation societies throughout China, run by the local gentry (Van der Sprenkel, 1962, p.114).

The hands of private government, receiving both criminal and civil cases, became highly skilled in an informal judicial process generally referred to as "mediation". This process of carefully directed head-knocking and compromise was the stock and trade of private justice in guild and clan alike (Cohen, 1968a, p.988). Mediation remains a crucial element of popular justice in the People's Republic of China. The Communist version of mediation will be described in the next chapter.

The first line of mediation (in imperial days) was the family. Members of the extended family (pao) were required under li to negotiate the settlement of family quarrels. If the quarrels were serious, such a settlement often called for the mediating efforts of the head of the family. The latter was generally the eldest male or a retired scholar-bureaucrat once again living among the family (Cohen, 1966, pp.1216-1225). Should family efforts fail or the crisis involve members of different families, the next logical step was the private government.

The practices of private justice were always influenced by the local traditions of the private government sponsor. Justice under the guilds was more "legal" (constrained by written law) than was the mediation of clans or village associations. The internal laws enacted by the guilds were, however, of a general nature and punishments were left open to decisions reached by mediation. The great weight of collective guild pressure fell upon deviants or conflicting members until they submitted their cases for mediation. Such mediation might involve only a few people in an informal discussion. In more serious cases guild members charged with offences, or engaged in dispute, generally met with special guild representatives. Some later guilds even went as far as establishing guild courts. The court or representatives worked out a compromise settlement or fixed punishments. Once the punishment or damages (often a fine paid to the guild treasury) had been set and accepted, the guilty person was welcomed back into the guild community (Golas, 1968; Jernigan, 1905).

The clans followed a similar pattern (of social pressure-mediation-reinstatement) for the resolution of conflict and disorder. Those clan members who attempted to by-pass private justice and go directly to the imperial magistrate were often punished by clan members, regardless of the merits of the case. Clan mediation was usually accomplished by the elder males or local gentry who provided the clan's political leadership. Mediation between members of different clans was accomplished by the private government of the village. In such a case the locally appointed village constable or village headman often decided the course of compromise and/or punishment (Cohen, 1966; Lubman, 1967). Like the guilds and clans, village governments were very reluctant to take cases before the magistrate's court (Hsu, 1963).

The intense social pressure brought to bear on guild or clan deviants could be devastating, given the dependence of the citizen upon private government protection. A craftsman or merchant who operated outside the guild for that business was subject to the co-operative hostility of all his competitors. The control of some enterprises, such as the salt trade, was absolute and recognized under imperial law (Jernigan, 1905). Likewise villagers who ignored the codes and dictates of the clan found themselves social isolates among villagers belonging entirely to one or two local clans. The tremendous reservoir of social pressure represented by guild, clan, village and family was a great deterrent to those who might violate norms and/or refuse the mediation or settlements of private justice. Though it was essentially a conservative arrangement emphasizing conformity, the mediation of private justice did at least spare the commoner from the horrors of the imperial courts.

The philosophy of private justice followed the imperial view of law as being essentially a political instrument and a rather clumsy tool at that. Legal codes were written in the language of Confucian morality (Legge, 1960), but neither private nor official justice claimed any divine origins or moral purity. The determination of wrongness and negotiation of punishments through mediation was not bound by legal codes. Like official courts, private justice followed the contours of power and wealth. Thus the decisions of clan, guild or village mediator-elites considered both the facts of the case and the wealth, prestige and political power of the conflicting parties (Cohen, 1966, Van der Sprenkel, 1968). The justice of private governments supported imperial rule through the dominance of ex-bureaucrats who were careful that local associations did not make large demands of the imperial order. Ironically, the tightly logical inter-connections of the Empire left it unable to adjust to new forces thrust upon it by the 19th century imperialist invasions (Hsiao, K.-C., 1961).

Social Consequences of Western Invasion and Over-population

Western invasion coincided with and further exacerbated a looming economic crisis. The Empire's conquest of the South, followed by the systematic culti-vation of high-yield rice crops, had enabled the country to support a far larger population than before. However, the determined resistance of the indigenous

Vietnamese, and the incursions of the French stopped the Chinese expansion in mid stride. Unfortunately, the population continued to grow at an enormous rate, labour became over-abundant and land became concomitantly more precious (Wakeman, 1975).

The landlord–peasant relationship was drastically affected. Landlords were no longer so concerned about good relations with tenants, who could be easily replaced, and began to squeeze the peasants to breaking point. Land speculation and usury became increasingly attractive, but this sort of profit-making further intensified conflicts between peasant and landlord. Increasingly the wealth and land was concentrated in fewer hands among the vast masses, especially in the volatile south of the country. The hard-pressed Empire neglected the repair of dikes and canals, with the result that agriculture declined as disastrous floods occurred. The local gentry sold their surplus grain at the city market, leaving the peasants with nothing in time of famine but debts and bad dreams. Speculation in this growing misery knew few bounds and desperate peasants even sold one child to feed the rest for another day. Wealthy landlords were drawn to the pleasures and Western goods offered in the city, or stayed within the walls of fortress-like rural homes. The material basis of mutual obligation within the clan evaporated, leaving only a remnant of sentiment and tradition too weak to contain mounting class conflict (Cheng li Chang, 1955).

It was within the cities that the penetration of Western capitalism was most dramatic. Cheaply manufactured foreign goods replaced Chinese handicrafts and employment at either Western or Chinese-owned factories became a necessary alternative. Within the massed labour system of the factories, the guild could not offer any protection to its members. The stability of urban residential communities was shattered by the massive migration of desperate peasants hoping to find work in the cities. The multiplication of stress and the collapse of old private associations proceeded at lightning speed in the urban areas, where social change, rebellion and repression were concentrated, and where the political and legal authority of the Empire was replaced by foreign "concession" governments on Chinese soil.

The Confucian code could not provide useful guidance for the emperors or their scholar-officials. There was neither time nor the capital to finance a rapid modernization of the economy, the educational system, or the national defence forces. More immediately, any such effort would have threatened the interests of the scholar-gentry and shattered the Confucian ideology that was the glue and lifeblood of imperial society. The survival of the Empire, even in the short run, depended upon a constant manipulation and appeasement of competing Western powers, the increasingly independent and unruly local gentry and even new armies of rebellious peasants like the Boxers. Given the pressures of the time it is surprising only that the imperial society struggled for so long during the long century of defeat and humiliation.

3   The Era of the Chinese Republic (1911–49)

The corrupt disinterest of the imperial government could not govern China under the pressure of foreign imperialism. The bureaucracy held fast to the abstractions of Confucian classics which had long since become irrelevant to the complex needs of the besieged nation. Last-ditch reform efforts of emperors desperate to save the fading order were stoutly resisted or ignored by the bureaucracy, revealing the weakness of shoulders wearing the "divine mantle" of authority. The imperial government, confronted everywhere by new domestic demands and blinded by the strange smoke of modern warfare, whirled about in elegant isolation to collapse dervish-like upon the rickety stage of Confucian ideals.

The End of the Empire and the Evolution of Private Government

The Empire operated a ghost government with ritual powers only in the final years (1880–1911). The abolition of Confucian examinations in 1905 and the drafting of new progressive legislation (part of a hopeless late attempt at modernization) did not lead to a strong central government (Meijer, 1949, pp.131–132; Tsao-Wen-yen, 1953b, p.8; Cheng, 1969, p.34). The old bureaucrats remained in their posts as the Western invasion sapped the last strength of the Empire.

Effective government control was limited to a few cities as bandit gangs ravaged the exposed countryside. These gangs, through bloody contest, merged into larger armies under the control of regional warlords. The warlord armies became the new "official" government for most of fragmented China.

In 1911 a revolution of intellectuals, students, workers, gangsters, merchants and industrialists toppled the imperial rule and announced its intention to reunite China under a modern government of the Chinese Republic. The KMT party created by this mixed lot of patriots reflected the internal contradictions of the revolution (Tan, 1963). Despite all of its broad national concerns, both the revolution and the KMT party involved only a handful of the people (Townsend, 1969, pp.26-27), and the revolutionary ideology of democracy never left the realm of theory.

The Revolution was an easy victory since the Empire had long since lost the support of several key social groupings. Sun Yat Sen, leader in 1911 and later president of the Republic, represented an energetic intellectual class (Chen, J. T., 1970), long disgusted with imperial corruption (Townsend, 1969, pp.26-29). Peasants supported the establishment of a strong central government as a hedge against the crop confiscations levied by rival warlord armies. Urban workers were angered by the fluctuations in employment and the miserable working conditions which were the outcome of backward-looking imperial policies. Secret societies formed by urban gangsters represented the political resentment of the city underclass (newly arrived ex-peasants) who found even the worst jobs to be very scarce (Lieberthal, 1973, pp.18-19).

Landlords and the rising class of merchant-industrialists also shared the peasant-worker-intellectual's interest in the re-establishment of domestic order and national integrity. National stability was essential to the protection of property, the successful growing of rent-crops and the free flow of commerce. The wealth of landlord-bourgeois classes and the muscle of workers, peasants and gangsters was strong enough to carry Sun Yat Sen's banner of reform and reunification across China. However, this programme was sacrificed and shredded by internal conflicts. The revolutionary ideals of "people's livelihood", agrarian reform and social justice remained an unfulfilled promise and one which ultimately prompted the Communists to continue the revolution, in leapfrog fashion, past the KMT.

Changes in urban private government

Long before the 1911 revolution the society of the nation had begun to show enormous changes. The cities were the most affected by Western intrusion. Under foreign influence new commercial and industrial enterprises began which displaced the craftsmen and merchants of older, simpler days. Peasants, displaced by changes in rural economy, poured into the cities, adding further to pressures of overcrowding and unemployment. Crime and disorder brought by poverty soon outstripped the capacities of the official justice agencies.

The small shops of merchants and craftsmen, forming the strength of the guilds, were beaten on many fronts by newly established factories and commerce companies backed by Western capital. The stability and cohesion of occupational groups, important to the maintenance of guild order, crumbled under the forces of capitalist development. Economic competition and the social disruption caused by new waves of ex-peasant immigrants resulted in the collapse of many old guilds (Schurmann, 1966b, pp.367-8). Those few which survived were weak, but alongside them arose new associations of businessmen, intellectuals, workers and criminals. Many of these new organizations developed new forms of private justice as a means of self-protection and internal discipline.

The establishment of China's first chambers of commerce (1902) in the closing years of the Empire signified the growing strength of the bourgeois merchant-industrialist class. While guilds were always a strictly local arrangement of people in a single trade, the chambers of commerce established links between cities and also included a wider range of businesses and occupations in their organization.

While broadening the scope of private government in a geographical sense, the chambers insisted that candidates for membership meet exclusive entrance standards of wealth and property. Thus the organization represented Chinese industry and commerce — but only through the interest of the bourgeois elites. By 1916 the top businessmen from over 195,000 old guilds had banded to form about 1000 chambers (Garrett, 1970).

The chambers established internal codes regulating competition and disputes among members. The various chamber of commerce courts conducted investigations into business practices and acted as mediator-judge when called upon. Greatly concerned about the maintenance of urban order, they frequently provided money and political support for police expansion and such improvements as street lights (Garrett, 1970).

Some years after merchants and industrialists formed the chambers of commerce, urban workers began organizing China's first trade unions (1919). The formation of the early unions was strongly supported by the intellectuals of the KMT and the movement expanded steadily despite the oppositon of local warlords and industrialists.

The unions, like the chambers, represent an early deviation from the non-political tradition of private government. Socialist (later communist) ideology was maintained by a large number of unions, and the emphasis on class conflict and social struggle was clear in the internal education and strike demands of unions (Hung, 1934). The unions did not seek to avoid contact with the Republican government, but rather attempted to bargain for protective labour legislation.

The old guilds were wrecked by the rip-tide of industrialization which tore away both the leading elite and the working masses from the old organization. In some cases new chambers of commerce established themselves in the old guild halls, while other guild memberships (such as the Shanghai Mechanics Guild) voted *en masse* to become trade unions (Hung, 1934). The remaining guilds became increasingly the representatives of employers in opposition to worker demands (Golas, 1968, p.7). The potential for conflict among these new private associations is obvious, especialy in view of the leftist union political ideology.

The Kuomintang government for a time supported the formation of both unions and the chambers. It was yet another strange and stormy KMT coalition. The early socialist ideas of Sun Yat Sen and other intellectuals permeated the Party, and the unions and chambers both provided support in the Kuomintang struggle with the warlords and the vestiges of the imperial order.

Changes in rural private government

The rural world of China remained under warlord control throughout the last years of empire and well into the Republic's early history. Many landlord gentry (especially in South China) left their home districts to live in the coastal cities, where contact with the West brought new luxuries and opportunities for profitable investment. The departure of this traditional elite middleman served to isolate peasant organizations further from the defunct central government (Moore, 1966, pp.180-1, 202-8). Another traditional landlord-peasant tie was broken when the country squire turned businessman and began to sell grain surpluses in city markets. These surpluses included the contents of emergency granaries, before always reserved for peasant use in times of famine (Chesneaux, 1972, pp.166-168).

Left to their own devices, and burdened by the confiscations of warlord armies, the private governments of clan and village (pao-chia) ceased collecting rents and serving absentee landlords. Peasants formed rural associations and village militia units to resist warlord gangs and rent collectors. Villagers co-operated in hiding crops, and authorities began to complain that the steady rural folk had abandoned the moral principles of Confucian thought.

The warlord armies far surpassed the casual brutality of the Empire and the peasants could no longer count on a set limit to taxes and crop payments. The arrival of a new warlord meant a second or even a third round of the yearly payments. The warlord demands were not bounded even by the traditional landlord's interest in maintaining a stable population of peasant tenants. Peasants driven from their lands by taxes, crop failures, famines and military confiscations formed local secret societies which resisted the warlords in armed contest. Those tenants remaining in the fields supported the secret society forces with food and money, and counted on them for protection against warlord troops.

The rural secret society, even more than the gangster syndicates of the cities, was a mixture of the Mafia and Robin Hood. In times of calm the society's demands for food and support sounded to peasants like extortion, and society leaders did on occasion forget their origins and establish themselves as new warlords (Chesneaux, 1972, pp.220-224). On the other hand, the societies did act to protect the peasants from warlords and the rent demands of landlords. When famine or warlord armies pushed the rural folk too far the societies sparked rebellions against the authorities. At such times members of societies like the Big Knives, Red Spears and Red Flags lead the poorly trained village militia into pitched battles (Chesneaux, 1972, p.139). Some societies became national powers, holding large territories in China.

A number of these large societies moved beyond military matters and developed the beginnings of government and political ideology. Generally the societies called for the reunification of the country under a democratic national government. Members of the huge Triad society were pledged to fight the imperial government to the last man. Not surprisingly the rural societies, like their urban counterparts, were closely allied with the Republican revolutionaries. Sun Yat Sen was himself a society member, and he worked closely with the Triad and Black Flag organizations (Chesneaux, 1972).

When the Republican armies marched into the countryside to face the warlords, they were joined by China's first "People's Army". The latter was composed of thousands of peasant militiamen led by the veterans of the secret societies (Chesneaux, 1972). The combined power of Republican troops and the People's Army was invincible and here can be seen the outline of the future People's Liberation Army of Communist-led peasants.

The rural secret societies were among the most sophisticated of China's private governments, especially when they controlled large chunks of territory. The Red Spears, for example, set up civil departments for finance, documents and judicial procedure, in addition to military defence. Chiao Ta-feng, leader of another huge society, conquered Human province and established a radical government which overturned gentry privileges and threw classics scholars out of office (Chesneaux, 1972).

A private justice was created by several societies. The Red Spears passed new legal codes governing their membership and the population under their control. Social reform was written into these codes which outlawed opium smoking and gambling. The societies established courts to deal with some violations, while others were handled by mediation (Chesneaux, 1972).

The private government and justice of rural secret societies was clearly beyond the narrow limits of the old clan and village (pao-chia) systems. The societies were the first government to mass the peasants for political and military action, though it must be added that these mobilizatons were limited to times of crises and were not systematically related to government. As many others have observed, the societies were a transitional arrangement. They were an organization of conflicts in a Chinese society about to split the thin skin of warlord rule.

The societies pulled together hundreds of village militia units to form the People's Armies. Society governments and justice systems initiated some reforms later picked up by the Republicans and finally expanded by the Communists. In the leadership skills and organizational ideas of the societies can be found shadows of the Communist mass line which would ultimately sweep across China. The mass line and the Communist People's Army would in the end destroy the secret societies mired at last in their own once progressive ideals.

The repression of private government

The Northern Expedition of 1927, led by Chiang Kai Shek, broke the independent power of the warlords as the countryside was brought under the Republic's authority. With the reunification of the country and the restoration of rural order, the Republic had met the desires of the landlord and the bourgeois classes. The rest of the 1911 revolutionary ideology called for social reform and the construction of democratic institutions.

At about this time Sun Yat Sen died and the class antagonisms long dormant in the KMT alliance split the party, as the landlord-bourgeois wing turned on the militant unions and the grumbling peasants. The newly emergent trade unions were no match for the combined power of the businessmen, landlords and Chiang Kai Shek's army. The Nationalist Government was henceforth to wear the old warlord costume as strikebreaker, rent-collector and extortionist. This latest in China's tradition of weak central governments was to be dependent upon the money of merchant and businessman (Barnett, 1962) and would, as before, extend no further than the garrison-town or the magistrate's office.

The Republic, now led by Chiang Kai Shek, began rule by assassination and intimidation as a means of forcing peasant and worker back into the subservient status of the imperial era. The landlords and bourgeoisie, backed by Chiang's army, reconsidered history and began to regard themselves as the legitimate successors of the mandarin-bureaucrats (Chiang Kai Shek, 1947, p.233). Unions and the revolutionary peasant associations were expected to return to their traditional passive roles in private government (Townsend, 1969, pp.33-4; Lieberthal, 1973, pp.1-2).

Social conflict again became an unpleasant disturbance of harmonious rule to be avoided or repressed. Confucian doctrines of submission to authority were selectively culled and tailored to meet the needs of industrial or agricultural work discipline. Chiang Kai Shek's remarks on nation-building recall both Confucian ethics and the ideology of European fascism, as follows:

In other words if the Chughua nation [China] is to be consolidated into a strong unit for national defence, as solid as a rock, it goes without saying that individuals cannot enjoy excessive liberty as if they are loose sand. Hence . . . excessive personal liberty cannot be allowed to exist either during wartime or in the post-war period (Chiang Kai Shek, 1947, p.208)

The revolution of 1911 was halted as the new ruling alliance of (absentee) landlords and merchant-industrialists sought to hold social development and private government within a tight new order of exploitation. Changes in the political economy of both rural and urban China, however, had blurred the lines of blood and business that marked out old private governments. The division of guilds along class lines and the departure of landlords from the villages had irreparably altered the static "harmony" of imperial days. The antagonisms represented by the formation of the chambers of commerce, trade unions and by the rural outbursts of secret societies and peasant associations could not be denied.

The revival of a psuedo-Confucian state ideology and the pleas for unity in the service of nationalism were not sufficient to maintain domestic tranquility after 1927. The bourgeois and landlord classes became increasingly dependent upon the armed might of Chiang's military for the collection of crop rents, the maintenance of factory discipline and the protection of commerce.

Military garrisons were posted throughout rural China and the soldiers of the Republic became rent collectors in the face of peasant uprisings and resentment. A large and expensive police state was established in cities, as poverty and union violence constantly endangered order essential to production and business (Moore, 1966, pp.194-7; Yang, 1945; Pepper, 1971). It is time to examine this imposed regimen of law and order which preceded the reconstruction of justice under Communism.

Republican Justice: Reform and Repression amid Civil War

The laws of the Republic show the tracks of the revolution, from hesitant liberal reforms in the early years to the police state of the last two decades. Sun Yat Sen's proposed social and political equality for women found a place in the early Law of Domestic Relations. A Kuomintang legal scholar (Hung, 1934, pp.7-8) in 1933 pointed at the law with pride, saying that: "The most attractive and courageous change that has been put forth by the legislature relates to the status of women".

An examination of this exemplary KMT reform reveals that it did not abolish, but only regulated such condemned imperial practices as the arrangement of marriages by parents, concubinage and wife-beating. Under KMT law, divorce could be granted (in the absence of the husband's consent) only on such grounds as bigamy, the imprisonment of the husband, incurable disease, a proven attempt on the life of the wife or extreme cruelty. Cruelty here was defined as wife-beating proven to be so severe as to require medical treatment and so frequent as to constitute a regular pattern and render co-habitation impossible (Hung, 1934, pp.166-8, 184-7).

The labour legislation adopted by the Republic wavered along the lines of the short-lived KMT alliance. Initially the KMT was able to win workers' support with promises and an appeal to nationalist sentiments; later the organization of unions prompted a reformist period of labour legislations. Ultimately the 1927 KMT split and Chiang's rise to power produced new repressive laws directed against union independence. The history of the unequal capitalist-labour alliance in the Republic closely parallels the history of Mussolini's fascism in Italy, where the bourgeois also turned upon the workers while waving the banner of syndicalism.

The Republic granted legal protection (and, of course, considerable political power) to the chambers of commerce in 1914 (Garrett, 1970). Ten years later the KMT held its first national congress and promulgated the trade union regulations. Until this time labour unions were only considered in a penal code entitled Law for the Preservation of the Public Order (1914) and the Provisional Criminal Code of 1912. These two laws prohibited workers' meetings in the following categories:

1. When they lead to a regular and collective stoppage of work;
2. When they lead to a strike;
3. When they lead to wage demands;
4. When they lead to public disorder;
5. When they organize action attacking good morals (Lowe, 1933, pp.82-83).

Workmen who violated these laws or combined in a strike were subject to imprisonment and fines.

The 1924 national congress headed by Sun Yat Sen repealed a number of these laws and promised to prepare a body of protective legislation in support of the strong new Chinese trade unions. Compulsory arbitration was established to settle labour-management disputes. Prior to this such disputes and strikes were settled by the chambers of commerce. The government's early choice of the chambers as official peacemakers fairly represents the influence of captains of industry within the KMT (Lowe, 1933, pp.82-88; Garrett, 1970).

The first shuffling movements of the Republic towards labour protection ended with the 1927 breakdown of the bourgeois-worker alliance. In 1928 a new set of laws were enacted to regulate the settlement of disputes and labour organizations (Meijer, 1949). These laws generally favoured the interests of the chambers. Strikes organized for political purposes were prohibited, as were any workers' societies of a "dangerous" character; but even the mild safety restrictions of the factory accidents ordinance and the guidelines restricting the right to strike in factory law were denounced by employers. These laws were attacked as idealistic, unreasonable and even communistic (Lowe, 1933, pp.89-90). The enforcement of even limited protective statutes was blocked by industrialists. The protection of labour, like the equality of women and other promised social reforms, was thus "postponed" until the forces of imperialism and communism were eliminated.

Republican courts and police work

In the early freshness of its victory the revolutionary Republic promised to overturn the bureaucratic corruption of justice of old China. New regulations were passed in 1913 which required judges to complete university training in law and to pass national law examinations. The Confucian classics were rejected as irrelevant, and the first steps were taken toward the construction of a specialized professional judiciary (Wou, 1971).

An study of the available figures shows that this reform, like others of the period, had little substance beyond the written word. A great many judges were granted special exemptions from training and examinations by higher officials in the government. Most other magistrates simply ignored the new laws and remained on the bench. In Hainan province, 10% of the judges were exempted and another 60% ignored the regulations. Throughout the Republican period, legally trained judges (with university degrees) remained in a minority (one third or less). Most judges held degrees in classical Confucian studies, either purchased or earned by examination (Wou, 1971).

The continuation of old training and recruitment patterns was accompanied by the continuation of old loyalties. Most of the Republic's judges were picked from the ranks of military tribunals which sat at the bidding of local warlords or generals serving the Republic. The judges were indebted to these patrons for their nomination to the regular judiciary and for the special exemptions which excused them from legal examinations. Judges were bound by family and clan ties and felt obligated to grant special privileges to relatives (Eastman, 1971).

The few fortunate law school graduates who won appointment as Republican judges found the old imperial courtroom rackets still very much alive. Even the most determined of the new professionals were unable to make much headway against the corruption that seemed to touch every member of their court staff. The clerks demanded special "writing fees" of any citizens lodging complaints or initiating lawsuits. The maze of forms and files required to process cases confounded the unassisted magistrates; and judges who fired dishonest clerks soon found it impossible to find necessary documents (Wou, 1971).

The careers and assignments of individual judges were often cut short by changes in political boundaries and the constant warfare between Republican and warlord armies. This high turnover rate made the judges insecure and even more dependent upon the old office hands who stayed on while the magistrates changed with every battlefield decision (Wou, 1971).

The police continued as leading racketeers under the Republic. Those sent to arrest and detain the accused returned empty-handed when well-oiled by rich gentry or prosperous bandit defendants, while innocent men who refused to pay the "shoe money" for runners' travelling expenses were often arrested. The Republican government would not support their lone magistrates with a body of professional paid policemen and so the judge was forced to rely upon these unpaid, untrained, unsupervised and notoriously predatory runners. These unofficial court officers handled arrests, subpoenas, and routine police work. A single court might have as many as 100 such semi-official volunteer servants of the law who survived entirely from the proceeds of bribery, blackmail and torture (Anonymous Magistrate, 1920, pp.5-10).

Republican jails were true to the rustic and informal patterns of Republican law enforcement. A contemporary judge recalled that:

> Upon arrival a prisoner is asked for bribes; if he refuses he is put in chains.
>
> Meals are later cut off [to prisoners refusing blackmail demands] and friends bringing food are kept out . . . Prisoners are, without a single exception, as thin as skeletons.

The judge also described how female prisoners were usually kept in the homes of jail matrons, where they were forced into prostitution by the matron in exchange for food. Many run-away girls ended up at these brothels which catered especially to the clerks and runners of the court staff (Anonymous Magistrate, 1920, pp.44-8).

Most judges glanced aside at such practices but even those who despised the rackets were helpless to prevent them. Magistrates bringing these abuses to the attention of their superiors were often disciplined or even fired. The Republic ignored corruption and would not pay for better help; the judge observed:

> The wages of jailers are too meagre for [the jailers'] food alone; so they have to take it out of the prisoners (Anonymous Magistrate, 1920, pp.3-5)

The hopelessness of reform under the Republican court arrangements prompted a number of progressive judges to take their complaints to the general public (or more accurately to urban-educated public). The judge quoted above prepared a series of muck-raking newspaper editorials which began as follows:

During the now defunct Ch'ing [imperial] regime I hated more than anything the corrupt and money-loving officials who never had any regard for the welfare of the country and the people . . . Therefore I determined not to enter officialdom as long as the Ch'ing dynasty existed. Upon inauguration of the Republic, I thought the conditions must be better than formerly, and so I accepted the post of Magistrate.

Officially some of the new magistrates have already reorganized their staff while others retain the old system. The so-called reorganized systems are only reorganizations in name, for beyond the names of the different departments no other reform can be found. When a Yamen [court] has given new names to its different departments and allotted its men to each of them, it sends a report to its superiors that a reorganization has been effected (Anonymous Magistrate, 1920, pp.3-4, 171)

The machinery of Republican justice, like that of the Empire before, ran on a fuel of bribery and blackmail. It was a fuel that few could afford. The judge quoted above finally despaired of reform and was unable to do more than echo the old imperial judges and counsel the people to avoid the official Republican courts. Throughout even the early progressive years of the Republic the law was bent to accommodate the wealthy and influential circles of city and countryside. Social reform legislation aimed at eliminating opium-smoking, for example, was not enforced in landlord, merchant, or industrialist homes, and gambling found a haven there as well.

In the midst of this period Roscoe Pound, Dean of Harvard Law School, was invited to evaluate the Republican legal system. After an on-site inspection tour of courts and jails he published an astonishing report which concludes in part as follows:

I have read much in [Chinese] lay periodicals, newspapers, and the English press in China of the inefficiency and corruption of Chinese judges. Careful observation has failed to disclose any such condition (Tsao-Wen-yen, 1953a, p.3)

The silent ruling class advantages of bribery and law-enforcement practices were written into the official magistrate's instructions after 1927. The Republican handbook of 1928 pointedly advises judges to maintain close relationships with the land-owning gentry of their court districts. The robed defenders of justice were encouraged to pay frequent visits to local gentry and to attend their weddings, funerals and social functions (Wou, 1971). The handbook was, of course, published after the 1927 split in the KMT over the issues of social reform. The Republican Constitution had by this date been shelved, and there was little remaining of the few trembling judicial reforms of the early Republic.

The failure of liberalism

The collapse of social reform was inevitable given the political weakness of the liberal strategy. The intellectual liberals who led the 1911 revolution simply did not have the broad political support and involvement of the Chinese people. The liberals kept to the cities and the small pockets of the intelligentsia and were unwilling to confront the landlords, industrialists and generals.

The only significant exception to this condition of liberal isolation may be found in the May Fourth Movement of 1919. All China reacted in spontaneous anger to the news of the Versailles Treaty ending World War I on that day. For a brief time the liberals enjoyed national backing in their denunciation of China's government for its diplomatic humiliation at Versailles (Chen, J. T., 1970, pp.75-79) Ultimately the study groups, demonstrations and published debates of the May Fourth Movement died down, having led to the formation of the Chinese Communist Party, but the liberals remained as isolated and power-less as before (Mao Tse-tung, 1969).

A clean-up and rebuilding of justice was possible only if the Republican government was willing to dismiss the political lackeys of generals and gentry, and instead pay for a staff of clerks and policemen bound by professional standards of liberal reform. Likewise, unless the Republic moved to simplify the ancient trial process and standardize files and legal forms, the rich and the corrupt would con-tinue to avoid the punishments of the law and would profit by the manipulation of legal procedures and corrupt court staffs. The isolated liberals could not bring the government to provide the money and legislation for basic reforms.

The old ruling classes of China, the landlords and the militarists, were com-fortable with the old legal system of ragged procedures and bribe-hungry officials. The liberals, even with the backing of some "progressive industrialists" (who were the latest and weakest addition to the ruling class circles), could not persuade the older aristocrats of sword and property to accept a new brand of justice. The sleek professional system proposed by the liberals would have favoured the capitalists over the older ruling classes and would have left fewer handles for the traditionally crude manipulation of justice by men of means. The old powers of gentry and generals were too set in their ways to learn the new skills of handling a professional justice, and too dominant with the ruling Republican circle to be pushed into the strange progressive reforms of the liberals.

The 1922 Coup and Chinese Fascism

The 1927 coup of Chiang split off the weak liberal influence from the govern-ment and forced the handful of progressive businessmen to accept the dominance of landlord and military leadership. Chiang called upon the official justice of courts and police to back up the army and the gangster forces in repressing all "subversive elements". The judiciary, true to unbroken ancient traditions, acted as the willing tool of the political champion. The enlarged police began huge political raids, and the courts called for the death and imprisonment of troublesome unionists, socialists, communists, student no-goods and over-zealous liberals (Pepper, 1971). Special laws were enacted for the "Suppression of Bandits" and these were used against political opponents throughout the country. Judges were given medals, merits and promotions for the capture, sentencing and execution of communists and other subversives. Secret police repressed dissent among students and workers in the cities (Wou, 1971, pp.34-36).

The government attempted to control unrest and disorder in the cities with a new urban version of the old village private government (pao-chia). Households were grouped in batches of 10, 100 and 1000 families with elected representatives who reported to the local police on all area activities. This urban arrangement was adopted from a similar one imposed by the Japanese invaders, and it did not allow for the influence of the local residents even in decisions concerning their own neighbourhood. The KMT government also organized voluntary self-defence bodies which, along with the pao-chia system, was designed to help the police hunt and destroy "bandits", and it had no voice in larger politics. The citizenry did not support this imperial-style private government and the pao-chia was not much help to the military government (Schurmann, 1966b, pp.410-412; Yang, 1945).

Chiang called also upon the secret societies of city crime syndicates to join in this government by force. The syndicates operated brothels, opium dens and extortion rackets, but drew most of their money and manpower from the poorest unorganized labourers. The syndicates controlled the unskilled labour pools of coolies and the gangsters recognized the independent unions as their bitter enemy. The gangster bosses, seeking to weaken unions and gain government bribes and favours, quickly joined the conservative forces of the KMT. The powerful Green Gang of Shanghai was responsible for many of the unionist-Communist murders ordered by Chiang in 1927. The secret gangster societies assisted the police state policies of the Republic in a number of cities. A great many KMT officials began their careers in the secret societies and maintained close ties with syndicates while in office (Lieberthal, 1973; Schurmann, 1966b, pp.368-70).

Despite the enormous concentration of law, monies, police and gangsters, the Republic was unable to hold China in check. The invasion of Japan drained off a good deal of the government's forces, but the post-war years were no easier for Chiang Kai Shek. The Republic was never to create a unified disciplined citizenry. Government control remained a spotty patchwork of police, army and gangster forces with but little recognition or assistance from the populace.

The dependency of the Republic upon the interests of landlord and industrialist put social reform, and therefore popular support, out of reach (Gillin, 1970).

The Republic of 1911 had indeed aged quickly. After only 16 years the KMT looked a lot like the sick old man of the Empire so rudely tumbled in 1911. Chiang's call for national unity under a Confucian ethic of submission seemed to echo from the walls of the Imperial Palace in Peking. The promised constitutional and judicial reforms were abandoned, and law remained the faithful servant of the privileged few. The corruption of the old Empire was easily equalled by the officials of the KMT (Eastman, 1971).

Unfortunately the old imperial robes did not quite fit the new rulers, for the fabric had shrunk a little in the wash of economic change. The Chinese people and their institutions of private government were not the same and no amount of coercion or propaganda could alter the changes in popular thought which had occurred.

The frustrations of the Kuomintang were closely watched by the exiles in the hills. Driven from the cities, these "bandits" were to draw strength from the very social changes which so enraged and bedevilled the Republic of Chiang Kai Shek. They carried the socialist ideology of murdered union leaders to the disgruntled peasants of the countryside.

The guerrillas of Mao Tse-tung were to form a new order, meshing mass politics with a Chinese brand of Marxism. Private government was mobilized and further transformed to be the political and economic mainstay of Chinese Communism. Short on arms, food and money the Red leadership would come to depend upon the will and energy of a peasant population which had for centuries been dealt with out of politics. It was to be quite a gamble.

Part II

The Dialectical Path of Justice in the People's Republic of China

4   *Popular Revolution and the Creation of People's Justice*

The decision to bring the public masses and their private governments into the affairs of national politics was crucial to the later development of popular justice in China. In 1928, however, it was a forced decision made by a mangled and unsure Communist Party. Earlier strategies of political manoeuvre and limited urban uprisings had ended with the slaughter of Communists throughout the country. The seven-year-old military government of Chiang Kai Shek remained unshaken and prospects for rebuilding the wrecked Party in the face of government repression were bleak.

Communist Strategy before Mao

Until 1928 the Party had largely followed the suggestions of the Soviet Russian Comintern, and had for many years worked within the KMT Party and the government of Sun Yat Sen's Republic. That uneasy arrangement ended with Chiang's military coup in 1927. The Nationalist Party, as a result of the coup, split into two hostile factions. Chiang's conservative wing was opposed by a leftist coalition of liberals and Communists. Both factions claimed to be the legitimate national government of China.

The Comintern ordered the Chinese Communists to remain "legal", and to seize control of the leftist government (then mainly in the hands of the liberals). The scheme was to stand behind the nationalist tradition of the old KMT Party, and to raise a new Red Army to oppose Chiang in the name of Sun Yat Sen's reformist programme. The Communists did not prove to be agile political acrobats. The take-over was badly botched, and the liberals reacted by expelling the Communists from the progressive KMT coalition.

The Communists, alone and unprepared for military combat, were an easy target for Chiang's armies. The liberals long remembered the attempted power grab by their ex-partners. Few liberals made any efforts to help the endangered Communists in 1927, or at any later time before the collapse of the military government in 1949. Chiang, on the other hand, could count on the generous backing of industrialists and urban gangster bosses who were quite ready to bankroll an attack on the militant trade unions which were the main force of the Chinese Communist Party in the 1920s.

The survivors of the 1927 anti-Communist and anti-union massacres staged a series of uprisings in China's major cities. This tactic was even more disastrous than the attempted power seizure within the KMT left wing. The Communist-led workers were poorly armed and their isolated revolts were easily crushed by Chiang's troops. Exhausted and discredited by failure, the Communist leadership turned at last, in 1928, to a new and unorthodox strategy of peasant revolution. It was a strategy long advocated and recently demonstrated by a minor leader called Mao Tse-tung.

While the main Communist efforts were concentrated on sparking the worker rebellions in the cities, Mao had been busy promoting revolution among the uneducated farmers of the countryside. He was able to establish base areas and peasant armed forces in a number of southern provinces. The collapse of the city revolution left Mao with the only significant Red strongholds, and the Party leadership was forced to recognize the possibilities and importance of the peasant revolution.

This peasant strategy, though ultimately successful, faced a number of serious problems. Mao described initial peasant reaction to the Communists as follows:

> Wherever the Red Army goes, it finds the masses cold and reserved, only after propaganda and agitation do they slowly rouse themselves (Mao Tse-tung, 1928, Vol. 1, p.97)

This peasant apathy ended when the Communists picked up the old Sun Yat Sen cry of "land to the tillers". People who had resentfully paid rent-crops to landlords and warlord armies were soon ready to fight for a chance at land ownership.

Enthusiasm for land reform would not be enough however to defeat the power of the military government. The inward-looking localism of peasant villagers and their inexperience of large-scale political efforts made it difficult for Communists to organize co-ordinated peasant action. Clearly the traditional Party style of leadership by ideological argument and tight revolutionary discipline would not work among the largely illiterate and village-centred peasants. It was, indeed, this cultural backwardness and political inexperience which prompted the old line Communist leaders to disregard the peasants as a leading revolutionary force. Such urban party leaders as Liu Shao chi regarded the peasants as "children" who needed workers and party leaders to "take them by the hand and lead them" (Schram, 1971b, p.3).

Mass Line, Elite Line and Revolutionary Politics

Mao and his handful of party cadres created a new style of political leadership in working among the peasants. This style carried the Communists through the Civil War and it remains today the central ideology of political practice in China. It has been fundamental to the creation and practice of popular justice and Communism. Mao and others who created the ideology call it the "mass line".

Mass line began in the countryside where Mao first recruited a few peasants into the weakened Communist Party. These new cadres found that the traditional Communist methods of tight ideological arguments and rigid party discipline (which worked fairly well among city workers and unionists) worked not at all among the historically apathetic and illiterate farmers. The party organizers soon abandoned the old tactics and tried new approaches which made use of their own peasant backgrounds.

The new mass line methods emphasized sensitivity to local conditions in the villages and party cadres lived among the farmers, sharing in local problems and village labours. Party members were required to move beyond the narrow confines of Party discipline, and would be a flexible and creative link between ideology and practice, between party leadership and villagers. The central importance of shared life styles and close Party-public communication is frequently discussed by Mao, who asserted in 1943 that:

> In all the practical work of our Party, all correct leadership is necessarily 'from the masses, to the masses'. This means: take the ideas of the masses (scattered and unsystematic ideas) and concentrate them (through study turn them into concentrated and systematic ideas), then go to the masses and propagate and explain these ideas until the masses embrace them as their own, hold fast to them and translate them into action, and test the correctness of these ideas in such action (Mao Tse-tung, 1943, pp.226-7)

The mass line is not only a leadership style, but is also an organizational method. The practice of mass line organizational principles enabled the Party to translate the peasant desire for land into a co-ordinated political movement. The basic strategy was to pull the farmers away from the narrow confines of traditional private governments (and private justice) maintained by village and clan. The Communist promise of land did the pulling, and great voluntary organizations of peasants were formed to replace old private governments and to mobilize the country folk for revolutionary action.

The most important of these voluntary public organizations were the "peasant associations". The mass line emphasis on direct public participation dictated that these associations be headed by elected peasant representatives and that the associations be granted considerable power. These mass organizations provided the people with political education made relevant to local culture and local needs.

The People's Government established in the Red-held areas also followed mass line principles of popular representation and decentralization. Village chiefs were drawn into larger politics as they were recognized as Communist officials with local powers. Peasant organizations also elected local representatives to serve in the government, and weekly meetings between representatives and constituents insured that politics would remain an intimate and active concern of the rural public.

To summarize briefly, the central goal of mass line is public political education and the total mobilization of the people for mass political action. The essential features of mass line as an organizational method are decentralization and popular participation. The central features of mass line as a leadership style are shared Party-mass life styles and a continuous Party-people flow of ideas. The development of an elevated political elite is contradictory to mass line, since it would undermine the mass-Party unity which is crucial to mass mobilization (Wylie, 1972, pp.8-11; Wheelwright and Macfarlane, 1970).

It must be pointed out that the mass line does not amount to direct popular democracy. Political initiative in such national matters as economic planning and political and military priorities remains largely in the hands of the top party and government leaders, but mass line principles do demand that the political leadership listen to the masses, understand mass needs and share the simple life style of the people.

Leaders who put on the elite trappings of special luxuries, exalted status and a bureaucratic working style mark themselves as targets for popular attack. Mass organizations of the people supervise the work of officials and periodically these voluntary citizens organizations mobilize their membership to criticize and remove incompetent or arrogant political leaders. Replacements for those elitist officials who violate the mass line and arouse this popular reaction are generally chosen from among the ranks of mass organization activists. Such are the rough and ready checks and balances of mass line leadership, which have caused not a few jolts and turns in the course of justice and politics under Communism.

Party discipline and the "bureaucratic" line

Opposing the mass line (though in a discreet fashion) were many traditional Party leaders who emphasized Party discipline and saw the ideal Party member as the passive instrument of his superiors. The Party member was to stand above the masses by virtue of his "high Communist morality" and his sophisticated political understanding. Liu Shao chi was such a traditionalist, hardened in long struggles as a union leader, and convinced that party discipline and tight party organization were the central necessities of revolutionary politics (Schram, 1971b, pp.4-6).

Liu's book on "How To Be A Good Communist" (1939) recalls the Buddhist code of "li". Liu and the Confucians both emphasize submission before authority and the moral superiority of political elites. Confucian codes and Liu Shao chi alike call for teaching through moral example, rather than the mass line method of "leading through close contact and Party-mass exchange of ideas". Liu described his notion of the ideal Communist as follows:

> A Party member's personal interests must be unconditionally subordinated to the interests of the party.

> He is the most sincere, most candid and happiest of men. Because he has no private axe to grind, and nothing he cannot tell others, he has no problems of personal gain or loss and no personal anxieties other than for the interests of the party and the revolution.

> For the sake of the Party and the revolution he can be most forgiving and tolerant towards comrades and can suffer wrong in the general interest, even enduring misunderstanding and humiliation without bitterness if the occasion so demands.

> Members of the Party are no ordinary people, but the awakened vanguard fighters of the proletariat (Liu, 1939, *in* Chai, 1969, p.211)

For Liu and the traditional party leaders the line separating the party from the public was inviolate. Liu argued that:

> If any Party member has an opinion about the leading organs of the Party, or any Party organization he can offer criticism only to the proper Party organization. He is not permitted to speak irresponsibly among the masses (Liu, 1941, *in* Chai, 1969, pp.211-12)

The political and moral "superiority" of such leaders has generally earned for them special luxuries and social privileges—in Communist China and elsewhere. This leadership style may be called the "bureaucratic elite line", and is basically a political and philosophical opponent of "mass line".

The conflict between these two lines was not fully resolved during the Civil War. The struggle over leadership ideologies has been a fundamental condition of Communist politics since Mao first challenged the unionist party leadership in 1927. Liu Shao chi, bludgeoned with his own words and thrown from power in the recent Cultural Revolution, was not the first casualty of this central struggle. There will surely be others in the future.

The stakes of the conflict and the distance between the two lines inevitably grow larger as China becomes more industrialized and more socially complex. The mass line aim of uniting all China for revolutionary progress becomes more difficult as state bureaucracies grow. Bureaucratic stagnation has been resisted, but bureaucratic growth seems to shadow economic progress and especially centralized industrial planning. The need for technological expan-pansion has threatened to widen cultural differences between city and country, between intellectual and worker. Political education and the deepening of popular confidence in socialist progress is crucial to the survival of the mass line, particularly among those whose education or political position makes them an elite which might demand special bureaucratic elite privileges.

Except for the Civil War period, the conflict between lines was relatively quiet and limited to contradictions within the Party. The simplicity of wartime government and the obvious need to mobilize public support gave the mass line a big edge over its opposing elite ideology. The Party and government established in the Red base areas closely followed the principles of popular participation, decentralization, Party-mass interchange and mass mobilization, all of which are the stock and trade of the mass line.

From Private Government
to Mass Mobilization

Upon arriving in a new area the Red Army usually found a great many grumbling peasants but very few landlords. Well-acquainted with the Communist custom of celebrating land confiscations with the hanging of a few class enemies, most of the esteemed gentry took occasion to pack shortly before the appearance of the first Red soldiers. Their absence simplified changes in boundary lines, but at any rate it would have been a simple matter for the new commissar to survey the area and dictate redistribution orders from his headquarters. In a matter of days the Red Army could thus grant land to the landless and win a great many friends among the local folk. The Communists chose *not* to do this.

The principles of mass line were considered more important than the obvious efficiency of a quick bureaucratic party decision. The Communists chose instead to put the tasks of land reform in the hands of the local masses. In this way the land reform programme could be more sensitive to local conditions, and the peasants would be introduced into revolutionary politics.

The recruitment of private government

The Communists called upon the local private governments of the countryside to organize the peasants and draw them into the business of land reform. Private government, as previously discussed, had undergone tremendous changes even before the Civil War. The traditionally passive clan and village organizations had begun to resist the authority of landlord and often hid crops from warlord soldiers. Ruined and landless peasants formed a number of secret societies and through them began a rag-tag military attack upon all sorts of local and regional authorities.

Communist success in attracting these local groups varied tremendously. The secret societies, promising allies because of their military experience, were tightly controlled by their individual chieftains. These leaders enjoyed considerable comfort from their positions, as they accepted "gifts" from the Chiang government, protection "fees" from the villagers and open bribes from local gentry and area warlords. The society bosses were unwilling to end this most profitable flexibility and embrace the Red banners in the interests of class solidarity. Communist agents who attempted to talk the society rank and file into the revolutionary movement were discreetly and efficiently murdered (Chesneaux, 1972, p.208).

The formation of mass organizations

The clan and village organizations were less hostile to the revolution, but were frozen politically by their superstitious beliefs and fear of government-landlord reprisals should the Reds leave. The Communists recognized these problems and began to organize a new type of private government, the peasant associations, which were closely tied to the politics of revolution. These peasant associations (also called "peasant unions") were charged with surveying landlord holdings and with sharing out confiscated lands to the villagers. Such an important responsibility, coupled with the backing of the Red Army, soon established the peasant associations as the leading local government in the Red base areas (Myrdal, 1965, pp.48-51; Van der Sprenkel et al., 1951, pp.160-164; Chand, 1958, pp.65-68).

The peasant associations became the workhorse of the revolutionary struggle. They pulled the rural population into mass campaigns and special projects aimed at strengthening war and production efforts. Such projects included warbond drives, the formation of producers' co-operatives and political education programmes (Townsend, 1969, p.50). Finally, these organizations served as the judge, jury and executioner in the attack upon landlords and counter-revolutionaries, and were the first institutions of popular justice (as will be discussed later).

The shortage of material resources in the besieged Red areas prompted the Communists to extend the principles of mass line to production as well as politics. The mobilization of masses of normally unproductive citizens was accomplished through new mass organizations of women, students and soldiers. These new associations formed work teams for farming, construction and political education, and enabled the base areas to survive despite poor soil, bad weather and a lack of industrial plants. In explaining Communist successes, the Chairman of the (Red) Border Region pointed out that by 1939 every citizen in the region belonged to at least one mass organization and many belonged to two or more (Selden, 1967; Lin Po Chu *in* Townsend, 1969, p.61).

The official Red government in the base areas, like the mass organizations, reflected the principles of the mass line. A three-level hierarchy of government stressed close public-government relations and direct popular participation in political affairs. The highest level of government was dominated by party members who were mostly ex-peasants. Mass organizations and village groups elected representatives to form the lower levels of government. These deputies were required to report back to the people every 10 days. With one representative for every 13 workers and every 50 peasants, government was an intimate part of village life. Village chiefs were drawn into larger politics as deputies of the Red government. Mass meetings were held to discuss policies and to mobilize mass support for important tasks. Party members were instructed by Mao to "attend to the daily problems of the masses", to adopt the life style of the people and to work alongside them (Waller, 1973; Townsend, 1969, p.48; Crook and Crook, 1959, pp.94-108).

In sum, the private government of rural China was transformed by the application of the mass line and the pressure of war and economic change. Clan and village groups were drawn into the new peasant associations and mass organizations by the promise of land reform. The historically apathetic and powerless peasants were pulled into the Red government and the politics of revolution, not by ideological argument, but through elected lay representatives, constant Party-public dialogue and participation in mass projects supporting production and warfare.

At the same time the party and the Red government stepped down to "go among the masses . . . and solve their problems of salt, rice, shelter, clothing and childbirth". Decentralization and attention to local conditions was stressed in creating a people's government closely tied to the masses. Party members and officials who governed in a bureaucratic manner, divorced from the public, were roundly criticized by the masses and the Maoist leadership alike (Mao Tse-tung, 1943, *in* Chai, 1969, pp.224-229; Mao Tse-tung, 1943, Vol. I, pp.147-150).

The politics of the Red base areas were clearly a break from over 2000 years of

Chinese national politics. Private governments of clan and village had been traditionally passive, village-centred arrangements, controlled by local land-lords, scholars and conservative elder males. The national government had for centuries been unconcerned with the welfare of the general public, and depended upon the support of landlord, bureaucrat and (most recently) warlord classes. Under Communism, mass organizations and peasant associ-ations replaced the passive private government. These new organizations mobilized the public and drew the masses into politics. The mass line directed the revolutionary government to reflect mass interests and to unite with mass organizations for political action. Together these changes form China's first popular government which, coupled with the promise of land reform, was an irresistible force.

Land Reform: Mass Action and Social Justice

The system of justice created in the base areas reflected both the principles of the mass line and the violent class struggle of the Civil War. The Communist Government, like the Imperial and Nationalist Governments before it, openly regarded law as a political instrument to be used for political education and political control. The primary task of Red justice during the Civil War was to find and attack the political enemies of the revolution. Landlords, agents of Chiang's government and others regarded as counter-revolutionaries were the targets of a justice which emphasized political ideology and class background over abstract legal notions of guilt and innocence. Crimes committed by workers or peasants and crimes of a non-political nature (e.g. theft) were often handled through mediation and were regarded as less serious offences.

Not surprisingly, the peasant associations played a central role in the new Red justice which aimed to destroy the political power and prestige of the landlord class. Upon entering a new region the People's Government and the peasant association prepared a complete census of the area, with a separate list for all known "evil gentry" and counter-revolutionaries (including both KMT agents and those who collaborated with the Japanese). The local associations set up "Committees for Settling Accounts" whose business it was to interrogate landlords and to organize demonstrations calling for the punishment of the former gentry class. The landlords were forced to kneel on the ground while peasants smeared them with cow dung and were paraded through the villages while wearing tall paper dunce caps. The effect of this preliminary street theatre was to shatter the aura of prestige which the educated gentry enjoyed among the largely illiterate peasants, and to dramatize the arrival of a new day in the countryside (Yang, 1945, pp.137-45; Pepper, 1971; Mao Tse-tung, 1927, Vol. I, pp.26-29, 37-38; Yu, 1964, pp.43-4; Wei, 1955, p.23).

Special tribunals — the courts of popular justice

The rural class struggle soon went beyond demonstrations as the People's Government established special tribunals and "adjudication committees" at all levels of government. These temporary judges investigated the history of local landlords or counter-revolutionaries and called mass meetings where peasants denounced these enemies. They were empowered to "exterminate local bullies and bad gentry", and records indicate that they were not bashful in this work.

Wartime justice is usually severe, and the intensity of the class struggle behind China's long Civil War prompted more than a few executions on both sides of the battle lines. There are few courtroom statistics from the Red base areas, but the Communists admit to the execution of 1822 landlords over one period of several months (Chung, 1957, *in* Leng, 1967, p.3).

While death sentences were passed on the most hated or most dangerous enemies, the vast majority of captured counter-revolutionaries and class enemies were spared and subjected mainly to intense criticism and political education. The police, courts and mass organizations devoted countless man-hours to the ideological re-moulding and social reform of "enemy classes". The often-repeated official policy toward political enemies was stated as follows in 1941:

> . . . with regard to traitors, except those resolutely unwilling to repent, a policy of magnanimity should be adopted toward them regardless of their past history. Efforts should be made to convert them and to provide them with a future in politics and livelihood. They should not be wantonly killed, manhandled, forced to give themselves up, or coerced into writing statements of repentance (Yang, 1957, *in* Leng, 1967, p.13)

No doubt class enemies and KMT officials were still roughed up on occasion, but the general emphasis was on education and political persuasion. The Communists had tremendous success in this work. It usually took only a few weeks to turn captured KMT soldiers around, and only a little longer to convert enemy officers and lesser KMT bureaucrats. Convinced that the Communist revolution was a necessary inevitability, these ex-opponents made excellent Red soldiers in the Civil War and later in Korea. Indeed, as Mao often pointed out, the KMT ranks were the chief source of army replacements. Class enemies, such as landlords, were more slowly reformed than KMT soldiers and ex-landlords were usually required to work as common peasants while attending lengthy political education and criticism/self-criticism meetings. After five years of good work and evidence of political reform, the landlord was eligible for full civil rights and "People's Status" as a citizen-farmer (Crook and Crook, 1959, pp.90-115).

Throughout the Civil War the Party leadership encouraged popular justice in both the punishment and educational reform of class and political enemies. Mao in 1927 explained the significance of the first popular justice campaigns in the provinces of Hunan, as follows:

> True, the peasants are in a sense "unruly" in the countryside. Supreme in authority, the peasant association allows the landlord no say and sweeps away his prestige. This amounts to striking the landlord down to the dust and keeping him there.

> [The peasants] fine the local tyrants and evil gentry, they demand contributions from them and they smash their sedan chairs. People swarm into the house of local tyrants who are against the peasant association, slaughter their pigs and consume their grain . . . At the slightest provocation they make arrests . . .

> Doing whatever they like and turning everything upside down, they have created a kind of terror in the countryside. This is what some people call 'going too far' or 'exceeding the proper limits', or 'really too much' (Mao Tse-tung, 1927, Vol. I, pp.35-39)

Mao turns aside objections to the "terror in the countryside" and asserts that popular justice under the mass line is indeed true and fair justice:

> The peasants are clear-sighted. Who is bad and who is not quite so vicious, who deserves severe punishment and who deserves to be let off lightly — the peasants keep clear accounts and very seldom has the punishment exceeded the crime (Mao Tse-tung, 1927, Vol. I, p.28)

This faith in the wisdom of common folk must be the starting point of any popular justice, be it Chinese or American. If justice is recognized as a clearly political institution then it logically follows that a democratic popular revolution should create a non-professional, locally controlled popular justice. The opposing emphasis on "orderliness" and professional standards follows from the view that law can be objective, and can therefore provide the basis for a scientific justice free from political considerations. The People's Government of the Civil War created a popular justice which was clearly politicized and which promoted class struggle between "unruly" peasants and landlord class.

Civil War Justice and Crimes among the People

A justice which emphasizes class conflict and openly sides with one class in attacking another cannot claim to be objective and, in fact, usually writes class differences into the law itself. Such was the case in Civil War China where two distinct brands of justice developed. While "local bullies, evil gentry and counter-revolutionaries" faced humiliation, mass trials and sometimes mass executions, the "people" were handled in a gentler way by another justice which emphasized persuasion and social pressure. This popular justice for the people, like that directed against class enemies, followed the principles of mass line and involved mass organizations and locally elected mass representatives.

The Communists meshed socialist ideology with the ancient practices of mediation in settling conflicts among the peasants and workers outside the courtroom. Quarrels between husbands and wives were brought before the peasant associations or the mass organizations of women (later the Women's Federation). On-the-job problems of labour discipline were handled through "comrades' adjudication committees" formed by local labour unions, while land disputes among the peasants were settled by the peasant association. Neighbours and family elders continued to serve as local mediators, but mass organizations replaced the old clan or village association as the social setting for mediation (Ma Hsi Wu, *in* Leng, 1967, p.12; Mao Tse-tung, 1927, Vol. I, pp.34-35, 44-45; Cohen, 1971, pp.297-299).

In resolving such conflicts "among the folks" the popular justice representatives emphasized persuasion rather than punishment. The Communists regarded these problems of internal order not as crimes, but as indicators of the unsuccessful social practice and incorrect political thought. The discussion and settlement of these problems was considered an important matter and mass representatives devoted a great deal of time and effort to mediation. The application of political ideology to such non-criminal matters transforms simple mediation into political education, and public meetings were frequently called to hear mediators discuss the application of socialist morality to examples of wife-beating, forced marriage or loafing at work (Lin Po Chiu, 1956, *in* Gudoshnikov, 1957, p.17).

Mediation was emphasized by leading party legal experts as part of the "New Democratic Working Style" of the mass line. Civil cases and minor criminal offences were increasingly resolved through mediation. The Communist People's Government reported that 18% of all civil cases were settled by mediation in 1942, a figure which had grown to 40% in 1943, and 48% in 1944 (Ma Hsi Wu, 1957).

Communist mediation does in some ways resemble the ancient practice of mediation under the Empire, in that both the Communists and those earlier peacemakers disliked punishment and instead relied upon directed social pressure and long discussions in settling conflicts. Mass organizations, like the private governments before them, called upon their members to criticize and pressure those who violated group guidelines. Both mass organizations and private government created their own internal arrangements for settling disputes among their membership.

The Communists clearly break with the past in their application of socialist ideology to decision-making in mediation. For the ancient mediator the aim of mediation was simply to soothe tempers and preserve the folkways of the local private government. The surest method in imperial mediation was compromise and submission. The Communist mediator is tied to socialist ideology, the Party and government, and compromise with those allegiances is out of the question. There is a right way dictated by "socialist" morality and a wrong way arising from the "incorrect thought of bourgeois ideas". The settlement of social conflict, like the decisions of production or politics, can follow only one of these lines, and thus Communist mediation comes to insist on struggle, persuasion and reform rather than settle for easy compromise (Lubman, 1967, p.1287; Lin Po Chiu, 1956, *in* Gudoshnikov, 1957, p.17).

The link between popular justice and the larger affairs of national politics was basic to land reform, the suppression of landlords and counter-revolutionaries, as well as to mediation "among the people". It is this political-legal linkage, along with the transformation of private government into mass organizations, which changed private justice into popular justice.

The Beginnings of Law and Bureaucracy

The development of popular justice was accompanied by the first hesitant motions toward the formation of a professional Communist justice system. The dominance of the mass line and the instability of Civil War politics slowed the growth of regular justice agencies, but a number of laws were passed and the skeleton of court police and procurate organizations was formed. These first semi-professional arrangements were not intended to replace popular justice, but were designed chiefly to regulate and refine the mass role in Red justice.

People's Courts and professional justice

Alongside the temporary special tribunals and local adjudication committees established by the peasant associations was formed a patchwork system of workers' and peasants' courts. These more permanent courts (later called "People's Courts") were created by the national People's Government in the Red-held areas. They were supervised by a Supreme Court of Chinese Workers and Peasants and later (1934) organized under a national Department of Justice (Gudoshnikov, 1957, p.10). These more regular and bureaucratically controlled courts existed alongside the temporary and popular tribunals throughout the Civil War. The People's Government sought to maintain some discipline in both popular and regular (People's) courts, and the central justice bureaux enacted regulations to prohibit the use of torture or corporal punishment (Leng, 1967, pp.7-8).

The People's Courts were, however, certainly not removed from the influence of mass line. Many judges were elected by the mass organizations, and sessions of the People's Courts were public and often attended by crowds of peasants and People's Liberation Army (PLA) soldiers. The spectators were encouraged to come forward and testify, question the accused, or address those assembled. Even these "regular" courts were seen as classrooms for mass political education (Townsend, 1969, p.59; Gudoshnikov, 1957, p.9; Cohen, 1968a, p.476).

The People's Courts also participated in the class struggle of the revolution and followed the class viewpoint of the temporary popular tribunals. The official law of the People's Government specified different sentences for people convicted of the same offence but belonging to different classes (Blaustein, 1962). Punishments for landlords or other class enemies were generally more severe than those imposed on workers or peasants.

The Chinese Reds borrowed rather freely from the Soviet Russians in the construction of their legal system. The creation of a body of People's Assessors was among the first of these imported practices, and it followed the Civil War emphasis on mass line. Mass organizations, army units and production centres in the Red base areas were entitled to elect a number of these unpaid assessors who were called to sit as judges alongside the "regular" professional judges of the People's Courts (Leng, 1967, pp.16-17; Gudoshnikov, 1957, p.14; Cowen, 1962). Assessors were often serving as special representatives in a given sort of case, thus trade unions elected assessors to deal with labour discipline cases, assessors from women's unions were called in for cases involving violations of the new revolutionary marriage laws guaranteeing women's economic, social and political equality, and peasant associations sent assessors to help decide land disputes (Cowen, 1962; Leng, 1967, p.16). In all cases the assessors were expected to serve as the direct representatives of the lay public and to familiarize the professional judges with local conditions.

Lin Po Chiu, Chairman of the Red Border Area People's Government, reported to the National People's Political Council in 1939 that all judicial organs based their work on the following three principles:

1) Absence of formalism in the judgement of cases; especially, accessibility of the trial proceedings to the people;

2) Trial publicity, participation of the people in the administration of justice through the organization of courts at public assemblies and the inclusion of people's representatives in the composition of courts;

3) Institution of political education for persons accused of perpetrating a crime in the conviction that this is the principal work of the court, and the strictist prohibition of torture and corporal punishment (Lin Po Chiu, *in* Gudoshnikov, 1957, p.14)

Clearly, the Civil War courts were a long way from the sombre ritual of professional justice which one encounters in a courtroom in a modern capitalist country, or even in the USSR for that matter. Even the regular People's Courts were quite "popular" in having open procedures and lay judges. Political ideology served as the supreme law of the land and class struggle was written into legal and courtroom practice. The Communists to this day describe law enforcement and adjudication as political-legal work. The dominance of ideology and the mass line ethic in the working style of the courts was nearly complete, and there is little evidence of scientific or objective judicial standards appearing in the decisions of even the professional judges.

Police work and the department of public order

Police work during the Civil War was largely in the hands of the revolutionary army (PLA), local militia units and the Department of Public Order officers. It is unfortunate that so little attention has been paid to the study of police work, since it is in China (as elsewhere) a central part of the criminal justice system. The army and militia were most active in border regions, while the more secure Red areas were patrolled mainly by Public Order personnel.

Like the judge, the Civil War policeman was most concerned with finding and crushing enemies of the revolution. Landlords and ex-landlords, as well as those who had served as officers in the KMT army or government, could expect to hear from the police of the Department of Public Order (provided the peasants did not get there first). Normally the police were responsible only for arrests, investigation of crimes and pre-trial detention of defendants. During periods of crises or military emergency (such as the 1931-43 time of the Long March) the police were directed to take whatever steps were necessary against enemy agents operating along the front (Leng, 1967, pp.13-5).

Those days past, the People's Government once again tightened the police powers through legislation in 1942. Police requests required court approval and a court appearance was guaranteed to all defendants within 24 hours of their arrest. The Department was also placed formally in charge of all prisons, labour camps and jails. It is probable, however, that in handling class enemies the police continued to step beyond the law on occasion. Throughout the Civil War the policemen of Public Order were generally recruited from the ranks of the PLA or the People's Militia (Leng, 1967, p.43).

The Procurate in the Civil War era

During the war years the Communists formed their own version of another borrowed Soviet legal office: the Procurate. The Nationalist Government had already experimented with this socialist invention in the years before Chiang Kai Shek's coup; but the KMT version of the office existed only in law books and a few municipal governments. The Procurate was picked up and renovated later by the Chinese Communists, but even then was limited to a few scattered offices. During the Civil War the Procurate was not an independent office, but individual procurators were attached to the various People's Courts where they served as state prosecutors. This most professional of the Communist legal institutions remained small and subordinated to courts and police (Li, 1969a; Gudoshnikov, 1957, p.9).

Written laws followed, rather than led, the development of Communist justice. New courts and judicial procedures were typically tried out on an experimental basis, to be written into law only later after they had been tested by practice. While Lenin and a number of leading Russian revolutionaries were legally trained, there were very few lawyers among the generals and commissars of the Chinese Red "bandits". Most Chinese lawyers' support of the KMT and the Maoist notion of continuous revolution is fundamentally anti-legal (Li, 1969a). The Communist leadership chose to rely on the popular justice of local peasant organizations and felt no pressure to turn out quickly a complete set of laws and legal institutions.

The principle of mass line and popular judicial practices argued against the establishment of a judicial system tightly defined and limited by written law. The Maoist Party leadership distrusted bureaucratic justice and was unwilling to "bind the hands and feet of the masses" with a set of rigid codes and procedures. The People's Government chose instead to make public a few "general principles", and to make room for the "direct mass action of the people" against class enemies and crime (Liu Shao chi, 1957, pp.82, 93).

Legislation and social reform

Nevertheless, a number of laws were written which followed and loosely regulated the course of justice in the liberated zones. These are of two basic types: organic laws and what may be called social reform laws. The organic laws established and described the various arms of the People's Government. Among them were the 1932 Temporary Regulations on the Organization and Procedure of Judicial Departments, the 1933 Organic Law of the Local Soviets, the Organic Law of the Central Soviet (1934) and the Judicial Procedure Act of 1934, all of which related to the organization and powers of People's Courts and the subordinate procurators' offices. The Department of Public Order was established and fleshed out by the 1931 Organic Regulations of the State Political Security Bureau and a few subsequent government regulations. The first attempts to regulate mediation work are recorded in the 1943 Border Region

Regulations on Conciliation Work (Cohen, 1971, pp.295-302; Leng, 1967, pp.16-18). In general organic laws signify the formal inclusion of offices and policies previously operating on an experimental basis.

The social reform laws are perhaps more important since they were closer to a direct statement of political ideology. They were often intended to stimulate or guide social change (while the organic laws merely record or describe existing organizations). Among the critical areas considered in these social reform laws were: women's rights and equality under the socialist marriage contract (1931 and 1946); the suppression of counter-revolutionaries and landlords (1931 and 1946); land reform, rent reduction and the redistribution of landlord holdings (1931, 1939, and 1944); and the rights and obligations of workers under Communism (1931) (Waller, 1973, pp.32-6; Leng, 1967, pp.10-14). Mass organizations and local governments were instructed to study and practise the social ideas put forth in these laws.

While laws were written and courts established, Civil War howled across the land. Parents buried children and then grandchildren, and after 20 years the war still continued. The cost to a nation already poor and weak from hunger was enormous, but the hard years trained both the Communist leadership and the peasants in the ways of mass line politics. The restricting bonds of the old private governments were loosened and the Communists found new revolutionary energy in men and women released from the absolute authority of family elders and the feudal marriage system.

Unlike the Bolsheviks, the Chinese Communists were to have a working government structure and a skeleton legal system on hand when final victory arrived. Justice was firmly established as a community affair, emphasizing political education and social pressure rather than legal procedures or punitive sanctions. The people of the countryside were effectively organized and became experienced in the new socialist version of mediation, investigation and volunteer peace-keeping. The war also pushed the development of this popular justice along the politically relative lines of class struggle and there was little place for an objective or professional legal system which ignored the obvious struggles for land reform and social equality. Finally, the People's Government was developed as an intimate part of the people's life and the peasants came to expect Communist officials to be sensitive workers for the local folk. Justice was likewise expected to be a simple matter open to public participation and popular understanding. The weight and importance of this Civil War experience was to become very apparent. A slicker, more complex and "professional" version of justice appeared later to challenge the mass line and popular justice. Throughout the Civil War, however, political thought was shaped by battlefield events and the revolutionary forces were united by their opposition to the KMT dictatorship.

5 Liberation: Class Struggle and Reconstruction

Over 30 years of Kuomintang rule ended in 1949 with the "battle of the feet". Chiang Kai Shek's last defensive lines evaporated as his long suffering soldiers defected or fled before the Red Army offensive (Gillin, 1970). Businessmen, landlords and the remaining Nationalist troops fought at the dockside for the last seats on boats bound for Taiwan. The Communists, long renowned for their forced marches, were for once unable to keep up with the enemy. On October 1st, the victors paused briefly to proclaim the inauguration of the People's Republic of China. The long siege of Yenan was finished.

The country won by the peasant army was in ruins. Ceaseless warfare had been China's political culture since the 1911 Republican Revolution, and the people ached from sacrifice and death. The coastal cities were devastated from the repeated invasions of warlords and Japanese. Highways and railway lines had been cut and sabotaged by KMT and Reds alike. The People's Army fought its way into the industrial heartland of Manchuria only to find that acres of factories and plants had vanished. Soviet Russian troops using blow torches had neatly cut away the machinery and shipped it across the border. The Chinese were left with long lines of jagged steel rising several inches above the cold Manchurian plains (Ashbrook, 1968, pp.17-19; King, H. H., 1968, pp.175-7).

The Communists were faced with the prospects of a national famine and were deprived of the heavy industry necessary to move beyond the shaky economy of peasant agriculture. Moreover, the new government was threatened by the United States Navy and by Chiang's regrouped army standing just offshore.

Mass Organizations, Mass Campaigns

Not surprisingly, the Communists relied upon the proven methods of mass line politics to get them over the rough years after liberation. The leadership expanded and developed mass organizations and soon was able to mobilize almost the entire population for production and rebuilding. Rather than tax the peasants and workers, the Communists chose to meet reconstruction and defence expenses by selling national bonds. The citizens' mass organizations, in addition to their production work, carried out these tremendous bond subscription drives. Wealthy businessmen and landlords on the mainland bought a good many bonds in the hope of gaining official favour and thus protecting their investments and their lives (Vogel, 1969, p.79; Barnett, 1964, pp.158-9). The political economy of recovery was an extension of Civil War programmes for mass action in production and class conflict.

The expansion of Civil War mass organizations

The mass organizations which carried out the reconstruction and popular justice tasks represent a new evolution in popular government. While the Civil War citizens' organizations were essentially local associations, the new mass organizations were connected by a set of regional and national offices, elected and maintained by the public memberships. Individual unions, for example, were formed into a national All China Federation of Trade Unions with a membership of over a hundred million and a national office closely tied to the National People's Government (Blaustein, 1962, pp.470-9; Harper, 1969, p.90). Likewise the local women's unions of Civil War days were pulled together into the national women's union with a stake and a voice in national politics (King, V., 1966, pp.8-13).

New mass organizations were created to co-ordinate public energies in the newly liberated cities. Artists and writers were organized into the All China Federation of Literary and Art Circles (Schurmann, 1966b, p.411). The old liberal parties of the intellectuals were mobilized to support the new government (Chi-shein Li, 1951, *in* Steiner, 1953, Vol.II, pp.198-9). Student groups merged into a national association and a Communist-led youth league. The rural peasants' militia established urban branches, and city workers began to participate in volunteer civil defence and street patrol work (KMJP, 9th April, 1953, *in* Steiner, Vol.II, 1953, pp.202-4). All youths between the ages of 18 and 30 had "the obligation and the privilege of joining armed (militia) units" (Central South Bureau CCP, 1952, *in* Steiner, Vol.II, 1953, p.159).

While great progress was made in these areas, the Communists were frustrated to note that many of the urban folk remained isolated in the narrow world of family and the neighbourhood. Children, old people, housewives and multitudes of the desperately poor urban underclass were still social and political "shut-ins". The mass organizations which had so totally involved the peasants in the revolution were unable to reach and organize these people. It was a problem not unfamiliar to American urban activists seeking to "organize the disorganized" poor in the United States.

The formation of residents' committees and street offices

The Party leadership is, to this day, troubled by the apathy and depressing fatalism of the urban shut-ins, but during the liberation years some important first steps were taken with the aim of bringing these isolated people into the larger affairs of the nation. New types of citizens' organizations were formed as the mass line reached into city neighbourhoods. Most important among these organizations were the "residents' committees" and the "street offices".

Immediately after liberation the Communists abolished the KMT neighbour-hood spy system (pao-chia) and encouraged city dwellers and especially the non-working women to form residents' committees (Vogel, 1969, pp.55-6; White, 1973, p.5; Cohen, 1968b, p.16). Each family elected one member to a street council, and the councils in turn chose representatives to form residents' committees (responsible for 40-100 households). The committees worked to bring the city folk into political action, and the Party leadership hoped that the urban stay-at-homes would gain some measure of political confidence and experience through their participation in committee work. Coastal cities, such as Shanghai and Tientsin, were the main sites for this new experiment in urban mobilization (Schurmann, 1966b, pp.372-3; Salaff, 1967).

By 1951 over 80% of the Shanghai population was organized into residential committees, and these committees were active in restoring order after the Civil War and also organized public support for the Korean War effort. Residential committees sold war bonds, worked in fire prevention, tutored the illiterate, collected materials and bandages for the troops, and sponsored political study classes which introduced socialist ideology to every family (Townsend, 1969, p.162; Salaff, 1967).

Popular justice action by the committees included the registration of new arrivals in the city, watching and reporting on known or suspected subversives and mobilizing residents for mass political trials and accusation meetings (Cohen, 1968b, p.16; Vogel, 1969, pp.370-74; White, 1973). The residential committees also established a less punitive justice among the people involving mediation work and the election of People's Assessors (lay judges) to serve in the People's Courts.

The residents' committees were enormously effective in political education and in co-ordinating public energies. However, the organizations failed to bring the urban shut-ins into the forefront of socialist politics and could not break the dark fatalism which lingered in the back streets. The long-silent housewives and the extremely poor only rarely served as officers or leaders in the committees, and usually did the legwork for the younger and more educated residents who ran the committees. These local leaders were also the nucleus of other mass organizations, such as the trade unions, the women's unions, the national Communist youth league and the urban militia. As the young neighbourhood activists devoted more time to other organizations, the energy and achievements of the residential committees dropped off.

A second problem in committee work was their organizational clumsiness. In the first years after liberation the committees grew at lightning speed. The thousands of new residents' committees, like the early peasant associations, reflected local differences and were so varied in organization as to make national co-ordination extremely difficult. The Communists responded to this classic problem of "popular" (or decentralized) politics by publishing some general directives and by creating yet another mass organization for the cities: the street office.

The first street offices were officially organized in 1952, and they were to be the link between the residents' committees and the regular bureaux of the People's Government. The street office would eventually have branch organizations in every city district. Like the residents' committees, the street office was manned mostly by volunteers, and the office carried citizens' complaints and requests from the committees to the regular government (Schurmann, 1966b, pp.326-7). The problem of slum-poor isolation also troubled this organization, and again it was the young and educated residents who held most of the top posts. Throughout the liberation period the urban population grew at an enormous rate (40% rise 1950-53), and the residents' committees and street offices likewise grew in size and importance (Townsend, 1969, p.159; Schurmann, 1966b, p.329; Ying Mao Kau, 1969, pp.32-3).

The sources and significance of mass action

The Party leadership called upon the national citizens' organizations for co-ordinated voluntary projects such as canal and dam building, industrialization and local defence. Lines of specialization were crossed and re-crossed as professional soldiers of the PLA were set to work in the fields and factories, while students went out from the cities to work as farmers and the women's unions organized militia units (Vogel, 1969, pp.77-8). The mass organizations also lightened the load of the official bureaux by forming volunteer auxilliaries to assist government census takers, health workers, teachers and police. Most important here is the role of these organizations as agents of popular justice; a role which will be discussed later.

The Party and government could count on the energetic support of the masses (through their mass organizations) only so long as the leadership remained true to its promised social reforms. Foremost among these was the land reform programme begun during the Civil War. The people also expected the elimination of feudal marriage customs and the establishment of women's rights. The city workers looked forward to better arrangements, as did the slum labouring class of coolies and ricksha-men. This urban under-class had been systematically exploited by the gangster societies which still remained after the fall of the KMT. Finally, the leadership was obligated to prevent famine and to defend the mainland against threats of invasion from Taiwan and later from Korea.

No Chinese government had ever before approached or even promised these goals, and the revolutionary programme must be seen as extraordinarily ambitious. The Civil War experiences in the Red base areas were of decisive value here, since the methods of mass line politics were applied to social reform, economic reconstruction and national defence in the years following liberation.

The national reconstruction programme was carried out—not by administrative orders or direct government action, but by a series of national "mass campaigns" including millions of citizens in the mass organizations. The mass campaigns of the People's Republic differed from the Yenan popular efforts in several important ways. To begin with, in re-united China a national mass movement would obviously involve a far larger number of people, but most importantly the mass movements after 1949 were more closely directed and co-ordinated by the national Party leadership than in the Civil War days.

The Communist Party did not, however, *create* the mass support for the campaigns. It has been the great and common mistake of scholars of China to equate co-ordination and direction with creation. The Party did arrange the timing and did set limits on the intensity of the mass campaigns, but the public energy and popular will to sacrifice and participate in such voluntary affairs could not be ordered or created by a tiny elite such as the Chinese Communist Party.

It has been reliably estimated that nearly every citizen in China was personally involved in at least two or three of the campaigns and aware of others (Townsend, 1969, p.88). Vast expressions of popular support on the scale of the mass campaigns cannot be "staged". Those who would argue so generally imply that the Chinese people are a batch of faceless puppets, dangling from the Party line. This analysis of Chinese politics as "mass psychological deception", "compulsive participation" or "controlled mob actions" (Barnett, 1964, p.135; Pye, 1969, pp.26–30) is but thinly disguised and cynical racism. The spokesmen for this view ignore the glaring fact that the Communists were the first and only Chinese government able to inspire such mass actions. Unless we are to believe that the ex-peasants who ran the Party were able to develop some mysterious hypnotic powers in the hills of Yenan, then we must regard the mass campaigns as voluntary expressions of political support and as an advanced application of the mass line. Political biases aside, one fact is clear: there were not (and are not) enough party cadres and rawhide whips in all of China to build one dam across the Yangtze.

Mass campaigns in politics and social justice

The mass campaigns and mass organizations may be seen as a sort of unofficial Popular Government paralleling the official People's Government. Both governments were explicitly and energetically committed to the Communist Party leadership and the Communist slate of social reforms. The popular government of mass action was called upon especially in times of crises for great national tasks such as reconstruction, the class struggle or land reform. In such times the written laws (few as they were) of the People's Republic were set aside. The mass campaigns, under Communist leadership, set their own guidelines and assumed many of the tasks assigned to official government in other socialist or capitalist states. Mass campaigns did not, however, amount to anarchy, as any violence or destruction was circumscribed and concentrated on set political objectives. Those guilty of serious excesses were often punished later by the regular agencies of government justice. The mass campaigns may be roughly divided into two categories:

1. Campaigns for production and reconstruction;
2. Campaigns for social justice, social reform and class struggle.

The second type of campaign is most important as part of popular justice in China. This type of mass campaign fits the previously advanced working definition of popular justice as *"the ideology and practice of mass action in the affairs of social control"*. Mass campaigns of the social justice type generally involve the creation of irregular popular courts (the popular tribunals) and irregular police forces (militia and the security teams of mass organizations) working alongside the regular justice agencies.

Mass campaigns are not usually intended to be a complete substitute for regular professional justice in the People's Republic. The campaigns are temporary events directed at specific sorts of "crime". The definition of crime here is *politically relative.* In this respect mass campaigns follow the oldest traditions of Chinese justice as discussed in the previous chapter. The popular justice of mass campaigns is even less restrained by written legal codes than are the regular justice agencies (which, during the liberation years, often favoured Party directives over written law in deciding cases).

The determined support of the Chinese people was the Party's greatest resource, and because mass campaigns provide a direct mass–Party exchange they have been favoured by the Party as a central political strategy. It seems worthwhile following the development of the campaigns as they moved beyond the local actions of the Civil War and became truly national popular movements. This chapter will consider some of the more prominent early campaigns of the social justice type, including: Land Reform (1949-51); The Suppression of Counter-Revolutionaries (1949-51); The Three Antis (1951-52); The Five Antis (1952).

Post-War Land Reform:
A Conflict of Lines and Classes (1949–51)

Land reform was the great recruiting officer for the peasant ranks of the People's Liberation Army, and liberation in 1949 meant the extension of that Civil War programme to all of China. There was some debate, however, as to whether land reform in the Republic should follow the same violent course as during the early years of warfare. A number of leaders such as Liu Shao chi wanted a minimum of disorder and were prepared to go easy on "class enemies" in the interests of stability and production schedules. Liu regarded the victory of 1949 as the end mark for class struggle, and he argued for a "peaceful land reform" regulated by written codes and government bureaux (Liu Shao chi, 1950, *in* Vogel, 1969, pp.95-6; Chen, T., 1967, pp.206-10).

The Agrarian Reform Law passed by the Republic in June 1950 reflected Liu's position and outlined a lenient policy towards the landlord class. Crucial passages of the law emphasize persuasion and reform, rather than punishment or social revolution, as follows:

> Landlords shall be given an equal share (of all confiscated land) so that they can make their living by their own labour and thus reform themselves through labour.

> Landlords who have returned after running away, persons who once worked for the enemy, but have returned to the countryside, and the families of such persons, should be given equal shares of land and other means of production equal to those of the peasants (Blaustein, 1962, p.278)

Liu and those who drafted the 1950 law sought to limit the role of popular justice in land reform. They were rather distressed at what they regarded as violent excesses and illegality on the part of peasant associations, and wished quickly to re-establish a stable and efficient agriculture in the countryside. Liu's proposals and the 1950 law would have closely restricted mass action and would have transferred power from mass organizations to regular government agencies. The conservative's programme for land reform amounted to a break with the Civil War tradition of decentralized peasant participation in the making of a revolutionary agriculture. Their proposals were a first step toward the "elite line" ideology of bureaucratic control and disciplined social stability (Vogel, 1969, p.95).

The initial prominence of the conservative's proposal was ended by the Korean War emergency. The national leadership called for active public support in the war effort, and the renewed enthusiasm for the mass line in defence work carried over into land reform. The conservative's position was also weakened by the development of a wartime mood which did not make for tolerance and forgiveness in dealing with landlords and other class enemies.

Some gentry reacted to land reform by attacking peasant activists and burning peasant homes. More often they tried to evade land confiscation through bribery and fraud. Landlords changed their names and attempted to register as peasants in the census. Others hid their possessions or "sold" their land to friends so as to qualify for peasant status. A number of the threatened rich attempted to soften the hearts of local accusers and Communist investigators with gifts of food, drink and well-endowed young women. A number of local scandals were uncovered and given wide notice in the press (Wei, 1955, pp.21-23; Vogel, 1969, pp.99-100).

The young Republic, threatened by new landings of KMT agents along the coast and the American fleet and air force in Manchuria, was hardly in the mood to tolerate such domestic resistance. Air raids from Formosa and the long Korean casualty lists were increasingly connected with landlord opposition in the popular mind of China. Mao Tse-tung's only son, a fighter pilot, was among those killed in action. As the first uneasy months of war passed, the landlords came to be identified as both counter-revolutionaries and exploiters of the peasants.

The campaign for land reform which began in that year showed little resemblance to the one outlined in the 1950 law. The Korean War brought instead a campaign of violent mass action against class enemies, largely unrestricted by laws or bureaucratic legal procedures. Leadership of the campaign would rest with peasant associations, PLA troops and travelling teams of Communist Party cadres. The courts and especially the written laws were subordinated to political ideology and political organizations. The land reform campaign which began in 1950 was frankly described as a class struggle and was linked to the war effort by the Party leadership (Yu, 1955, pp.44-45; NFJP, 26th December, 1951). Teng Tzu-hui, Director of the Rural Work Department and a member of the National Central Committee of the Communist Party was both an economic planner and top administrator of land reform. In a December 1950 broadcast he pointedly criticized suggestions for a "peaceful land reform" in the following message:

> Some comrades look upon agrarian reform as the simple matter of redistributing land, which in turn is considered a simple technical job; and thus

understand the problem of agrarian reform merely as a means of developing production. This view is incorrect.

The current campaign to Resist-America, Aid-Korea is developed to oppose imperialism. The agrarian reform campaign, on the other hand, is the last and fiercest battle in the series of systematic class struggles for the wiping out of feudal influences.

We all know that the landlord class, this feudal force which stands together with our great enemy, Imperialism, is not a weak and effeminate form but has a history of exercising deep-rooted authority over the country for over 2000 years.

We realize that it is no easy task to wipe out this cruel and stubborn foe, the landlord class. The job must be done with fierce class struggle . . . (Teng Tyu Hui, 1950, *in* Steiner, 1953, Vol. II, p.11)

The land reform campaign of 1951-52 developed alongside the national campaign for the "suppression of counter-revolutionaries". The language of the 1951 and 1952 Laws Against Counter-Revolutionaries condemns "reactionary" or "stubborn" landlords together with traitors and spies, and all received similarly severe punishments. Temporary People's Tribunals were established to judge cases against landlords and counter-revolutionaries alike (Blaustein, 1962, pp.222-3,237).

People's Tribunals and mass organizations in land reform

These irregular courts followed the Civil War practices of mass line and marked another step in the evolution of popular justice. Most of the tribunal judges were non-professionals elected from the ranks of local mass organizations. The remaining judges were appointed by government bureaux such as the regular People's Courts and the police (Gudoshnikov, 1957, p.88).

Investigations of landlords were assigned to the peasant associations with the assistance of a few travelling party investigators. The associations, as in the Civil War period, completed a census of each village, classifying all residents as landlord, rich peasant, middle peasant or poor peasant, and thus prepared the way for the trial and punishment of class enemies and "local tyrants" (Chand, 1958, p.66; Kiang Wen Han, 1952).

The peasant associations called large "accusation meetings" in which the People's Tribunals heard testimony against landlords. The procedure at these crowded popular trials followed the openly political and informal practices of Civil War land reform. Neither lawyers nor rigid codes of legal procedure regulated the tribunal's process, as peasants came forward to bite, kick and spit upon the assembled gentry. Witnesses and spectators frequently numbered thousands and entire villages left the fields to participate in the business of social justice (Lo Jui lung, 1951; CFJP, 28th August, 1951, *in* SCMP No.167, 1951).

Judicial opinions were phrased in the common language of mass line politics, and the supreme law was class struggle and Maoist ideology. Sentencing was immediate and often severe. The Party was determined not to allow the landlords to use their greater education, wealth and knowledge of the law to advantage and so procedure was rough, lawyers were generally absent and legalistic arguments were cast aside in favour of common sense and popular opinion (Lee, L. T. C., 1961, p.338; Hsia Tao-Tai, 1967, pp.46–47; Ta Kung Pao, 24th August, 1951, *in* SCMP No.165).

National statistics on land reform are spotty, but the Communists recorded some 143,761 cases against landlords and counter-revolutionaries over one six-month period in Central-South China alone (NCNA, 3rd May, 1951, *in* SCMP No.102, 1951). Though national sentencing figures are unavailable, it may be fairly assumed that executions of landlords numbered at least several thousand, and tens of thousands were most likely fined or placed for several years in forced labour camps. In one South China county a total of 400 counter-revolutionaries and landlords were shot. This number included fully 20% of the local gentry. Observers noted that it appears to have been a government policy to shoot at least one landlord in every village (Barnett, 1966, p.30; Vogel, 1969, pp.111–14).

Suppression of Counter-Revolutionaries (First Campaign 1949–52)

It is sometimes difficult to distinguish land reform clearly from the (first) campaign to suppress counter-revolutionaries which occurred at about the same time. Those arrested as counter-revolutionaries in the countryside were forced to share accusers, judges and firing squads with the landlords; but urban subversives were provided with separate facilities. Throughout China the campaign against counter-revolution followed the principles of mass line popular justice with public participation mass trials and procedures which were more political than legal.

The suppression campaign stands out as easily the most violent period in the history of popular justice and Chinese Communism since liberation. It is also remembered as the first mobilization of the city populations, which were controlled by the KMT until the final months of the Civil War. A number of new mass organizations were formed in the course of the campaign with the aim of bringing the city dwellers at last into the affairs of national politics.

The threat of counter-revolution in 1949–52 was not a manufactured illusion, conveniently projected by the Communists in order to unite the people through fear. Counter-revolution against the new Republic was very real and was especially grave in the newly liberated provinces of South and East China.

The suddenness of the KMT collapse in South China left thousands of Nationalist troops, anti-Communist individuals and organizations stranded on the mainland. A number of these soldiers and civilians were yet armed and bands of them operated in the countryside, where they murdered isolated Communist officials and leaders of peasant associations. Special agents with explosives came from Taiwan to organize subversion and sabotage in coastal cities. There were also a number of commando raids by Chiang's troops which were assisted by informers and spies in China. Finally, there were a large number of ex-landlords, KMT officials and assorted war criminals hiding in the South China cities where they found refuge with relatives and anonymity among the throngs of newly arrived war refugees (Northeast People's Daily, 12th November, 1950, *in* SCMP No.189, 1950).

The Korean War and government policy toward counter-revolution

The Republic's policy toward these active and potential subversives was, like the land reform programme, deeply affected by events in Korea. Until the American invasion the People's Government generally combined alert self-protection with a policy of leniency toward most former enemies. This relatively peaceful and tolerant attitude was consistent with the philosophy of reunification laid out by Mao Tse-tung in his 1949 treatise "One New Democracy". Even such a source as the US Air Force staff (during the Korean War) observed that

> At first, and for nearly a year after they proclaimed the Central People's Government at Peking, [the Communists] used methods of persuasion rather than of force; and all report they were comparatively lenient in their treatment of the Chinese people . . . (Chen, W. C., 1955, p.5)

The war changed things. The Chinese entry into the war, forced by threats against the industrial resources of Manchuria, reopened political hostilities between the Party-led public and those who had supported Chiang. Fresh landings of KMT raiders (encouraged by US naval support) and the possibility of foreign invasion in the North, stirred up domestic conflicts and Civil War memories.

The People's Republic, with little navy or air force, could not prevent landings of agents and supplies, especially in the devastated and newly won South China area. Over 6000 incidents of sabotage and over 650 cases of espionage were reported by the government in a 12-month period of 1949–50 (Wei, 1955, p.28).

Likewise the Communists could not easily eliminate the problems of informers and subversion, since the Reds were compelled, by their own inexperience in city matters, to keep a great many ex-KMT administrators in employment. These threats and the new war made the Communist leadership sensitive to national vulnerabilities and forced them to take counter-revolution more seriously.

Several weeks after the start of the Korean War, Mao reversed the tolerant philosophy of "New Democracy" and called for the "resolute elimination" of "all bandits, spies, despots and other counter-revolutionary elements" (Mao Tse-tung, 1950, *in* Steiner, 1953, Vol. I, p.166). Later, the People's Government prepared a number of directives to guide a national suppression campaign and ultimately passed a set of legal regulations in February 1951. The 1951 "Regulations for the Suppression of Counter-Revolutionaries" overturned the lenient policies outlined for most counter-revolutionaries in the 1949 Common Programme of the Communist Party.

While the 1949 Common Programme promised that "Feudal landlords, bureaucratic capitalists and reactionary elements . . . shall be given some means of livelihood . . .", the 1951 Regulations emphasized punishments and the dangerousness of counter-revolutionaries. The term "counter-revolutionary" was defined most broadly and without concern for Western legal style. Niceties like *ex post facto* and those who had opposed the revolution were now subject to punishment unless they had done "meritorious service to atone for their crimes after liberation". The 1951 Regulations also specified prison terms of more than three years for "provocation and instigating acts with counter-revolutionary intent". This category of crimes included:

> Alienating and splitting the solidarity between the Government and the nationalities, democratic classes, democratic parties and groups, and people's bodies.

> Conducting counter-revolutionary propaganda and agitation; fabricating and spreading rumours (Blaustein, 1962, pp.218-19)

The practical guidelines provided by the Party leadership and the legal codes advanced in the 1951 Regulations stress political and not behavioural or "legal" definitions of counter-revolutionary crime. The crime of "counter-revolutionary intent" is a rather flexible category, and "alienating and splitting" the people is clearly a question of political practice rather than overt sabotage. The suppression campaign emphasized political education and mass action, at the expense of tougher legal procedures and the due process rights of defendants.

The national leadership called upon the entire population to stand by the war effort, and to seek out, accuse and punish all counter-revolutionary elements. Mass organizations in city and countryside were to play a central role in mobilizing the population for the suppression campaign. The application of mass line to the problem of counter-revolution resulted in a vast national struggle involving millions of citizens in an attack on political enemies. The national campaign was drawn along class lines, rather than along "legal" lines, as guilt and innocence were largely determined by wealth and social status. Those who wound up in the defendant's post included many ex-officials or soldiers of the defeated KMT, former "yellow" (anti-Communist) union leaders and the bosses of the secret gangster societies. The scale of the campaign, its emphasis on class struggle and political ideology and the central role of the mass organizations of popular justice are all consistent with the earlier pattern in China.

The rural campaign

The suppression campaign developed quickly and with tremendous force in the countryside, where the Communists could count on the well-organized peasant associations. Counter-revolution in the countryside was generally more open than in the cities and therefore easier to eliminate. The mainland press reported pitched battles with isolated KMT units and "bandit gangs" in Hunan and Kuangsi provinces. The bandit forces of one Kwantung province battle were said to number 36,170. During one period of several months (in 1951) some 4512 enemies were reported killed and another 3436 captured. In Szechuan province (South-Central China) the police confiscated over 200 rifles and uncovered numerous counter-revolutionary organizations. Bandit gangs were said to be responsible for poisoning wells, political assassinations and numerous attacks on the offices of peasant associations (NCNA, 4th May, 1951, in SCMP No.103, 1951; NFJP, 19th September, 1952, in SCMP No.134, 1952).

The rural hostilities were quickly ended by military and police action. The volunteer peasant militia units played a part in these mop-up operations, particularly after many of the regular troops were sent to the Korean or Taiwan fronts. Counter-revolutionaries found few hiding places in villages as the peasant associations kept a close watch on travellers and recorded all new arrivals. Generally those who had opposed Communism and land reform were well known, and the associations prepared local registers of all such political enemies.

The Communist strength in the countryside did not help the position of former KMT village chiefs or the officials of the KMT pao-chia system. The peasant associations quickly assumed the tasks of local government in liberated zones, and former Nationalist servants and pao-chia spies were unnecessary, unwanted and soon under investigation by the Associations and the police force. At the suggestion of the People's Government, local villages and associations elected "Committees to Suppress Counter-Revolutionaries". These committees co-ordinated local investigations and mass accusations, but their primary purpose was to relate socialist ideology and broad national goals to individual cases and trials for subversion. Political education was a part of every step in the mass campaign (Crook and Crook, 1959, pp.30–32, 118–120).

The People's Tribunals for land reform handled cases against counter-revolutionaries and followed the same popular justice style used against landlords. The Tribunals were candidly described by the People's Government as a political arm of class struggle. As in the land reform movement, there was little desire to create an "independent" judiciary governed by bureaucratic procedures and specialized professional standards. The representatives of the government, peasant associations, women's unions and militia units which made up the Tribunals regarded themselves as leaders of a mass movement, not as an elevated or "impartial" elite of law-givers.

Trials were crowded affairs to which the mass organizations called their memberships as audience and witness against the accused. At one such trial 380,000 people followed the accusations against Osman Bator, a "US armed spy" and his several accomplices, all captured after landing from a KMT vessel. Ten thousand peasants watched the executions which immediately followed the Tribunal's decision (NCNA, 5th May, 1951, in SCMP No. 102, 1951). Ex-KMT officials in the countryside were to remember land reform as a time of death and suspicion. In one South China district 80% of the village pao-chia chiefs were shot before the assembled peasant associations (Barnett, 1966, p.30).

The urban campaign

Suppression of political enemies in the city was a much tougher job than in the countryside. The Communists were not prepared or trained to take over city government and had little choice but to keep KMT administrators, teachers and judges on the payrolls. These ex-KMT officials still held over 70% of Shanghai's municipal government posts some two years after liberation. The urban public had long been under KMT control, and private government, such as the unions and the urban pao-chia system, were led by people hostile to Communism. A number of isolated strikes were sparked off by surviving KMT "yellow" union organizations (Barnett, 1966, p.30).

The national leadership, lacking both a reliable urban government and the support of strong citizens' organizations, was compelled to rely heavily on the services of the Red Army. For some months the cities remained under martial law and the Military Control Commissions co-ordinated the first stages of the suppression campaign. The overall strategy of the city campaign was to rely on military courts and on police recruited directly from the army until new mass organizations could be established and "new" city governments sounded out (White, 1973, p.5; Vogel, 1969, pp.53–4).

The suppression movement concentrated public energies against three specific groups. Those caught in sabotage, espionage and similar acts of treason were quickly tried and despatched at the wall. High Nationalist officials and lesser figures in KMT organizations who were regarded as individual criminals by the populace were also rudely handled. Finally, the Communists exposed and punished the leadership of secret gangster syndicates which had for so long controlled and exploited the unskilled labourers of the slum towns (Gudoshnikov, 1957, p.30; Cohen, 1968b, p.4).

The campaign followed popular justice principles and was openly designed to promote mass participation in political education and political struggle. While a number of laws and government directives were passed to guide the movement, it remained an affair of neighbourhood meetings, crowded trials, elected worker-judges and an "irregular" courtroom language of the street and factory. It was the first unruly experience of city populations with mass line politics, and the first popular justice action by the newly formed mass organizations of city folk.

The residents' committees and street offices were only half-formed and were limited to a few scattered districts at the time of the suppression movement. The trade unions made some efforts to support the movement, especially in the attack on gangster societies, but the national union leadership angered the party by its readiness to seek compromise and avoid class struggle. The most important mass organizations were the urban militia and the security defence committees. These volunteer police units helped patrol the streets, guard factories and (along with the police) arrested suspected counter-revolutionaries.

Those suspected of counter-revolutionary acts or anti-Communist politics would become quite familiar with the local security defence committees. These specialized committees were set up throughout China's cities at the start of the campaign. They were the active arm of popular justice and were linked to larger mass organizations of residents and city workers. The Provisional Regulations authorizing the committees read in part as follows:

> Article 1. For the purpose of mobilizing the masses to help the People's Government in anti-treason, anti-espionage, anti-bandit and anti-arson activities, and in stamping out counter-revolutionary activities — thereby protecting the state and public order — security committees shall be set up in all cities after the campaign for the suppression of counter-revolutionaries begins and in all rural districts following the completion of agrarian reform.

> Article 3. Security committees shall be established in cities on the basis of (public) organs, factories, enterprises, schools and streets as working units . . . They shall consist of 3 to 11 members, depending on the number of people in the base organizational unit . . . (Ministry of Public Order, 10th August, 1952, *in* Steiner, 1953, Vol. II, p.161).

These volunteer committees worked closely with the police and also co-ordinated registration and surveillance work undertaken by their parent mass organizations (such as residents' committees, unions and youth leagues) (CFJP, 29th August, 1951, *in* SCMP No. 166, 1951). Like many other political-legal institutions in the People's Republic, the security defence committees were supervised by both the local police and their parent mass organizations (Ministry of Public Order, 10th August, 1952, *in* Steiner, 1953, Vol. II, p.162). This double administration follows from the dual function of socialist justice as both social control and mass political education.

Without the aid of mass organizations and the mobilized public it is doubtful whether the police and the army could quickly have ended counter-revolution in the cities. Typically the policeman on the beat worked closely with the leaders of local popular justice, including the chief of the militia, the chairperson of the local residents' committee, the union officers in nearby factories, the branch officers of the youth league and, most especially, with the security defence committees. Through their mass organizations these leaders could call out the general population for political study, mass accusation rallies, and surveillance of active or suspected counter-revolutionaries (Cohen, 1968b, pp.15-16).

The attack on the secret gangster societies

The suppression of organized crime syndicates presented some very different problems and the police were virtually on their own here for some time. The syndicates were based on the total control and exploitation of the unskilled city slum labour. There were no unions for those who sweated as ricksha-pullers and coolie dock workers. Instead they were compelled to pay "protection fees" to the secret gangster societies who arranged for all work contracts.

The Communists set out to break the power of the syndicates by organizing the first coolie and ricksha-men's unions. The workers were at first reluctant to join the unions and were intimidated by the threats of the racketeers. A number of assassination attempts were made against the union leadership. The police provided bodyguards for the union leaders and protected new members from the attacks of thugs. Within a few months the unions had organized most of the unskilled workers and the People's Government was satisfied that the suppression campaign was a success (Lieberthal, 1973, p.9).

Three months later it was obvious that the syndicates were not beaten. The gangster bosses, failing to prevent the formation of unions, had ordered their henchmen to join them. The police, unfamiliar with the faces of workers and gangsters, had enrolled all applicants in the new organizations. The coolie unions were soon under complete syndicate control and the protection rackets were booming.

The Communists were compelled to begin again and to re-examine every union member's background. This screening was placed in the hands of the few labourers who had demonstrated their integrity and loyalty to the new unions. These workers identified syndicate members to the police who arrested and punished syndicate bosses, warning the hoods to leave the unions alone. Mass rallies were called by the unions to accuse and punish mobsters. In one case Li Tch sheng, boss of wharf labourers, was denounced by over 1000 dock workers in a mass trial (CFJP, 28th August, 1951, *in* SCMP No. 167, 1951). By the autumn of 1951 the government policy on secret societies had hardened. Those who still refused to resign syndicate membership and cease their secret activities were rounded up by police and publicly executed (CFJP, 29th December, 1952, *in* SCMP No. 232, 1952). Nearly two years after the suppression movement began the syndicates' power had been broken (Lieberthal, 1973, pp.25-30; Vogel, 1969, pp.64-65).

The courts and the campaign

The People's Government of the liberation era learned an important lesson from this near fiasco: social reforms are not workable without strong popular support and strong mass organizations. Police officers cannot match local mass organizations for sensitivity to local problems (such as gangster syndicates). Police work, no matter how thorough, is no substitute for popular justice with public participation.

The public were to be drawn more closely into government affairs through the work of mass campaign activists in political leadership positions. Thousands of the most active volunteers in the land reform and suppression movements would be invited into paid government service. Most of these citizen activists received a few months of training before joining such agencies as the police, public schools, city administration, or the People's Courts. By 1952 the number of government workers had grown from 720,000 to 3,310,000 (Kau, 1969, pp.20-27).

The courts established for the suppression campaign did not involve the public nearly as much as the police did. Those accused of counter-revolution were brought before three types of courts which were "popular" in varying degrees. The Military Courts were first established by the Military Control Commissions, and those judges were chosen solely by the army and Party leadership. These first courts called mass trials with thousands of spectator-accusers, but judgements were entirely in the hands of the appointed military judges.

The most serious cases of gangsterism and subversion were brought before the Military Courts and the sentences were severe. During the first 10 months of the campaign the Military Courts of Peking sentenced to death 211 of 505 defendants, while in Shanghai Military Courts heard evidence against 272 accused counter-revolutionaries, and sentenced 62 to death and another 208 to imprisonment (CFJP, 28th August, 1951, *in* SCMP No. 167, 1951). China's Minister of Public Order, Lo Jui ching, recalled that these early trials were accompanied by some 26,626 mass meetings involving over three million citizens in political study and in the denunciation of counter-revolutionaries (Lo Jui ching, JMJP, 23rd May, 1951, *in* SCMP No. 154, 1951).

People's Tribunals were later established which allowed for greater public participation. The new mass organizations of the cities elected a number of judges to sit alongside the magistrates chosen by the Party. These courts were also known for their severe sentencing and were responsible for the bulk of the 800,000 counter-revolutionary cases handled in 1951 (Shen Chun-ju, JMJP, 30th October, 1951, *in* Cohen, 1965, p.977). In Canton 676 counter-revolutionaries were executed in May 1951 (JMJP, 6th May, 1951, *in* SCMP No. 150, 1951). That same year China's greatest city, Shanghai, was enlivened by a particularly colourful summer suppression campaign with over 38,000 cases. On the night of 27th April, the entire police force was massed and sent into the streets to round up subversives. In May some 11,400 enemies were denounced and 485 executed. Within one month the citizens and police had found another 432 counter-revolutionaries and, of these, 30% were sentenced to prison and were permitted to watch the remaining 70% stand before the rifles of the Shanghai militia (CFJP, 28th August, 1951, *in* SCMP No. 167, 1951; CFJP, 19th July, 1951, *in* SCMP No. 159, 1951; White, 1973, p.7).

The first "regular" People's Courts were established in the cities during this period. These courts were rather quickly organized and were entrusted with few serious cases. The Wusih (Shanghai area) People's Court heard cases against 331 counter-revolutionary criminals in 1951, 142 of whom were released and only 40 received death or prison sentences (TKP, 10th August, 1951, *in* SCMP No. 165, 1951). A large number of ex-KMT judges sat on the People's Courts, and the Communists were reluctant to place the suppression campaign in their hands (Gudoshnikov, 1957, p.32; Cohen, 1968b, p.4).

In the summer of 1950, the People's Government called the "First All-China Conference of Judicial Workers", and most of the judges from all types of courts attended. The conference stands out as the first move toward the creation of a national court system. Leading Party officials instructed the lay and professional judges in the importance of mass participation in political-legal work. P'eng Chen, then a member of the Party Politburo and national Party Committee on Political and Legal Affairs, reminded officials that:

> Administrative and legal work is not merely routine and documentary work to be performed in an office. It must be extensively combined with the mass movement, linked directly and closely with the masses (P'eng Chen, 11th May, 1951, *in* Steiner, 1953, Vol. II, pp.101-102)

The conference served to outline government recommendations for the suppression campaign. The national policy promised lenient treatment for those who confessed openly to past crimes, and even greater leniency towards those who aided the People's Government in discovering other enemies—but those who resisted or attempted to elude justice would be severely punished.

The Conference also introduced local judges to the national judicial leadership. Shih Liang, the first Minister of Justice, spoke at length regarding the need for a trained body of judicial workers, and proposed a five-year training programme for new legal cadres (Shih Liang, 1st August, 1950, *in* Wei, 1955, p.14). The President of the Supreme People's Court, the Minister of Public Security and the newly independent Procurator General addressed the conference and outlined the national policies of their respective agencies. All stressed the unity of justice and politics, and there was great condemnation of a legal system based on "judicial independence" or on written legal codes. Shen Chun-ju, President of the Supreme People's Court, stated that "Our judicial work must serve political ends actively, and must be brought to bear on current political tasks and mass movements." (Shen Chun-ju, JMJP, 30th October, 1951, SCMP No. 2229, 1951).

Trials before any of the courts were a grim experience for those charged with counter-revolution. Even the highest Communist officials ignored legal routines while encouraging open public participation. The Minister of Public Security and the Mayor of Peking did not hesitate to order the execution of 220 subversives after the assembled audience shouted "shoot them" at a mass accusation rally in Peking (JMJP, 3rd April, 1951, *in* Wei, 1955, p.34). On May Day 1951 the Procurator General of China mounted a platform in the Shanghai stadium to read indictments against nine more "counter-revolutionary agents". Ten thousand citizens strained to hear the evidence in this trial-by-loudspeaker and then screamed for the death of the nine accused (Leng, 1967, p.14).

Labour reform

Lesser officers from the KMT army and the smooth-faced middle bureaucrats of the Nationalist Government were usually spared the trip to one of Shanghai's six execution grounds. These "serious but less dangerous" criminals were sentenced to either "mass control" or "labour reform". Mass control generally allowed the convicted to remain at home and on the job, with curfew and travel restrictions and the loss of civic rights. Mass organizations were responsible for watching these "bad elements", and the residents' committees, unions and security defence committees prepared regular "control" reports for the neighbourhood police. Control usually ended officially after several years, but the "bad element" label would devil former KMT supporters for years afterwards (White, 1973, p.9).

Labour reform was also intended for the avowed purpose of political control. The People's Government made no pretensions to a primary concern for "offender treatment" or "rehabilitation". Lo Jui ching, Minister of Public Security, discussed the politics of labour reform in a nationally published editorial as follows:

> The subjugation of counter-revolutionaries to labour reform is an indispensable method for the liquidation of the counter-revolutionary class, as well as a basic policy for the thorough reform of the culprits into new human beings. This sort of reform is a combination of political reform coupled with labour reform, as well as a combination of punishment and education . . . (Lo Jui ching, JMJP, 1st October, 1951, *in* Ong, 1955, pp.5-7)

The Communists have consistently avoided the wide use of Western-style enclosed prisons. Instead they created mobile labour reform brigades which were assigned specific work tasks. These brigades were established in every major city and most rural districts during the suppression campaign. Sentences were generally from one to five years with a few life sentences. There are no reliable figures for the national prisoner population or for lengths in sentences. The labour brigades did include thousands of the more serious surviving "counter-revolutionary elements" (King, H. H., 1968, p.68; Schurmann, 1966b, p.411).

It is clear that, whatever their exact number, the labour reform brigades were sizeable (probably several hundred thousand), and they made a significant contribution to reconstruction and production. Labour reform workers cleared new lands, built dikes and roads in rural China. By the end of 1951 it was reported that the majority of convicted counter-revolutionaries in South West China had been assigned to labour reform (KMJP, 18th October, 1951, *in* Wei, 1955, pp.53-54; Yu, P. C., 1951, p.22; Barnett, 1964, pp.64-67).

The easing of the Korean situation and the gradual decrease in sabotage prompted a lessening of suppression activities. Most of the leading KMT officials had been captured in the first months of the campaign, and sentences against the lesser enemies were lighter. Chou en Lai remarked that:

> By the end of last spring (1951), the movement for the suppression of counter-revolution reached a high tide throughout the country. We have [now] adopted a policy of pronouncing on those criminals who have merited the death penalty, but who owe no blood debt, and whose crimes against the nation's interests, though serious, are *not* in the most serious category [lesser sentences of imprisonment] so as to see how they turn out (Chou en Lai, 23rd October, 1951, *in* Wei, 1955, p.57)

In another year the gangster syndicates had been finally crushed and the last mop-up operations against rural "bandits" carried out. The first and bloodiest suppression campaign ended, but the potential danger of counter-revolution and violent reaction would remain as long as China was afflicted with the siege psychology of an isolated and threatened nation.

The "Five Antis" Campaign (1951–52)

The merchants and industrial capitalists watched nervously as mass movements and class struggles developed in the liberation period. Early in 1949 many of the top executives fled with the company kitty to Formosa or elsewhere, leaving the managers and clerks to deal with the Communists. The People's Government did not imprison those remaining behind, but kept private enterprises open while a new socialist management was trained. Rather than nationalize private firms, the Communists chose to limit their profits and regulate their investments. The new government even provided low-interest loans to enterprises wishing to repair war damages.

The vulnerability of mainland capitalists

Despite such government assurances, the capitalist bourgeoisie could not but shiver as other "reactionary classes" were dragged before People's Tribunals and punished in mass campaigns. The landlord class was wrecked by land reform and the ex-KMT officials were badly mauled in the suppression movement. The future of the bourgeoisie was uncertain.

Mao had listed the "petty bourgeoisie" and the "national bourgeoisie" with the friendly classes of "the people", but he also denounced capitalism and listed "reactionary capitalists" among the "enemy" classes (Mao Tse-tung, 1949, in Chai, 1969, pp.264–6). The difference between friendly and enemy capitalists was a matter of political relativity, as these categories were not defined by laws or constitutions. The business community felt vulnerable with the execution grounds of the mass movements clearly in sight, and businessmen were only too willing to "donate" money or buy government bonds in the hope of protecting their investments and their lives (Cohen, 1965, p.308; Hughes and Luard, 1959, p.83; Barnett, 1964, p.158; Dunlap, 1956, pp.59–63).

The political heat was turned up in early 1951 when the managers of industry and commerce were repeatedly accused of corrupting government bureaucrats. Available figures indicate that many businessmen were able to buy favours from local Communist officials or they avoided taxes by padding their books and bending regulations (TKP, 26th August, 1951, in SCMP No. 165, 1951). Two vast national campaigns were begun in 1951 to control and punish such corruption. These two were the "Three Antis" movement (against illicit gains in government) and the "Five Antis" movement (directed against five forms of business malpractice). The latter included bribery, tax evasion, cheating on state contracts, theft of state assets and stealing state economic information (Hsiao, G., 1965).

Five Antis developed in the popular justice tradition of earlier mass movements. Class struggle by way of mass organizations, mass rallies and public action were to dominate this campaign, while written laws and "regular" legal procedures were as yet unformed in China. The movement began in April of 1951 and it soon reached every major city and involved millions of citizens.

This was to be a new sort of class struggle and popular justice. Unlike suppression and land reform, this movement did *not* seek to destroy the target revolutionary class; it sought only to weaken it. There was little physical violence, few executions or imprisonments, but businessmen paid a great many fines (Barnett, 1964, pp.139-140). The Communists cut the purse strings and not the heads of the capitalist class.

The role of trade unions in "Five Antis"

The trade unions emerged from the campaigns as a powerful and reliably radical mass organization. There were at first some hot arguments between Party leaders pushing for class struggle and old line unionists who wanted a quietly efficient economy with high wages and a minimum of management-labour tensions. A number of union bosses were fired and the reorganized trade unions became the leading popular justice force in Five Antis (Harper, 1969, p.99).

The unions were called into the campaign after the Party had become dissatisfied with the self-policing and self-criticism practiced by the All-China Federation of Industry and Commerce. The Federation was established shortly after liberation and included most of the members of the capitalist class. It was supposed to report all corruption or tax evasion among private business or commercial firms, but the business organization was slow to probe the affairs of its members and was accused of "softness" in punishing law-breaking employers. The government asked the unions to send representatives to Federation meetings and the workers' organizations took over the leadership of the Five Antis campaign (Barnett, 1964, pp.144-5; White, 1973, pp.28-29).

Unions in local factories, stores and shipping firms formed "strike the tiger" teams. These volunteer teams carried out political education and urged other workers to investigate and denounce corrupt employers. Groups of workers and other city dwellers formed People's supervision committees which collected complaints and accusations and helped the unions and "tiger teams" mobilize people for rallies against business men (Harper, 1969, p.99; Hughes and Luard, 1959, pp.83-93; White, 1973, pp.27-8).

The People's Government did not, however, simply begin the campaign and then drop it in the hands of local unions. A number of new laws were passed to guide Five Antis action and government officials, especially police, were often involved in arrests and accusation rallies. The general effects of the government's efforts were to increase pressure on businessmen and to intensify conflicts between labour and management, while limiting the use of physical violence.

Classification of crime in private enterprise

The close-knit business community of China was torn apart by the pressures of class struggle and the policies of the People's Government during Five Antis. The Party leadership called upon trade unions, "strike the tiger" teams and other mass organizations to help prepare investigations and reports on over 450,000 businesses in China's nine largest cities (Schurmann, 1966b, p.318; CFJP, 9th, 22nd March, 1951, in Chen, W. C., 1955, pp. 63, 71).

The private firms of China were then sorted into one of five offence categories on the basis of these reports. The courts were not involved in this process, but assignment to a category carried the weight of a judicial decision. A few months after the campaign began the government formalized the arrangements in the special 1952 Statute on Corruption (Blaustein, 1962, pp.22-228). The five legal classifications for private enterprise were as follows: (1) law abiding; (2) basically law abiding; (3) semi law breaking; (4) seriously law breaking; (5) completely law breaking.

Chinese businessmen have been historically skilled in bribing and eluding government bureaucrats and they might have succeeded in avoiding fines collected by government agencies, but they could not turn aside the investigations conducted by workers in their own companies. The businessmen sweated out the first months of Five Antis while their employees looked over the company books and denounced the bosses in open shop meetings. The initial judgements which placed a firm in one of the five offence categories was made on the basis of the total worth of goods misappropriated or "stolen" by the enterprise in question. The government ended this uneasy waiting period with the publication of the "five category" judgement lists in March of 1951. The executives were relieved to find that the great majority of enterprises were judged to be "basically law abiding" or "semi law abiding" with very few firms condemned as "seriously law breaking" or "completely law breaking". The law on corruption spared most of them the inconvenience of prison and required instead that they pay large fines (Barnett, 1964, pp.140-2; White, 1973, p.28).

Five Antis was not to be a routine mechanical matter of computing fines from a tabulation of illegal profits and hidden company assets, however. Mass line politics and class struggle were extended beyond investigation as workers were also involved in the interrogation, trial and punishment of executives accused of corruption.

The psychology of defendant pressure

Throughout the interrogation the unionists made a special point of urging the bosses to reveal business conspiracies and demanded that executives denounce one another. Those who exposed the crooked ways of their business associates were often given lighter sentences. This psychology of defendant pressure was written into the national Statute of Corruption. So strong was the pressure to confess and denounce fellow capitalists that a great many bosses wrote out long and elaborately false denunciations and confessions. True or false, such statements served to create feelings of mutual distrust among the businessmen. The capitalist class was divided by fear, suspicion and by the lines of the five offence categories (Dunlap, 1956, pp.147-169; Chen, W. C., 1955, p.44).

The familiar popular justice practice of bending legal codes to fit political needs also increased the pressure on businessmen during Five Antis. Bosses who stubbornly resisted the demands of "tiger teams" or unions and those who refused to pay their assigned fines risked being reclassified into a more serious offence category. On occasion employees burst into offices, handcuffed the management and berated them until the exhausted employers admitted their crimes and agreed to pay fines. A number of executives were paraded through city streets in their underwear and were spat upon by thousands of citizens (Barnett, 1964, p.139).

More than a few overseas offices of mainland firms received frantic calls from executives facing the Five Antis storm. The overall strategy behind Five Antis worked, as money stashed in American, Swiss and Hong Kong banks was sent back to pay the heavy fines imposed for business corruption.

The courts and "Five Antis"

Only a few of the employers charged with corruption were actually brought to a formal trial. The courtrooms were reserved for the most serious cases and fines were usually collected by the unions or the police. Those charged with grand theft or active resistance were brought before temporary People's Tribunals. Fraud and grand theft were punishable by death under the 1951 Corruption Law. The unions selected a large number of the assessors who sat with the Tribunals, and thus formalized their role as the leading popular justice agent in Five Antis (Barnett, 1964, pp.136-142).

The unions called out thousands of workers for the free-wheeling mass trials of criminal bourgeoisie at the Tribunals. The court was often held at the place of the accused's enterprise and procedures followed the rugged pattern of popular justice in earlier mass movements. The Tribunals incorporated political education into the judicial process and the unions (and other mass organizations) sponsored smaller meetings to discuss the political significance of the Five Antis corruption trials.

Court statistics for Five Antis are scarce, and there are virtually no systematic figures for the thousands of cases handled outside the Tribunals. It is likely that at least a few thousand businessmen were sent to labour reform camps, and that several score were probably shot. The economic importance of the fines paid during the campaign is certain. In Shanghai alone it is estimated that merchants and industrialists paid more than $250 million in US dollars to the government (about 15% of total intake in the campaign). Fines and back taxes were collected on a retroactive basis (Chen, W. C., 1955, pp.68-70; Barnett, 1964, pp.158-60).

The campaign ended strong private enterprise in China. Many banks and a number of companies closed after Five Antis, and the state-owned share of the national industry jumped from 34% to 53% during the 1949-53 period (Tang and Maloney, 1970, pp.184-221). While some private firms were to hang on until 1956 and the Great Leap Forward, the management was never to regain the composure and capital necessary to play an aggressive role in the national economy. The campaign outlined the political weakness of the bourgeoisie class and served notice that the capitalists were earmarked for gradual removal.

The campaign provided a much needed source of fluid capital for socialist construction. The Communists were reluctant to tax peasants or workers and were not prepared to nationalize private firms. The mass action of Five Antis squeezed funds from the capitalists and helped the government avoid heavy public taxes. Inflation which had developed from the huge government expenditures of 1951 was eased by the payment of fines, which pulled millions of yuan from the bloated economy (Vogel, 1969, pp.80-81; Barnett, 1964, pp.158-161).

Finally, Five Antis may be seen as the end of an era in popular justice. It was the last great movement of class conflict and it established the party, peasants and urban workers as the undisputed ruling forces in a socialist republic. The movement brought the trade unions into national prominence alongside the residents' committees, women's unions, militia, peasant associations, security defence committees, and the People's supervisory committees. The cast of mass organization was, for some time to come, complete. The judicial arms of popular justice, the People's Tribunals, were to be put at rest after the simultaneous Five and Three Antis movements. The days of mass trials, mass accusation rallies and free-swinging court procedures were to return briefly in 1954-55, but the Tribunals would not lead national justice again until 1957.

The nation was, by the close of Five Antis, back on its feet and moving ahead. The Korean crisis had passed and China felt confident after its victory there. The national leadership turned its attention toward the less threatening crimes against public order and to the problems of running a huge government apparatus while at the same time maintaining close ties between bureaucrats,

Party and people. It was to be a tough job and one requiring a new sort of mass line politics.

Street Crime and Liberation Justice

Since the Civil War the Communists had consistently identified imperialism and capitalist exploitation as the source of street crime in China. The evidence of opium wars and organized crime in the foreign concession areas of Chinese cities certainly lends some support to the Communist analysis of crime. The People's Government directed the main force of justice against what they regarded as the sources of social crime. The Minister of Justice and other officials repeatedly stated that the (previously discussed) mass movements against class and political enemies were the first concern of both popular and professional justice during the liberation period.

Despite the priority given to political offenders and "system" crimes (such as capitalism), the Communists did devote some considerable attention to the control of ordinary street crime. Aside from the combined trade union and police attack on organized crime syndicates, there were some serious moves against individual non-political offenders and also some medium-sized campaigns against certain categories of ordinary criminals. Generally these local urban campaigns followed a gentler course than the mass actions against landlords or counter-revolutionaries. The Communists preferred to use persuasion, social pressure and public demonstrations, rather than violence or imprisonment, in dealing with common criminals. The public would be actively involved as the agents of social pressure and informal social education.

The co-operation of police and mass organizations

In Canton the police worked closely with the residents' committees in organizing hundreds of neighbourhood discussion meetings, a few large demonstrations and accusation rallies—all of which were directed toward the elimination of street crime. One such local campaign concentrated on drug abuse and began with a city-wide educational programme in which opium smoking was discussed and denounced as a social indignity inflicted on China by European imperialists. Opium smokers were sought out by local residents and warned to clean up in no uncertain terms.

Some weeks later the residents and local police rounded up nearly 5000 people who continued to use opium. The entire crowd of smokers was paraded through the city streets in a humiliating public demonstration. At the end of the parade a huge bonfire was prepared and confiscated pipes were burned along with large amounts of opium. The opium smokers were finally required to sign a public oath in which they vowed never to use the drug again (Vogel, 1969, p.65). The Communists put opium fields to the torch all over rural China and there is today no evidence of a significant drug abuse problem in the country.

Initially the police were rather sympathetic in their handling of petty thieves. A number of policemen were publicly criticized for confusing "the proletarian viewpoint with the thief's viewpoint". In several publicized cases the police turned robbers loose with all or part of their loot when it was discovered that the victims were better fed or better dressed than the thieves. This sort of selective law enforcement is not surprising given the open class preference and political relativity of Communist justice; but higher officials ended such practices and reprimanded the police (Wei, 1955, p.13).

Public order was viewed as a necessity and campaigns like the anti-opium action were begun to control other problems such as drunkenness, gambling, prostitution and theft. Residents' committees again played a central role as crime prevention and crime control forces. It is difficult systematically to defy the law if the local population supports a vigorous popular justice programme which can act against crime in its earliest stages with persuasion, social pressure and, if necessary, force (Vogel, 1969, pp.48-49; SWJP, 22nd August, 1951, *in* SCMP No. 167, 1951).

Minor offences and popular justice

A huge number of social disputes and minor crimes like juvenile delinquency were resolved by the mediation teams created in mass organizations (especially residents' committees). During 1952-53 alone some 45,960 mediation teams were established or reorganized and these teams involved some 300,000 citizens in mediation work (CFJP, 1st February, 1953, *in* Leng, 1967, p.43). Thousands of cases, piled up during the confusion of Civil War, were worked out by the mediation teams.

The enforcement of the Communists' tradition-shaking Marriage Law opened up thousands more cases as couples unwillingly married before 1949 sued for divorce under the new government. The tight controls of clan organizations, which backed up the feudal marriage customs, were eliminated as the Marriage Law destroyed all legal basis for such kinship groups and ended the authority of clan elders. The violation of women's rights to political, economic and social equality became a criminal offence and this led to more charges and court cases. Despite the avalanche of legal work loosened by the new laws, the Communists were determined to push ahead and in 1951 and 1953 they launched two national mass campaigns on behalf of women's rights (Gudoshnikov, 1957, pp.124-5; Johnson, 1969, p.21).

The police and the courts, acting alone, would have been hard pressed to maintain order and also push social reforms. The radical redefinition of marriage and sex roles is probably beyond the capabilities of any regular judicial bureaucracy. The mass organizations, and particularly the national Women's Union, were essential to this work and the Union continues to make the womenfolk an important force in China. The continued support of mass line Communism by Chinese women is in no small part due to the determined action of government popular justice on women's behalf during the liberation years (Johnson, 1969, pp.21-2).

The "Three Antis" Campaign (1951-52)

The "Three Antis" campaign ran alongside the "Five Antis" movement and is important as the first popular justice struggle against a bureaucratic run-away in government. Three Antis was not an across-the-board confrontation between mass line and the opposing bureaucratic-elite line; but the movement did mark out some of the political boundaries beyond which bureaucrats dared not trespass. Three Antis was the crucial first round in a dialectical conflict between mass line and bureaucratic growth, matters of justice and government in general. Mao, as both a Communist and a former Taoist, recognized the existence of such fundamental political contradictions, and the course of the People's Government affected by the forces and philosophies emerging from the charged dialectical synthesis of Three Antis.

The movement developed as a concerted attack on three serious malpractices of the People's Government (hence the term Three Antis). These three were waste, corruption and bureaucratism. Po I po, a member of the Party Politburo, announced the opening of the movement in January 1952, a few weeks before the start of Five Antis (Po I Po, in Chen, W. C., 1955, p.49).

In 3000 years of national history no Chinese government had ever seriously attempted to curb bureaucratic corruption. Graft had been an integral part of political culture and bribery an essential skill for all officials. The Communist philosophy of mass line politics called for an end to the official rackets and demanded that government consciously avoid bureaucratic or arrogant attitudes in its relations with the people.

The mass line dictated that the struggle with corruption not be a behind-the-scenes political purge, but rather a public event directly involving the common people. This campaign, like those before it, created and encouraged new mass organizations. Spokesmen for the People's Government described the new Three Antis campaign with pride as follows:

> This is a movement of historical significance. Never in any period of China's past has there been such a movement; nor was a movement of this kind

possible. Only democratic rule of the people under the leadership of the
Communist Party could dare to initiate such a mass movement to uproot,
once and for all, the rotten legacy of centuries of reactionary rule. Only a
People's Democracy can stand the vigorous test of such a movement and
thereby further consolidate and strengthen itself (SWJP, 8th March, 1952,
in SCMP No. 39, 1951)

In practice, the movement was to mean intensive political study and internal
housecleaning for the staff of government bureaux. The people were also to
participate in popular justice action against corrupt or arrogant officials and
many cadres were thrown from office.

The targets of "Three Antis"

Those most often in trouble during Three Antis were the bureaucratic "holdovers", i.e. men who had served the KMT as petty officials and who were no
longer wanted now that more reliable help could be found. During the initial
Three Antis action in East China, fully 42% of those purged were holdovers
(White, 1973, p.29). Soon after liberation the Communists set up huge training
institutes to prepare candidates for government service, and most of the students
were chosen for their work as activist volunteers in the earlier land reform and
suppression movements. The graduates of the training centres were to replace
many holdovers.

A number of Party members and Party-appointed officials were also charged,
denounced and fired during Three Antis. Some of these had accepted bribes
from wealthy families in exchange for protection during the class struggle of the
suppression and land reform campaigns. The charge of "bureaucratism" was
lodged against other ex-guerrillas who had been too impressed by their new
powers as officials of the new government (Wei, 1955, pp.50–52; Gudoshnikov,
1957, p.103).

The Party's determination to keep government in touch with the people was
a basic part of the Common Programme prepared in 1949. The Common
Programme served as the supreme national law in the years before the 1954
Constitution. Article 4 of the Programme commanded that:

All State Organs of the People's Republic of China must rigorously maintain
a work demeanour that is pure and frugal and that serves the people. They
must severely oppose the bureaucratic demeanour that causes the organs to
separate themselves from the people (Blaustein, 1962)

Some corruption was inevitable from the very size of the People's Government, but the level of corruption uncovered in Three Antis was particularly
serious in view of China's stretched finances, the pressures of the Korean War

and the need to modernize the country. Po Yi po hinted at the extent of official rackets and bureaucratic arrogance when he announced the discovery of 1670 cases of corruption in 27 government agencies, with a total loss of over 200,000 million JMP ($US 10,000) for Canton city alone. Later reports indicated some 4500 Canton corruption cases (Barnett, 1964, p.138). It is probable that Shanghai had an even larger number of cases with a greater loss in revenue. It has been estimated that by the end of Three Antis, over 4·5% of all government officials received some form of punishment for misbehaviour (Schurmann, 1966b, p.318; Kau, 1969, p.49).

Charges were usually lodged against *individual* officials, but there are some clearly visible patterns in the Three Antis cases. The great majority of defendants came from two specific branches of government: finance and justice (White, 1973, p.29). Many cadres were accused of involvement in kickback rackets or protection deals with city capitalists. The police and especially the regular People's Courts were linked with corruption and favouritism. The numerous KMT holdover judges were denounced for graft and for their failure to change their arrogant and elitist working styles (Li, 1969b, pp.10-11).

A number of top justice officials were pulled down. The Director of Police in the huge South-Central China region and his Deputy Director were dismissed. The Chief Procurator for this same region was also fired along with the Mayor of Wuhan. These and other officials were publicly disgraced and accused of "screening corrupt elements" from the people's justice (URI, Vol. I, pp.40-41). More than a few police officials were punished for black market rackets. In Tientsin 21 police were convicted of illegal buying and selling, and a ranking police chief in Nanking was caught operating gambling houses (JMJP, 8th September, 1950, *in* Wei, 1955, pp.50-51).

Typically the national Party leadership called upon government agencies to conduct political study and criticism sessions aimed at producing an extensive self-examination. The national Party leadership sent special "investigation teams" to spur Three Antis actions inside government and local party branches (Schurmann, 1966b, p.315). As in earlier campaigns, the Communists worked the "defendant pressure psychology" into the strategy of the campaign. Those who voluntarily confessed or implicated others were treated leniently. Agency heads were held responsible for the failures and offences of their subordinates.

These practices are rather un-Western but they are not strange to Chinese political history, and they served to widen the impact of Three Antis investigations. It was hard for bureaucracies to "scapegoat" their way out of public and Party criticism since bosses could be punished for the failings of scapegoats. Three Antis put sustained pressure on municipal government bureaux and especially the regular justice agencies. In several cities the entire police force entered into study and self-criticism programmes which uncovered not a few crooked policemen and ultimately forced many of these and even some district police chiefs to resign (White, 1973, p.30).

Supervisory committees and "Three Antis" action

The public added to this intense pressure and agency-surveillance, again through their mass organizations. A few associations of volunteer agency-watchers were established and officially recognized as People's supervisory committees. Thousands of these local committees were set up, each with a dozen or so members. They were frequently elected by the local core organizations (residents' committees, unions, youth leagues and women's unions). The supervisory committees were initially created on a local basis to watch the performance of area officials (such as police, teachers, financial administrators and judges). The committees were considered so important to the maintenance of responsiveness in government that the organizations were included as part of the 1949 Common Programme (Blaustein, 1962, pp.41–42; T'an P'ing shan, NCNA, 4th August, 1951, *in* SCMP No. 163, 1951).

During the course of Three Antis the national Party leadership urged the supervisory committees to enter national politics as a co-ordinated popular force. The first All-China Conference on People's Supervisory Work was called in April 1951 in Peking. The hundreds of committees represented at the conference had already handled over 7000 cases against both counter-revolutionaries and corrupt officials. P'eng Chen, Member of the Party Politburo and Vice-Chairman of the National Council on Political–Legal Affairs, addressed the conference. P'eng called on the citizens' supervisory committees to watch officials and to mobilize the people against counter-revolution and corruption. Other speakers urged that local committees install suggestion-and-criticism boxes and work to encourage public criticism of malpractice in government (NCNA, 29th April, 1951, *in* SCMP No. 101, 1951).

The expansion of the supervisory committees led to the creation of regional and national People's supervisory offices. The local committees were also linked to the national Party leadership through co-operation with the "special investigation teams", and were provided with funds from the national budget. Ultimately these committees against corruption and bureaucracy became the street arm of a new agency, the Ministry of Control, which would itself be attacked later as a stagnant and elitist bureaucracy. This piece of political dialectic calls to mind a tale from West Texas about a black snake that swallowed itself to stay warm, but that is another story and one most relevant to the more recent history of China. During those first few years of the Republic the committees worked effectively in hearing accusations and preparing charges against offending bureaucrats.

Most charges of corruption or bureaucracy were made during the heated study and criticism sessions arranged by each agency for internal policing and sanctioning. In other cases the wayward officials were singled out and accused by the citizens' supervisory committees, usually by way of reports sent to the accused's superiors. Few of the defendants were formally convicted before a court. Most were investigated and cleared, or denounced, disgraced and fired upon the advice of their co-workers and the decisions of higher government authorities (Li, 1969b, p.40; Schurmann, 1966b, p.318).

Three Antis was not, however, an entirely lawless affair of citizens' complaints and office confrontations. The People's Government closely watched and guided both intra-agency struggles and the actions of popular justice.

In April 1952 the government prepared a special "Statute on Penalties for Corruption in the People's Republic", which set the punishment for the most serious Three Antis cases. This special law sounds rather Western in that prison terms were based on the value of goods embezzled, but the Chinese also wrote their "defendant pressure psychology" (so effective in the suppression and land reform campaigns) into this law. Thus sentences initially set by the worth of goods stolen could be reduced if the defendant made a voluntary confession or if he/she exposed other offenders (Blaustein, 1962, pp.227–233).

The courts and "Three Antis"

The People's Tribunals which enforced this statute were similar to the Tribunals which handled the land reform and suppression defendants. The Party leadership was at this point still reluctant to rely on the regular People's Courts for political-legal leadership, especially in view of the large number of KMT holdover judges and the numerous judges under suspicion in the campaign. These temporary courts had the advantages of being more open to popular justice action and were more politically reliable than the People's Courts. As was often noted, the Tribunals "were more flexible and closer to the people, capable of resolving a great number of cases related to the movement" (White, 1973, p.29).

The Tribunals were chaired by army officers or regional government officials, while public representatives chosen from Three Antis activists and mass organizations also served as judges with equal voting rights (Gudoshnikov, 1957, p.108). The Tribunals followed the popular justice pattern of mass rallies and loose procedures in trials that were as much political education as judicial events.

Sentences passed by the People's Tribunals were not nearly as severe as in the earlier campaigns. In one period at the end of Three Antis some 332 recorded cases ended with 6% death sentences, 73% labour re-education terms and 21% lesser sanctions (Kau, 1969). Again it should be emphasized that only the most serious cases went to trial, but taken together with the vastly more numerous dismissals and public censures of bureaucrats, it was clear to everyone that Three Antis was a serious business.

It should also be pointed out that a Three Antis dismissal for malpractice did not necessarily mean the end of an official's career. Those removed could and often did work their way back into government service. While Communist and non-Communist officials seem to have been fired in about equal proportions, the Communists had a better chance of recovery and reassignment after a period of reform through education and punitive labour. Generally those dismissed and sent to labour re-education camps remained on the organizational tables of their agency and often continued to receive a percentage of their original salary. The government generally sent enough funds to meet the expenses of their families while the ex-officials were "away" (Kau, 1969).

This pattern of accusation-dismissal-reform-reassignment is found in the career lines of many Communists and not a few non-Communist officials. Later mass campaigns against government abuse, such as Judicial Reform (1952-53) and Anti-Rightist (1957) had much the same effects as Three Antis. Throughout these actions the intent was not to destroy individual careers, but to make officials more sensitive to public demands and more aware of their own political vulnerability.

The net effect of the campaign was to support and expand mass line politics. Strong national government and industrial growth was not to mean an automatic bureaucratic lock-up of the revolution. The purge of KMT holdovers made bureaux more reliable, and their replacement by citizen activists drew popular politics more closely into official government. New and old bureaucrats alike were warned, by widely publicized case examples, against arrogance and elitism.

The new People's Supervisory committees and the mass actions of Three Antis are important events in the development of popular justice. For the first time mass organizations were actively opposed to bureaucrats and certain official policies of government. The committees were the first institutional recognition of the conflict between mass line and bureaucratic growth in China.

Three Antis was also the first instance of a clearly *political* struggle after earlier mass movements which emphasized *class* struggle. It is not surprising that agencies of justice should be among those singled out in the campaigns, for justice had historically been a subject of political struggle. Differences between mass line and the bureaucratic-elite line are especially visible in the operations of justice, where conflict is the subject of government. Three Antis would not be the last occasion for popular action in political contests over the policies and institutions of justice.

Judicial Reform (1952–53)

The Three Antis campaign made clear the Communist determination that new government officials remember mass line principles and avoid the corrupt and arrogant traditions of bureaucrats before them. The Judicial Reform Movement of 1952-53 was to strike at old bourgeois concepts of law and especially at judges who still sat with the stiff elitist posture of magistrates in old China.

In the three years since liberation the Party had built a national structure of regular People's Courts; but many of these courts were run by ex-KMT judges who valued legal procedures and "professional" standards above popular participation and socialist ideology. The Communists needed agile and politically sensitive judges who were in touch with the common people and the great class struggles against landlords, counter-revolutionaries and capitalists. The old legally trained judges of the People's Courts stood aside and watched as the serious business of class struggle and mass movements was handled by the street-trained jurists of the People's Tribunals. Now that questions of class power were resolved in favour of workers, peasants and Party, the Communists were anxious to make the People's Courts into the permanent institutions of a more regular and orderly judicial system. The Party called for a national judicial reform campaign to set the political course of a new professional justice (Cheng P'u, JMJP, 1952, in CLG, Vol. I, No. 3, 1968, pp.72-73).

It was a feminist and not a party member who announced this reform campaign and opened it for popular justice action. Shih Liang, the first Minister of Justice, criticized the work of the People's Courts and called for a national judicial overhaul in her August 1952 report to the People's Government. She described the intent and organization of the new campaign as follows:

> It is both necessary and opportune to raise now the question of the thorough reform and reorganization of all grades of the People's Courts along with the consolidation and deepening of the Three Antis movement. With a view to carrying out this reform so that all grades of People's Courts will be enabled to preserve and enhance their political, organizational and ideological purity, we propose the following views:
>
> 1. We must first of all reshuffle and dispose of the responsible cadres, from top to bottom, who have already degenerated, displayed bad working style or persisted in the old judicial viewpoints. At the same time we must eliminate from the judicial departments the unworthy elements among the retained (ex-KMT) personnel. In principle, retained personnel who have not been thoroughly reformed and undergone severe tests should not be permitted to act as judges.
>
> 2. The various grades of the People's Courts must be supplied with necessary cadres . . . Particular attention should be paid to the bold promotion to important posts of activists from among the cadres of People's Courts . . . and who were hard workers during the Three Antis and Five Antis campaigns and during their previous work.
>   Next the People's Courts should be complemented in strength by a group of elites supplied from the cadres of the People's Tribunals, from revolutionary [PLA] servicemen assigned to [socialist] construction

work, from workers', peasants', youth and women's (mass) organizations.

3. The thorough reform and reorganization of the different levels of the
People's Courts is an important measure . . . This is not only a question
of reshuffling personnel within the People's Courts, but also a question of
clearing away the remnants of reactionary judicial ideas and working
styles of the KMT. For this reason, it is necessary to begin—by
mobilizing the masses from top to bottom in a planned and systematic
manner . . . (Shih Liang, JMJP, 23rd August, 1952, *in* Steiner, 1953,
Vol II, pp.115-6)

The overall strategy of Judicial Reform was to draw the energies and working
philosophy of popular justice into the regular justice system of the People's
Courts. The central leadership could quite easily order the purge of all ex-KMT
judges, but Judicial Reform was meant to be more than a change in courtroom
casts. The revolutionaries wanted nothing less than a clean break with 2000
years of judicial culture. They called for a mass effort in changing the people's
traditional distaste for courts and enlisted popular support in an attack on old
elitist courtroom practices. It was an ambitious task and was probably impossible
without the concentrated energy of a mass campaign. Judicial Reform involved
millions of citizens, judges and police in rethinking judicial philosophy and
courtroom procedures. A complete new set of mass organizations was created for
the campaign and the older permanent formations of workers, students, women
and peasants all contributed to the making of the national People's Court system.

    The dismissal of judges unresponsive to the needs of socialist justice was the
first and easiest of Shih Liang's reform goals. A long hard look at the staff of the
People's Courts had already begun with the Three Antis movement. The
government's special investigation teams and the People's supervisory committees had turned over a good many benches and fired many judges and police
chiefs for bribery, corruption and elitism. This examination continued well into
Judicial Reform and the newspapers carried numerous accounts of judges
dismissed and prosecuted for courtroom rackets and such excesses as the rape
and torture of defendants (KMJP, 18th September, 1952; JMJP, 21st July,
19th August, 1952, *in* Leng, 1967, p.39). The elimination of such practices
might seem a simple muck-raking operation to those more familiar with Western
courts, but it must be remembered that this sort of judicial behaviour was
unofficially regarded as routine and appropriate among more than three-score
generations of pre-Communist judges.

    The new movement placed particular pressure on the ex-KMT holdover
judges. Despite Three Antis attacks a large number of holdovers remained on
People's Court payrolls at the start of Judicial Reform. In the Shanghai courts,
84 of 104 regular judges had served the old regime, while in T'ienching 46 out of
120 were holdovers (JMJP, 30th August, 1952, *in* Gudoshnikov, 1957, p.37;

Li, 1969a, pp.18-21). Shih Liang reported that 6000 or 22% of the People's Court jurists were retained from KMT service (Shih Liang, JMJP, 13th August, 1952, *in* Leng, 1967, p.90). The holdovers were denounced individually and as a group. Party spokesmen attacked them for their failure to integrate legal practice with Communist political-legal philosophies as found in such works as Mao's "On New Democracy". Moreover, the judges of the old school seemed unable to shake off their feudal ideas concerning women, and were charged with failure to understand and enforce the new Marriage Laws (Rickett and Rickett, 1964). The Communists asserted that 60 to 80% of the holdover judges were "opposed to Communism and the Communist Party". Not surprisingly, the Communists chose thoroughness over delicacy in dealing with holdovers, and by the end of the campaign around 80% of the ex-KMT judges were ex-judges (KMJP, 31st August, 1952, *in* CNA No. 203, 1952; CCJP, 24th August, 1952, *in* Leng, 1967, p.42; Cohen, 1968a, p.978).

Mass line and Judicial Reform

Judicial Reform also developed into a "fierce political and ideological struggle" between bourgeois and socialist legal theory and practice. New judges and hold-overs alike were criticized for their preoccupation with the technicalities of legal procedure. The People's Courts were supposed to be a school for socialism and an active force in the reordering of society. The Communists would not be satisfied with judges who confined themselves to hearing and settling disputes and maintaining order. Judges were urged to leave their chambers and take justice and courts into factories and fields. For the Communists, as for every previous Chinese government, law was politics; but the Communists wanted justice to be an active revolutionary force and not a passive political instrument (NFJP, 22nd October, 1952, *in* CNA No. 245, 1952; JMJP 5th September, 1951, *in* SCMP No. 168, 1951; Cohen, 1968a, pp.977-8).

The Communist emphasis on political ideology and popular participation at the expense of orthodox legal procedures was clear in the work of the People's Tribunals as described in the land reform, Suppression and Five Antis movements. Judicial Reform was to bring this sort of legal practice into the regular People's Courts. The Communist mass line perspective on the political role and daily practice of courts was well described before Judicial Reform in such national editorials as this:

> The judicial system and working style of the People's Courts are aimed at advantage for the masses, connection with the masses, and service to the people. On no account do they conduct hearings simply on the strength of complaints, depositions and defence, but lay stress on on-the-spot investi-gation and study, on acquainting themselves with all the true facts of the case

and on obtaining adequate evidence before passing judgement according to law . . . At the same time, contrary to all reactionary and backward judicial systems which passively await for charges to be brought up, and then simply mete out punishment, our people's courts always attach importance to propaganda—education on the laws and adopt appropriate methods to conduct it.

> The People's Courts regard judicial propaganda work as an important part of the judicial process. Propaganda—education on the laws and discipline— will result in greatly elevating the awakening of the broad masses and in enabling them to avoid the occurrence of offences and disputes; conse- quently, judicial work will be enabled to seize the initiative and to pass from the passive to the active (JMJP, 5th September, 1951, *in* Steiner, 1953, Vol. II, pp.16-17)

The editorial continues on to attack bourgeois legal theory for its false separation of law from political ideology. The Party leadership regarded the courts as but "another arm of the people's democratic state power" and regarded the administration of courts by higher agencies of government as a logical feature of socialism. The Party spokesmen criticized some judicial workers of the old school for:

> . . . the premature emphasis on the independence of the people's judicial organs from the interference of local people's governments, and the subjective demand for something that is called an orthodox system that divorces itself from reality (JMJP, 5th September, 1951, *in* Steiner, 1953, Vol. II, pp.16-17)

The "reality" of which the editor spoke was the condition of class conflict which still existed, though with reduced violence, at the time of Judicial Reform. As long as the suppression of class enemies was regarded as the first task of Communist justice the courts would be tightly controlled by larger government and judicial decisions would speak of ideology before law. Judges who failed to bring mass line and socialist ideology into judicial practice were criticized and often fired during the reform campaign. Even the old Communist judges from the Civil War days were vulnerable to Judicial Reform pressure and were required to move beyond bureaucratic procedures, changing the language and practice of justice to meet public needs.

The mass line also demanded that justice and law be written in the language of the people. Unless the judges and legal officials adopted street language, the value of the court as an educational institution was limited. The Peking Municipal People's Court published a judge's handbook in 1950 which stressed that:

> A judicial decision is a document meant for the public. It should be written so as to be understood not only by the litigants but also by people not involved in the case. Therefore, not only must the facts be clearly

presented in a decision, but the language used must be in a popular style. Ordinary stereotyped expressions for legal documents . . . should be avoided (Hsia Tao-Tai, 1967, p.15)

The handbook's instructions were repeated many times in pointed criticism of judges trained in the "old working style" of Western or KMT law. The Communists were determined that even the regular People's Courts be so simple in language and procedure as to be intelligible to the man on the street. Laws were to be brief and simply written, even if this meant a sacrifice of some legal precision. Throughout the Judicial Reform campaign, judges with law degrees and/or KMT experience were roundly criticized for their failure to "keep law simple".

Mass organizations in the campaign

The actual mechanics of the campaign were true to the pattern of popular justice action noted in earlier mass movements and especially in the Three Antis. The central government, through Shih Liang, initiated the campaign and directed county and city branches of the government to establish local "Judicial Reform committees". These committees were composed of volunteer representatives of local government bureaux (including reliable court personnel), members of the local Party branches and representatives of mass organizations (NFJP, 22nd October, 1951, in SCMP No. 182, 1951).

The Judicial Reform committees heard complaints against judges and prepared charges against ex-KMT and Communist jurists alike. Great numbers of common citizens participated through the committees or the mass organizations. The committees prepared only a few criminal charges, as the most serious cases of judicial corruption had been resolved during Three Antis. For the most part erring judges were censured or placed in political education programmes, while those dismissed were mostly the ex-KMT holdover judges. The total purged from the judiciary was probably around 7000 (of 22,000 judges).

The Party had very few law-school-trained cadres on hand to replace judges fired in the campaign. Instead, most of the new judges were chosen from those workers and Party members who had served on the temporary People's Tribunals during the earlier mass movements (Li, 1969a, pp.11–12; Shih Liang, TKP, 25th August, 1950, in Wei, 1955, p.11; KMJP, 31st August, 1952, in CNA No. 203, 1951). Some 6505 new people were brought into the judicial system, including 1707 women. The new judges were not well versed in the intricacies of legal procedure, but they were close to popular movements and were politically reliable. Over 70% of them were members of either the Communist Party or the Communist-led Youth League (Shih Liang, NCNA, 12th May, 1953, in Leng, 1967, p.43).

China's law schools were also shaken up by the Judicial Reform action. Law departments and political-legal training institutes in Shanghai, Peking and Wuhan were reorganized and new departments were established. Curricula were reconstituted to connect legal theory and professional practice to mass line principles. Students were urged to stay in close contact with the people and their mass organizations (Cohen, 1970, p.58; Lee, L. T. C., 1961, p.343).

The end of Judicial Reform was marked by the Second National Conference held in April 1953. The conference stands out as a turning point in the history of justice since it ushered in a new era of legal consolidation and professionalism. The delegates adopted resolutions calling for the regulation of popular justice functions such as mediation, investigation and adjudication. The informal system of People's Courts was firmly established and new professional standards were set for the judges. Finally, the conference urged the drafting of a national constitution and asked for more law schools and government legislation to guide the judicial system further (Gudoshnikov, 1957, pp.46-47). The liberation period of mass political-legal action was ending in a surge of industrial growth and national judicial legislation.

6 The Constitutional Moment and the Drive to Professionalism

By 1953 the debris of Civil War was cleared and new Russian locomotives rumbled over rebuilt rail lines hauling the fuel and materials for Chinese industry. The mass movements of liberation had pushed aside the old ruling classes of landlords, capitalists and bureaucrats, and the country was ready for a time of peaceful progress. The Communists, after Three Antis and Judicial Reform, were at last comfortable with their political and legal bureaux and were ready to assign them greater powers in the Socialist Reconstruction period of 1953-57.

The Political Economy of Industrialization

The First Five-year Plan, begun in 1953, was a deliberate departure from the political economy of the Civil War and liberation years. The plan depended on social stability and centralized economic controls, and the new emphasis on a quietly efficient economy required a more systematic government of laws and regular bureaucratic procedures. The collectivization of agriculture and the rapid build-up of heavy industry, were to be accomplished at the same time. The Communists poured billions of Soviet roubles and Chinese yuan into the two tasks and set up enormous government bureaux to manage industry and agriculture. The mobilization of vast human resources, as in earlier mass movements, was *not* to be the central idea of the new political economy. The ideology of mass line was still the language of government, but the Five-year Plan would count first on massed capital rather than massed labour (Johnson, 1969, p.52).

The Russian influence was important in the decision to shift the gears of political economy. The Soviets had long ago sacrificed popular support to bureaucratic control and were convinced that total centralization was essential to socialist development. In 1957 Djilas well described the development and power of the centralized Soviet bureaucrat elite in his book "The New Class". While the Maoist leadership did accept a great deal of Soviet "enlightenment" there were, even in 1953–54, a number of Party veterans who disliked and distrusted the Russian political style and who, like Djilas, worried about the appearance of a bureaucratic monster behind a centralized industrial economy.

Rural change and the First Five-year Plan

Collectivization in the countryside was a fairly successful mixture of Soviet strategy and Chinese methods. Stalin had relied upon travelling propaganda-leadership terms from the cities and the persuasive effects of fixed bayonets to "raise peasant consciousness" and establish collective farms on schedule in 1935–37. But the Chinese Communists had begun their revolution among the farmers and felt no need to use brute force in their 1955–56 collectivization drive.

The peasant associations of the Civil War and liberation period sparked the collectivization campaign and through them the Communists were able to complete a popular and peaceful socialization of agriculture. In 1950 20% of the peasants were organized into collectives, by 1952 the number had only reached 25%, but over 60% of the farmers had joined by 1955 (Bernstein, 1967, pp.1–4). There were no great massacres of middle-class peasants as in the Soviet slaughter of the "kulaks". The Chinese proceeded gradually through collectivization and made considerable adjustment for local differences among the farmers.

Tractors and technological aid were the great persuasive arguments used by peasant associations to draw the country folk into farm collectives. Machines, co-operative child care centres and community kitchens could increase the labour force and ease the individual farmer's work load; but these things were only possible in higher collectives where resources were pooled.

The Chinese, with Soviet aid, were able to build or purchase hundreds of tractors, but the government refused to put the machines directly in the hands of those who would use them. The Russians had persuaded their comrades that the peasants were incapable of properly maintaining and efficiently using the new equipment. The tractors were kept in government garages and rented out to the peasants for day use.

This sort of bureaucratic chauvinism did not go down well with the more radical supporters of the mass line. One of these, Kang Sheng, returned from a tour of Russian farms in 1954 and noted that:

Collective farms in the Soviet Union have many machines but production is nevertheless low and costs are high (Kang Sheng, *in* Gray, 1970, pp.122-3)

Like many other Chinese Communists Kang Sheng disliked the government tractor station arrangement and he angrily wrote:

This is a problem that must be solved: how to link the tractors to the peasants . . . If tractor stations continue to be run in their present form . . . they will become disguised tax-collectors, and will hold the peasants to ransom, as the Soviet tractor stations do . . .

The centralized control of agriculture was the subject of long argument and tension between mass line radicals and those who believed the tight control of technology and planning was a necessary government duty (Gray, 1970, p.123).

The politics of industrialization

Industry boomed as the government spent huge sums on new machinery and on the wages of industrial workers. The Chinese were determined that technology and heavy industry should quickly expand to provide China with a modern economic base. Soviet arguments and the need to develop industry fast and far prompted the party to create a system of material incentives to encourage increased production. Wage gaps between individual workers widened as each labourer was paid on a piece-work basis. Industrial workers as a group were better paid than farmers; but the best-treated were the professionals, scientists and government bureaucrats who received huge wage increases and special privileges (Hoffman, 1963, pp.97-99).

These policies were an effective way to recruit workers and intellectuals into industrial work, but the system of material incentives threatened social equality and the mass line ideology of voluntary mass action. The decline of mass political participation and the renewal of competition among workers weakened mass organizations and the sense of shared social community. Unions became increasingly concerned with wages and fringe benefits rather than socialist ideology and mass political participation (Harper, 1969, pp.12-13, 30-31). As will be noted later, popular justice declined as a political–legal force during this period.

Though costly in terms of popular politics, the Five-year Plan did carry China a long way toward a socialist economic system. Steel production had plodded along from less than a million tons in 1949 to about 1·35 million tons in 1953; but the Five-year Plan boom brought production to 5·35 million tons in 1957. Petroleum output tripled and electric power doubled during this period (Barnett, 1962, p.54; King, H. H., 1968, p.187).

The state, by means of legal and financial pressure, completed the take-over of private enterprises (still staggering from the effects of the Five Antis campaign), nationalizing all remaining capitalist firms by 1956. Capitalist owners were given bonds in exchange for their businesses, but dividends from these were described as a "revolutionary measure, not a fixed or codified right" and so the capitalists remained vulnerable to political pressure and the threat of financial loss (Hsiao, G., 1965, pp.5–6).

The growth of the state share in China's economy is illustrated by the shift in sources of government revenue. During the liberation period the Communists had drawn only 17% of their funds from state-owned industry, another 39% from taxes on private firms and 41% from the unpopular and politically costly public grain tax. Midway through the Five-year Plan, the government could count on its own state enterprises to the tune of 64%, the weakened capitalists for another 15%, and was able to reduce the load on farmers by drawing only 13% of government revenue from the grain tax (Tang and Maloney, 1970, pp.56–9).

The growth of the bureaucrat–technocrat elite

Centralized planning, the expansion of government functions and the emphasis on production efficiency contributed to the emergence of a new elite of bureaucrats and the beginnings of a "bureaucratic elite" political line. The bureaucracy grew into a mammoth, expanding from 720,000 workers (0·13% of the population) in 1949 to 5,170,000 and 0·86% of the population in 1955. The cost of government was high, the payroll amounting to about 10% of the national budget. Most of the new lower and middle-level officials were recruited from the ranks of citizen activists in mass campaigns, but centralized economic planning and the bureaucratic structure of government worked against their background and eroded their belief in mass line politics. Moreover, a good many ex-KMT officials yet remained in the government and these people had plenty of reason to prefer bureaucratic "consolidation" over continued mass political action and class struggle (Kau, 1969, pp.27–37).

Near the top of the government were a group of "planners" who lived by a new ideology of "efficiency", "professionalism" and centralized political control. A large number of the newly recruited, ex-citizen officials accepted the planners' ideas as the most reasonable style of leadership for socialism. The old pre-Mao Communist leadership of the 1920s was staging a national comeback. Party "organization men" like Liu Shao chi had never been comfortable with boisterous mass campaigns and mass line politics which sacrificed party discipline for mass participation; but they were skilled in industrial organization and bureaucratic operations. Liu and the Party conservatives sought out the politically lukewarm technologist-intellectuals and, through persuasion and material inducements, pulled them into the planning councils of government. Together, these technologists were to be the junior members of a new conservative political elite especially prominent during the First Five-year Plan of 1953-57.

Both the origin and the political power of the new elite were tied to the use of centralized industrialization as an economic strategy. The new bureaucratic elite was strongest in the unions and the bureaux of industrial management. Their less powerful technological elite partners were drawn mostly from fields of practical value to a centralized industry, such as engineering, economics and the physical sciences. It should be stressed that the technological elite did *not* include most of China's "intellectual" class. Artists, poets, scholars and most teachers were left outside the circles of power. Even those intellectuals invited into the government bureaux were not granted power and influence equal to the Party bureaucrats. Tension between the Party and intellectuals (including both the more favoured technologists and the ignored artists and scholars) continued. Admission to the new conservative elite depended on one's potential contribution to industrialization and the fortunes of the elite are, to this day, tied to development of centralized industry in China.

The bureaucratic-technological elite of 1953-56 wanted a sharp curtailment of the messy and often embarrassing business of militant popular justice. They well remembered the painful days of Three Antis, when public scrutiny and charges of corruption or elitism threatened the independent power of officials throughout the country. Few had forgotten the humiliation of struggle meetings where the general public and the mass organizations had denounced bureaucrats for arrogance, corruption and elitism, and the accused officials were not even permitted to reply (Barnett, 1966, p.11).

The rising bureaucratic-techological elite wanted assurances that agency stability and their own political careers would not be disturbed by more such mass actions. Not surprisingly, they wanted to close the book on class struggle and popular justice. Spokesmen for the new elite dutifully praised the mass line achievements of liberation years but they repeatedly stressed that China should turn her attention to production since the era of class conflict was over.

All but the most ardent radicals were for a time affected by the new conservative political mood. Indeed it should be pointed out that bureaucratic "consolidation" and the development of a regular justice system were national policies fully approved by Mao and the central Party leadership. Soviet assistance was crucial to Chinese development and the deep contradictions between the Maoist faith in popular politics and the conservatism of the bureaucratic elite were not as obvious in 1954 as they were in 1967 or even 1957. Chou en Lai, always a lithe political tumbler, stood beside the bureaucratic elite and called for more conciliatory social policies. He argued that:

> The representatives of the state should co-operate with those (non-reactionary) representatives of the capitalists and give them free scope to use their special knowledge and their initiative and, in the process of working with them, make efforts to re-educate them, help them overcome their bourgeois ideas and style of work and gradually turn them into working people in the real sense of the term . . . (Chou en Lai, 1956a, Vol. I, p.309)

> We should not discriminate against them.

Some indication of the new elite's growing strength may be seen in the 1955-56 revision of entrance requirements for the Communist Party. Throughout the Civil War and the liberation period the Party made special efforts to recruit the poorest peasants and city workers, and had established a special, more open admissions procedure for these struggling social elements. The new conservative elite regarded the revolution as essentially complete with the First Five-year Plan, and admissions were tightened with more "objective" standards that favoured the educated middle class. Liu Shao chi explained that the new admissions policy was reasonable since, "the former classification of social status has lost or is losing its original meaning". The conservatives opened the Party to the intellectuals who Liu claimed, "have now come over politically to the side of the working class" and who of course spoke the language of the bureaucratic-technological elite. (Liu Shao chi, 1957, Vol. I, pp.172-5; *see also for contrast*, Constitution, CCP, *in* Steiner, 1953, Vol. I, p.66).

The high point for this new ideology of disciplined production and elite control came in 1956. The Eighth National Party Congress was held in that year and Party conservatives basked in the warm light of the economic success. Liu Shao chi delivered a major address which stands as one of the clearest expression of the social stability ideology and its implications for popular and professional justice. Liu reviewed history and economic developments as follows:

> The Party programme for a democratic revolution has been carried out in nearly all parts of the country, and its programme for a socialist revolution has, in the main, been carried out. The present task is to complete the socialist revolution of the country, building China into a mighty socialist industrial country.

> During this [liberation] period, the chief aim of the struggle was to liberate the people from reactionary rule . . . The principle method of struggle was to lead the masses in direct action . . . Now, however, the period of revolutionary storm and stress is past, new relations of production have been set up, and the aim of our struggle is changed into one safeguarding the successful development of the productive forces of the society, a corresponding change in the methods of struggle will consequently have to follow, and a complete legal system becomes an absolute necessity (Liu Shao chi, 1957, Vol. I, pp.208-209)

Liu spoke for the Soviet advisers and the growing ranks of career bureaucrats who wanted stability and political protection guaranteed by a professional legal system. This conservative elite would not attempt to eliminate mass political participation, but would seek to subordinate mass action to central government and would, over a time, almost disarm popular justice. If mass organizations could be reduced to the status of dependent, political auxiliaries and if popular justice could be bound within professionally controlled bureaucracies, then the fortunes of the bureaucratic-technological elite would be assured. The Constitution of 1954 was to come near to the desires of this elite and the Russian advisers gazed upon the new Chinese legal system with the pride of parenthood.

The 1954 Constitution and the Structure of Professional Justice

Work on a new socialist constitution had begun as early as 1948 when the Judicial Commission of the Communist Party Central Committee began the preparation of an All China Law on the Judicial System. The Commission looked closely at judicial experiences in Civil War liberated areas and studied Soviet legal literature, especially the Soviet Constitution (Cohen, 1968b, p.5; Gudoshnikov, 1957, p.28). Even during the liberation period some justice professionals had called for a tighter regulation of court procedures and an upgrading of professional standards among judicial personnel (Wang Fei jan, *in* Wei, 1955, p.11). Despite these efforts and urgings the Communists did not enact much in the way of codified law and did not establish strong professional justice bureaux in the early years of 1949-53. The resistance to a more systematic justice was at this time more pragmatic than ideological as Party spokesmen later recalled:

> . . . during this historical stage, a detailed and perfect legal system divorced from actualities could not and should not have been instituted to bind the feet and hands of the masses (Ginsbergs and Stahnke, 1964, p.23; JMJP, 21st May, 1954, *in* SCMP No. 201, 1954)

As the country moved into the Socialist Construction era of the First Five-year Plan, however, the pressure to develop a professional law-bound judicial establishment increased. The Soviets joined the government careerists in demanding a more regular justice. There were in Russia over 100,000 jurists trained in law and the Soviets were convinced that justice should be "legal" and removed from the arena of party politics. The popular justice aspect of the Soviet system was (and is) limited to public lectures by judges and the weak routine involvement of public representatives as lay judges (assessors) in the lower courts (Berman,

1970, pp.316-7). There were no bodies equivalent to the People's Tribunals, mass campaigns, or People's supervisory committees and Soviet bureaucrats were not (and are not) vulnerable to public scrutiny and the pressure of mass line politics.

The Soviet legal system looked attractive to a China which had already imported Soviet industry and Marxist ideology. Soviet justice looked especially good to the security-minded bureaucrat-technocrat wing of Chinese Communism and in September 1954 a People's Constitution was ratified which looked very similar to the Soviet model of 1936 (Johnson, 1969, pp.32-34). The two most important features of the new constitution were that justice would only be administered by the regular People's Courts, and that the courts would be politically independent and subordinated only to the law. Article 73 of the Constitution eliminated the People's Tribunals and deprived mass organizations of all judicial powers. Article 78 put the courts off limits to direct political pressure from either the Party or the influence of mass campaigns and mass organizations (Blaustein, 1962, p.92; Gudoshnikov, 1957, pp.50-51, 64-65).

The 1954 Constitution and the "organic laws" of government which followed in the same year decreed a new three-pronged legal system for China. There were to be three great judicial bureaucracies: the People's Courts, the police and the Procurate, and each of these would be formed as a multi-layered organization of local, regional and national offices. The constitutional system also spelled out checks against the abuse of judicial power: firstly, the responsibilities of the agencies were so arranged as to create some bureaucratic competition, and secondly, the public was allowed to elect representatives to serve *within* their structures.

There was nothing particularly surprising or revolutionary about the constitutional arrangements. The People's Courts, Department of Public Order and the Procurate had been on the books since the days of the Civil War. As early as 1946, the Communists had specified that the police were to make arrests, the People's Courts were to hear cases and the Procurate was to prepare investigations and watch for any wrongdoings by police, judges, or other government officials. The Constitution confirmed and clarified these early job assignments, but it was the 1954-56 expansion of the three bureaux which showed that the People's Government was at last serious about setting up a more "regular" system of justice.

The courts and professionalism

The People's Courts had been freshly overhauled in the Judicial Reform Movement and were expected to play a more active role in justice after the liberation years. The Constitution eliminated the People's Tribunals and the investigative bodies of mass organizations as competing judicial institutions. Article 78 of the Constitution went so far as to put the courts beyond Party influence and political ideology by declaring that: "The administration of justice by the People's Courts is independent, subject only to the law". This judicial independence clause was not strictly observed, and Party leaders continued to "advise" judges on sentences and procedure in cases of political significance. The great majority of non-political cases, however, would be decided by court-room evidence through "legal" channels as the People's Courts moved closer to the Soviet model of a code-bound judicial bureaucracy (Cohen, 1968b, pp.6-8; Waller, 1971, p.110).

The path to professionalism was, even in 1954-57, not a sunlit highway. The Party continued to play a major role in the selection of judges at the People's Congresses, and the four-year judge's term of office could be ended by the Congress. A judge could be removed from office for "violation of the law or neglect of duty". The mass line survived at least in the language of government directives which cautioned judges to avoid a bureaucratic style which might separate them from the common people, and the Party still urged that political ideology and socialist education be woven into court decisions and judicial arguments. A large number of cases were handled by direct police action or the mediation teams of popular justice, and these were obvious limitations on the "judicial authority" granted to the People's Courts. The supreme political authority of the Party was unchanged as the courts had no power to declare any government laws or Party directives "unconstitutional" (Waller, 1971, p.110; Wei, 1955, p.2).

Yet despite all these limitations, the judges of the 1954-57 Socialist Reconstruction era were generally free to decide cases on "legal" issues and the People's Courts did move a long distance toward the stable legal bureaucracy outlined in the Constitution. Advocates of judicial independence argued that only a judicial bureaucracy based on law could provide the "social predictability" essential to social stability and greater economic production (Wang Hai, JMJP, 16th October, 1954, in Cohen, 1968a, p.982; Lee, L. T. C., 1962, p.344).

Along with the stabilization of judicial procedures and the greater political insulation of judges came an upgrading of technical training and professional standards. The formation of the National Institute of Law of the Chinese Academy of Sciences began in 1956-57 and law schools across the country were expanded and geared to a more technical curriculum. Judges were provided with short-term specialized courses at legal institutes and more legal research technicians were trained at universities and at the institutes (Cohen, 1968a, pp.50-51; URI, 1963, pp.122-123). There was also a rapid growth in the number of professional legal journals, the number of publications increasing from 11 in 1951 to 21 in 1953, 46 in 1955 and a peak of 53 in 1957 (Cohen, 1970, pp.27-30). The 1957 "Lectures on the General Principles of Criminal Law" (published by the Institute of Criminal Law in Peking) are representative of this cautious new professionalism among legal scholars and judges. After re-affirming the importance of class conflict and mass line ideology in justice, this leading national legal text goes on to describe a new justice based on bureaucratic procedures and fixed legal categories all in a language not unlike the technical speech of Western lawyers (JPRS No. 1331, 1957). The inconsistency between the opening chapters on ideology and the main body of the text is obvious, and this professional-political contradiction is reflected also in the internal conflicts of the regular justice agencies in the 1954-57 period. The new professionals were most likely aware of their political vulnerability in crossing the mass line to build a quiet, stable judicial bureaucracy.

The Constitution brought defence lawyers (called "legal advisers") into the People's Courts, and these new members of the professional bureaucracy soon organized lawyers' associations to promote orderliness and professionalism in legal practice. By 1957 over 2700 lawyers were organized in local People's Collectives serving defendants without fees (Leng, 1967, p.49). Legal advisers were quickly appointed in 22 provinces (178 offices) and in Shanghai alone, five advisers defended 160 clients in criminal cases, handled 121 lawsuits and prepared many legal documents (KMJP, 6th July, 1956, in SCMP No. 1336). They were instructed to remain in close touch with their clients and the needs of the larger community. Nevertheless, the presence of defence lawyers working cases through technical legal procedures did inhibit public participation in courtrooms which were increasingly marked by the rigidity of these procedures and the specialized language of legal professionalism.

The Procurate and "due process"

The People's Procurate was first organized during the Civil War in the areas held by the Red Army. Funds were then provided to hire a national Procurator General and a staff of a dozen or so assistants. By 1951 the Procurate had established offices in 51 out of 352 Chinese cities and more local branches were set up in 1953.

For the most part, however, the Procurate was a paper agency with few workers and little prestige. It was certainly in no position to "supervise and regulate" the thousands of police, judges and government officials. The average citizen probably did not even know that this small judicial agency existed (Ginsbergs and Stahnke, 1964, pp.12-18). Throughout the liberation years procurators were limited to preparing evidence against important counter-revolutionaries and the Party and mass organizations were the most important restraining influences on the police (Ginsbergs and Stahnke, 1968, p.101; Ginsbergs, 1965, p.53).

The constitutional emphasis on regular justice brought new energy and financial support to the skeleton procurate bureau. The new 1954 Organic Law of the People's Procurate ordered the establishment of a national procurate system with the following powers:

1) To see that the resolutions, orders and measures of local organs (such as police or courts) conform to the law, and to see that the law is observed by persons working in these organs and by all citizens.

2) To investigate, prosecute and sustain the prosecution of criminal cases.

3) To see that the investigating of investigation departments [police] conforms to the law.

4) To see that the judicial process of People's Courts conforms to the law.

5) To see that the execution of judgement in criminal cases, and the activities of [police] departments in charge of reform through labour conform to the law. (Blaustein, 1962, p.145)

Clearly the writers of the Constitution and the 1954 Organic Law meant the Procurate to be a great and powerful agency. Even the highest leaders of the Communist Party were to be bound by the laws and the various Procurates were to "exercise their functions and powers independently, and not subject to interference by local organs of state (Blaustein, 1962, p.45). The Procurate would be the new internal check on government and it would be a predictable, legal replacement for the rather unmanageable and threatening mass actions of popular justice. Only a strong centrally controlled Procurate bound by professionalism and written codes could guarantee the due process of law and thus preserve the stability of a centralized bureaucratic government.

For a time the Procurate did grow and prosper. Shih Liang stated that in the one year following ratification of the Constitution the staff of the Procurate increased from 7000 to 12,000. There were procurators' offices in most major cities by 1956. Many of these personnel were law school graduates but most were citizen activists briefly trained in one of the new political-legal institutes (Shih Liang, 29th July, 1955, in Lubman, 1970, p.28; Ginsbergs, 1965, pp.58-60, 75-81; Ginsbergs and Stahnke, 1968, pp.103-104).

While the Procurate did grow in size and prestige as the theoretical overseer of government, it remained the smallest and weakest of the three justice agencies. The Procurate was effectively under "dual" supervision, with each procurator answerable to both his agency superior and the local committee of the Communist Party (Ginsbergs and Stahnke, 1964, pp.28-29; Ginsbergs, 1965, pp.85-86). The bureau did show some strength in its review of arrest warrants and indictments prepared by the police. During the 1954-57 Constitutional period the Procurate review was a serious matter and a substantial minority of cases were influenced by Procurate action or by the Procurate's rejection of police recommendations (Hsia Tao-Tai, 1967, pp.49-53; Chang Ting-ch'eng, *in* Lee, L. T. C., 1962, p.340). Still, the Procurate was only able to act on cases put before it by the police or the courts. The large number of out-of-court judicial matters were beyond the influence of the Procurate. The Procurate was never able to fill its constitutional role as the aggressive protector of due process.

The Department of Public Order under the Constitution

The police, under the control of the Department of Public Order, remained the largest and by far the most important judicial agency. While the Procurate did step into a number of cases by rejecting warrants and police reports, this inter-agency competition amounted to a periodic Procurate veto, rather than regular Procurate supervision of the police. The police remained in control of labour reform and the jails with little interference from the courts or Procurates. The new laws of 1954-57 probably had more effect on law enforcement than did the other two justice agencies. Articles 89 and 90 of the Constitution protected citizens from unlawful search or seizure and the 1954 Regulations of Arrest and Detention further circumscribed police powers (Cohen, 1969, pp.6-8; Blaustein, 1962, p.145).

The tightening effect of new legislation and Procurate review was *not* however, accompanied by a large-scale move toward police professionalization. The police for the most part continued to be recruited from mass organizations and from the People's Liberation Army. While law enforcement practices did become more regular, there was no great call for political independence and the Party was careful to retain firm control of the police (as will be detailed later). The difference between police, Procurates and courts over the question of profession-alism was to be important to the future of the police leadership in the next round of political crises and judicial reform. But for the moment of 1954-57, bureau-cratic justice ruled and popular justice was the object, rather than the agent of political change.

The Regulation and Control of Popular Justice

The prominent new conservative bureaucratic elite sought to control mass politics without losing popular support so valuable to production. In the realm of justice the professionals tried to extract the political initiative and legal teeth from popular justice institutions quietly without unduly disturbing the larger mass organizations. The Constitution eliminated People's Tribunals and the justice professionals hoped to draw the popular justice leadership into a more manageable role as assessors in the People's Courts.

The assessor system

Assessors had been attached to People's Courts since Yenan days, but they had served only when called as special advisers on certain types of cases. The trade unions sent assessors to cases involving labour violations, the women's unions elected assessors to serve on marriage law violations and so on, but there was no regular national assessor system. The duties and powers of these early lay judges were unclear and assessors were not a regular part of the People's Courts (Gudoshnikov, 1957, pp.30-33).

The Constitution ended direct popular participation through the Tribunals and it became politically important to settle the status of the assessors so as to draw popular energies behind the new regular courts. The 1954 Organic Law of the People's Court as well as the Constitution incorporated assessors into the courts on a systematic basis. Two assessors were to sit with every regular judge and were to have equal voting rights on all cases (Blaustein, 1962, pp.142-143). The assessors were selected for 10-day terms by mass organizations and were drawn from all sectors of the labour force. The Communists made a special effort to recruit women for this work (URI, 1958, pp.83-85). Their numbers grew steadily from 127,260 in 1955 to 246,500 in 1957 (Leng, 1967, p.49; KMJP, 12th July, 1956, in SCMP, No. 1336, 1956).

The Communists were for a time well pleased with the assessor system. The People's Courts were said to be more sensitive to the needs and problems of the common people and assessors also helped to encourage public respect for the law. The enthusiastic evaluations of 1954-56 began to wane in 1956-57, however, as newspaper editorials increasingly complained that regular judges treated the assessors with contempt and assigned them the tasks of errand-boys or court clerks. Professional judges criticized the assessors for their poor understanding of legal principles and for their failure to follow proper courtroom procedures (Townsend, 1969, p.141; KMJP, 12th July, 1956, in SCMP No. 1336, 1956).

The assessor system was cracking and could not stretch between popular justice traditions and the new judicial professionalism. The public became discouraged by the lack of authority and prestige given to their lay representatives, and ultimately those elected assessors began to see court work as an extra burden rather than an opportunity for political leadership (Leng, 1967, pp.90-92).

The restriction of mediation

The regular justice agencies also sought to regulate the work of mediation teams during the constitutional era. Some moves had been made in this direction as early as the Civil War but, as in the case of so many other professionalization efforts, the regulation of mediation only began in earnest after the economy and government became more centralized in 1953-57. The Second National Judicial Conference of 1953 called for the drafting of mediation rules and the creation of a national "system" for mediation work. The central government urged that People's Court judges take an active leadership role in mediation work and failures in mediation work were attributed to the absence of professional leadership in these affairs of popular justice. The professionals criticized the local mediators for their practice of bending laws in resolving disputes through compromise (JMJP, 23rd March, 1954, *in* SCMP No. 46, 1954). The judges and People's lawyers insisted that mediation be limited to only the most minor cases and were angrily opposed to the "mediation instead of court" options of popular justice. The move on popular justice shifted from regulation to elimination in the 1953 "Five Too Many" campaign when a large number of mediation teams were abolished as an unnecessary waste of the people's time. The new judicial bureaucracy left only the smallest place for mediation by commoners (Cohen, 1971, p.302; Lubman, 1967, pp.1317-18).

A national set of Mediation Rules were passed in 1954 to guide the work of the remaining mediation teams. The Rules declared that the People's Courts were to be the major arm of Communist justice and the undisputed final authority on legal matters. Mediation was explicitly limited to minor civil and criminal cases and any individual could bypass mediation and take his case directly to the court. Mass organizations would no longer have the authority to impose mediation on their members, as mediation could not be employed without the consent of all involved parties (Cohen, 1971, pp.303, 314; Cohen, 1969, pp.125-7).

Despite all of these efforts to systemize mediation, it remained an informal locally managed affair of compromise and community social pressure. The professionals were serious enough in their desire for a more "legal" mediation, but the country was simply too large and the professional justice agencies too small to do without mediation or even to regulate it closely. The 1954 Regulations were more a statement of professional ambition than a tight legal code. The articles were vague and while they outlined the *need* for a more regular mediation, they stopped short of actually *defining* such a system. The newly weaned People's Courts and Procurates were not strong enough to supervise the thousands of local mediation teams, and the People's Government needed the mediators' contribution to public order in the vast country.

The subordination of residents' organizations to government

The mass organizations which supported and maintained popular justice would also be affected by the new legalism of the Socialist Reconstruction period. The residential committees were encouraged to grow but their political independence and powers of initiative were reduced. New legislation brought the committees under the control of an expanding semi-bureaucracy: the Street Office. The street office was staffed by both citizen volunteers and people on the payroll as full- or part-time government workers (hence the designation "semi-bureaucracy"). This agency played a double role as both an "autonomous mass organization" and an arm of the People's Government. It transmitted policies from the government to local residents' committees and was to be the active link between neighbourhood policemen and the volunteer peace-keeping forces, such as the security defence committees. The street office was also to guide mass action and popular justice along the orderly legal path set by a People's Government now anxious to maximize production with a steady-state society (Townsend, 1969, p.160; Cohen, 1972, pp.315-316).

The new street office bureau surged ahead and by 1956 had caught up with the mass organizations it was to supervise. The growth of the official government bureaucracy was paralleled by the swelling of this semi-bureaucracy of "street cadres". By 1957 there were 150,000 such full- or part-time civil servants in Peking alone (accounting for 3·7% of the city's total population). Another 65,000 worked in Mukden, while Shanghai supported 100,000 more. The street cadres comprised over 2% of the total population in China's five largest cities where they totalled almost 400,000. Street offices were established in 129 major cities by August 1955 (Kau, 1969, p.34; Townsend, 1969, p.160).

The street office was not by any means limited to action in criminal justice matters. It was, like the residents' committees, an all-purpose social agency active in public health, education and general social welfare. The street cadres did, however, regard the neighbourhood constable as an especially important co-worker, and the policeman counted heavily on the local street office for information and support in the community (Salaff, 1967, pp.4-8). A typical street office would supervise about 15 residents' committees. Each of these committees represented 500-600 families and together the organizations could theoretically speak for everyone in that city district. The families also elected representatives to serve on "residents' small groups" which were sub-organizations of the larger residents' committees. It was to be a huge and yet intimate urban arrangement which could reach into every street and mobilize the millions of city folk. Canton, for example, was by 1955 peppered with residents' organizations. There were in that city of 1,717,000 some 6992 security defence small groups sponsored by 675 larger security defence committees and supervised by the residents' committees and 54 street offices (NFJP, 4th, 6th December, 1953, *in* SCMP No. 201, 1953; Vogel, 1967a, p.21).

In 1954 the National People's Congress incorporated the residents' organizations into the political-legal system of the country and empowered the mass organizations to:

> . . . lead public order (police) and protection work of a mass (popular justice) character.

> . . . mobilize the residents to respond to government appeals and to respect the law.

> . . . reconcile disputes (mediation) among the residents.

> . . . supervise the work of government organs (Townsend, 1969, p.160)

Like a lot of other constitutional period legislation this directive was more a statement of political ambition than a description of social reality. The residents' committee did not have anything like the strength necessary to "supervise" government workers effectively and were hard pressed to mobilize the city people in support of government appeals. The more energetic and educated citizen activists had left the residents' committees to join trade unions, women's unions, the youth league, government bureaux or the street offices. While all citizens were urged to participate in committee work, only the unemployed were really pressured. The residents' organizations became associations of "the very old, the very young and the female, especially the female" (Salaff, 1967, pp.10-14). The committees organized work for the idle, helped in sanitation projects and political education work, but were essentially passive and impotent as a political force. Residential small groups were henceforth the setting for gossip but little political action (Salaff, 1969, pp.54-58).

The small groups and larger committees did process citizens' complaints regarding unpopular policies and government staff but there was no mass confrontation with the bureaucracy over the question of bureaucratic elitism. Mass campaigns and the free application of mass line to politics and justice halted in the Constitutional period. The residents' organizations withered as participation in the committees became a social ritual with little force or substance. The justice professionals could not attract energetic public support while avoiding all political power.

The displacement of mass supervision by the Ministry of Control

The People's supervisory committees were another political casualty of Socialist Reconstruction. These committees had sponsored the "strike the tiger" teams of the Three Antis movement and were regarded as unruly and potentially threatening by even those bureaucrats who gained advantage in the storms of earlier mass campaigns. In 1954 there were still over 100,000 unpaid "supervisory correspondents" who received citizens' complaints, worked on supervisory committees and prepared charges against corrupt or elitist officials (URI, 1957, Vol. I, p.86). Not surprisingly, the justice professionals and the conservative career officials moved immediately to "consolidate" people's supervision work during the 1954-57 Constitutional era.

In 1955 a major shift began with the creation of the Ministry of Control, which was to watch and regulate other government bureaux. Citizen volunteers continued in supervisory work, but they were now directed by the Control bureaucracy and the volunteers passed citizens' complaints directly on to Control officials. The "correspondents" were no longer so closely linked to mass organizations and they no longer sparked mass popular action for political reform. The tie between centralized government industrialization and professional justice was present in the courts and Procurates, but it is especially obvious in the case of the Control Ministry. Control officials served on economic planning boards and they were the inspectors of industry, checking the accuracy of production reports and the quality of products (Hughes and Luard, 1959, p.37).

Just as important as the *organizational* changes in the check-and-balance system, was the change in the *philosophy* of government-watching. The Ministry of Control, like the Procurate, was to see that government officials obeyed the *laws* and written *production standards* of the Republic. This was a very different and more limited sort of "supervision" than was provided by the earlier popular justice arrangements which had attacked officials for "arrogance", "bureaucratism", "commandism" and elitism as well as for corruption, incompetence, or law-breaking.

The creation of the Control Ministry, like the expansion of the courts and Procurates, was designed to stabilize the revolution and channel public energies into support for the regular bureaucracies. This was an essentially conservative strategy which closely followed Russian advice and the experience of Soviet Communism. In terms of regulations the rising bureaucrat-technocrat was quite successful in "consolidating" justice and politics under the control of the professionals. The conservatives were far less successful in the actual practice of justice, however, and the professionals were compromised by the mass line ideology including community organizations in many judicial matters. The strategy of conservatism and centralized regulation was costly in terms of political support. The mass line was not so easily coiled and hung on the rack of bureaucratic convenience, and neither the public nor the Party radicals were prepared to accept a freezing of the social revolution — even if it brought Soviet aid and socialist "legal respectability". For the time being, however, the new professionals surged ahead toward an unsteady prominence in the 1956 Party Congress and the sharp crescendo of One Hundred Blooming Flowers.

The Uneasy Calm and the Eighth Party Congress

The Communist Party had, of course, been deeply affected by the events of Socialist Construction. The tiny liberation party of peasants and soldiers had expanded to include thousands of workers and intellectuals (Liu Shao chi, 1957, Vol. I, pp.64-65). The old veterans were unfamiliar with the problems of centralized industrial planning, bureaucratic organization and urban govern-ment; but they had serious differences with the new bureaucratic-technological elite which was assuming leadership in these matters. The 1956 Eighth Party Congress, held in Peking, reviewed the recent triumphs of the new elite but it was for them a cautious celebration threatened always by a revival of mass line politics.

The second campaign against counter-revolution

The professionals and conservative careerists had felt several such threatening resurgencies even in this era of legal consolidation and social stability. In 1954-55 a second campaign for the Suppression of Counter-revolutionaries swept across China. It was directed against both active subversives and officials or Party members with a "bad class background". This was not generally a violent movement, but there were many mass accusation rallies, and not a few "unreliable" Party members or government officials were sent for short terms to labour re-education programmes (but rarely to prisons or the more punitive labour reform camps).

This second campaign was designed for the purpose of political education rather than for the defence of a government imperilled by treason, as was the case in 1951-52. Far fewer individuals were arrested or punished, and press coverage was heavily concentrated on these events. In one case television crews and radio announcers accompanied police as they followed and arrested a "KMT agent". The "agent" was filmed cashing large cheques and doing "routine subversion work" prior to the arrest. This bit of staged political theatre was widely viewed on both the mainland and in Hong Kong, but it was poorly received by foreign critics who thought it unconvincing (NCNA, 9th June, 1956, *in* SCMP No. 1316). A few weeks later about a thousand Japanese prisoners of war were dragged out for public trials and were formally sentenced as counter-revolutionaries some eleven years after their capture (NCNA, 21st, 22nd June, 1956, *in* SCMP No. 1317).

In South China the Party leadership began a general investigation of new Party members, taking a hard look at those "with historical problems". Some 34,670 cadres were reviewed and 3670 were pronounced "counter-revolutionary" to some degree, either because of their own past affiliations or because of the past political posture of their close relatives (Vogel, 1969, pp.134-36). Those singled out were confined to their places of work and were forced to write out personal confessions. A large number of these Party members spent six months in labour re-education camps where they did manual labour and attended political education classes. It should be pointed out that they were not generally dismissed from their party or government posts and these sanctioned individuals continued to receive all or part of their salaries while in the camps.

The newspapers generally described the actions of the campaign in legal terms, but the available literature shows that the laws were set aside by the campaign. People's Tribunals were re-established in a number of places such as Mukden, where defendants faced a mass trial before 30,000 peasants. Local governments called mass accusation meetings and the procedures of trials and rallies resembled those of the more violent earlier campaigns (URI, 1957, Vol. I, pp.83-88).

The psychology of defendant pressure also reappeared to replace some regular legal procedures. Police or other government officials frequently demanded confessions before trials began and encouraged mutual denunciation among accused "counter-revolutionaries". Those who remained silent or those who attempted to defend themselves through constitutional procedures risked tougher sentences. As in previous movements, those who co-operated were assured more lenient treatment (Liu Shao chi, 1956, Vol. I, pp.82-83; JMJP, 26th May, 1956, in SCMP No. 1305, 1956).

Alongside the suppression campaign there was the national Su Fan campaign. Su Fan was directed at Party members who had moved too slowly in the 1954-55 agricultural collectivization and at others who wanted "a return to capitalism". A number of justice professionals were dragged from office in both Su Fan and the suppression campaign. The Vice-Director of Public Order in Shanghai, Yang Fan, was charged with counter-revolution and arrested along with a few lesser police officials (Bernstein, 1967, p.3; URI, 1957, Vol. I, p.42).

Professional justice and the second suppression campaign

Both campaigns served to warn officials not to forget the mass line and the need for continued social change. The two movements showed that the potential for class conflict still lingered to threaten any tight rule by law or the bureaucratic elite. The new professionals could not resist these movements and they rolled with the punches, hoping to regain their political footing later.

The leadership of the People's Procurate was concerned lest their fledgling agency get caught in the crunch of these national movements. Chang Tiu Cheng, Chief Procurator of the Supreme People's Procurate, ordered that:

> All counter-revolutionaries and other criminal elements should be arrested, should be placed under arrest without hesitation.
>
> The present deviation in certain places of refraining from arresting and trying those who should be arrested and tried and of passing light sentences on those who have perpetuated high crimes, should be thoroughly rectified and overcome (Chang Tiu Cheng, 1952, *in* Ginsbergs and Stahnke, 1964, p.128)

The Chief Procurator went on to make clear the precedence of politics over legal procedures in the suppression campaign. He warned his subordinates not to carry professionalism and legal stability too far in times of political crises, as follows:

> Among some procurate cadres, because they are complacent over the past success of the movement to suppress counter-revolution . . . there grows among them a most dangerous sentiment to be lethargic and to under-estimate the enemy.
>
> [Procurators] make mechanical use of the provisions of the law, bog them-selves down with intricate red-tapism and estrange themselves from the present actual struggle.
>
> This is due to . . . their lack of working experience . . . and the inadequate leadership of political ideology in the work of the People's Procurate.

The People's Courts were also worried by the new national movements and the judicial leaders were determined to avoid a political confrontation with popular justice and mass line ideology. Shih Liang, Minister of Justice, praised the movement, and the People's Courts under her direction processed some 364,604 suppression cases (Shih Liang, 1953, *in* Leng, 1967, p.49). Early in the campaign the President of the Supreme People's Court, Tung Pi Wu, described the suppression action as "a new Chinese advance toward socialism". He sought to line up the regular courts alongside the new movements and thus maintain the position of the People's Courts as the supreme and leading judicial institution. Like the Chief Procurator, the Chief Justice was prepared to sacrifice some degree of professionalism in order to hold intact the power and the relative independence enjoyed by the People's Courts. He cautioned his subordinate judges as follows:

> A major [problem] is that in handling cases of counter-revolution, some People's Courts have passed either too light or too severe sentences . . .

The chief reason for these shortcomings and mistakes is the rapid development of the political situation in China since the latter half of last year (1955)
and the failure of some judicial officials to keep their understanding abreast
of these objective developments. In handling cases, they were not adept in
executing the state policy in light of changes in the country's political
situation . . . (Ginsbergs and Stahnke, 1964, p.128)

A study of suppression cases in 1955 showed that in one province only 3·57%
of the 4000 accused of subversion were acquitted by the People's Courts. In
Tsingtao only 0·78% of the defendants were found not guilty (Ginsbergs and
Stahnke, 1964, p.126). Official political-legal magazines praised the judge Lu
Hsu as an exemplary enemy of counter-revolution. Lu Hsu was known for his
hard sentences and his refusal to allow mercy, peace-making, or mediation in
cases involving counter-revolution. He suspended legal procedures and advised
his fellow judges to use the law against accused counter-revolutionaries as though
they were "beating a mad dog in the water" (*Hung Ch'i*, 1966, *in* CFIA-EARC,
1970, pp.287-9).

The courts and the Procurates were obviously not going to cross with Party
policy or mass line movements even during this period of new judicial independence and rising professionalism.

The Eighth Party Congress of 1956

The Eighth Party Congress began shortly after the national movements of
1954-55 and the suppression and Su Fan actions were yet fresh in the minds of
the delegates. Though the bureaucratic elite demonstrated their strength
throughout the conference sessions, they still felt it necessary to re-state their
support for the mass movements and mass line ideology. Liu Shao chi, the most
prominent of the new elite opened his rather conservative speech with a properly
fierce attack on counter-revolution, saying:

The counter-revolutionaries are bent on undermining the security of the
people. It is the duty of our State [justice] organs to weed out and suppress
counter-revolutionaries. In 1950 we led a nation-wide struggle for the
suppression of counter-revolutionaries . . . In 1955 we carried out another
struggle against counter-revolutionaries in the Country at large and we
ferreted out counter-revolutionaries hidden in public organizations throughout the country (Liu Shao chi, 1957, Vol. I, pp.82-83)

However, Liu wanted to end direct public action and the irregularity of
popular justice. He was determined that the newly created justice monopoly
of the state bureaucracies be protected. He continued:

> Our Public Order [police], courts and procurates must continue to wage a determined struggle against counter-revolutionaries and other criminals. But, as has been mentioned before, this struggle must be conducted with strict observance of the law and in accord with the new situation which obtains today.

Lo Jui ching, Minister of Public Order, was more hesitant to call for a new justice of laws and professionalism. The national police chief stressed the importance of close public–police co-operation in keeping with the mass line. Lo did hope to see an end to mass movements of popular justice, which he regarded as a mixture of confusion and arbitrary extremism. He felt that the time for such public militancy was past:

> It is now virtually impossible for the counter-revolutionaries to stage a come-back in China, and it is also more difficult than ever for them to sabotage and create disturbances.
>
> The period of intense class struggle in our revolution is past (Lo Jui ching, 1956, Vol. II, p.100)

Tung Pi Wu, President of the Supreme People's Court, also addressed the 1956 Congress and he delivered perhaps the clearest statement of the new legal professionalism. Tung made almost no mention of mass movements or other aspects of popular justice in his review of Communist legal progress. He regarded law and regular legal institutions as the highest goal of socialist justice. The state bureaucracy and its written codes were, in Tung's mind, the only strong and just guardian of liberty. He stated:

> Every freedom our people are entitled to has been given a firm guarantee in the shape of the People's democratic legal system (Tung Pi Wu, 1957, Vol. II, p.83)

Like Liu, Tung believed that the age of revolutionary change was over for China. He sought to stabilize and "consolidate" the revolution under the control of the state bureaucracy and the legal system. The Chief Justice also pushed the new legalism even further than Liu when he demanded that the Communist Party itself recognize the supreme authority of the Constitution and the legal system. This would mean a sharp break with nearly 30 years of Communist political tradition in which the laws had followed political developments, rather than vice versa. Tung, of course, understood this but he believed the legalized social stability a political and economic necessity. He sought to end the flexible independence of Party leadership by binding political action to legal codes. This was the unmistakeable meaning of his address to the Eighth Party Congress which read in part as follows:

I think that we also have another serious question to deal with: that is, a few of our Party members and government personnel do not attach much importance to the legal system of the State, or do not observe its provisions.

The Party guides the state organs through its own members and its own organizations, but does not take the affairs of state organs into its own hands . . . some Party committees used to issue orders themselves and take into their own hands part of the administrative work of the local governments.

We oppose all arbitrary illegal acts and anything which departs from the regulations (Tung Pi Wu, 1957, Vol. II, p.95)

In the area of justice, Tung, not surprisingly, emphasized professionalism and procedural correctness as part of his strategy for tight centralized political leadership under the new laws. He criticized both regular and popular justice organizations for procedural sloppiness as follows:

It must be pointed out here also that sometimes when a person has violated the law or committed a crime, attention is concentrated on whether he is guilty or not, but no attention is given to seeing that legal procedure is strictly observed.

It must also be pointed out that our jurists have not yet produced a single fairly good book explaining the legal system of our country — a book written with knowledge of the theories of jurisprudence and in accordance with the Marxist-Leninist point of view. Up to the present all we have is a few pamphlets! Jurisprudence is an important branch of social science.

Legal work is a kind of specialized work, but the personnel engaged in legal work have not yet been given the kind of treatment that should be given to personnel working in the legal field (Tung Pi Wu, 1957, Vol. II, p.90)

Finally, the Chief Justice noted that popular justice was fundamentally incompatible with a tight professional justice. Tung blamed the mass movements and other popular justice practices for the weakness of professional justice and the low prestige of regular justice agencies. He reviewed the history of popular justice with due respect but hoped to close its career with the following criticism:

In the first few weeks after liberation we carried out a succession of mass movements, and the results achieved in all these movements exceeded even our expectations. But as mass revolutionary movements do not depend entirely on law, they are likely to bring a by product — encouragement of an indiscriminate disregard for all legal systems. This is another factor that has increased the difficulty of the Party and the state in overcoming this sort of public attitude (Tung Pi Wu, 1957, Vol. II, p.92)

The Soviets were warmly encouraged by the developments at the Eighth Party

Congress and were especially sympathetic towards Liu Shao chi, Tung Pi Wu and other leaders of the conservative bureaucratic elite. The Eighth Congress deleted the standing Chinese Communist tenet that the "thought of Mao Tse-tung" was to be the "theoretical foundation of the Party", and the new legalism of the conservatives also weakened the position of "mass line" ideology. Russian Communists ruling their country from the top of an elitist bureaucracy and a professionalized legal system were heartened to see the Chinese revolution "consolidated" under a brother elite committed to Soviet-style justice, politics and economy. The Soviets did most clearly regard the Eighth Congress as the most striking and positive event in the life of the Chinese Communist Party or the People's Republic as a whole (Burlatsky, 1968, p.43).

The Russians joined the Chinese conservatives in calling for the prompt codification of tighter laws and encouraged the Chinese to develop a still more "regular" legal system. The leading Soviet jurist Lunov warned the Chinese that legality was essential to the development of a respectable socialism (Lunev, *in* Berman, 1970, p.316-318).

The growing strength of the conservative elite and their ideology of legalism, professionalism and social discipline was a clear threat to the forces of popular justice and the principles of mass line socialism. The radicals were, however, far from beaten, despite their acceptance of more centralized government as a means to quick industrialization. Soon their grumbling resistance would break out into an open attack on the power and ideology of the new conservative elite, prompting angry Soviet advisers to board the last trains to Moscow, but in these last months of the Constitutional era, the radical complaints were still muffled and political attacks were indirect. The One Hundred Flowers episode of 1957 marked the end of such political subtlety, since the tensions and conflicts released in this shocked observers and demolished the screen of political serenity which had largely hidden Chinese politics since liberation.

Rectification and the Sound of One Hundred Flowers

While the rising bureaucratic elite showed its strength at the Eighth Congress, the lesser technological elite began to flex its ambition in the One Hundred Flowers episode in 1956-57. Action began in May 1956 when Mao called upon intellectuals to widen China's cultural horizons by engaging in free exchange of ideas (that is of ideas not hostile to the Party or the ideology of socialism). Initially an academic affair, One Hundred Flowers became a political action in the spring of 1957 when Mao invited the intellectuals to help lead a national "Rectification" campaign designed to criticize elitism in the Communist Party.

In general, One Hundred Flowers amounted to a long nervous conversation between the intellectual community and the political leadership. There were a great many published articles and speeches by both Party bureaucrats and non-Party intellectuals. Many of these publications concerned legal issues and the theory of socialist justice, but only in the final weeks of the 13-month episode was there an open political conflict; and at no point did the public act in much other than an observer's role. Thus One Hundred Flowers *cannot* be considered a popular justice action, but it did have an important overall effect in setting the limits of professional justice. It was a high water mark for the conservative ideology of social stability and rule by law and a bureaucratic-technological elite.

Political subtleties in the first blooms

One Hundred Flowers remained a relatively quiet academic debate throughout 1956, with intellectual arguments growing warm over *implied* political meanings in literature. Throughout this year (as in the previous two years) the Party courted intellectual favour and provided scholars with even better homes, salaries and privileges (Hoffman, 1969, p.99; Goldman, R., 1961, p.138). The learned minority was well aware, however, that luxuries were no substitute for power, for advantages given by the Party could be just as easily taken away. For the most part the intellectuals were carefully calm and stayed close to Party instructions regarding research and teaching (Chen, T., 1960, pp.112-126).

The spokesmen of the Party bureaucratic elite were not nearly as reluctant to "bloom and contend" (i.e. speak out) as the intellectuals. Throughout 1956 the advocates of social discipline, material incentives and legal social stability argued for their version of Soviet-style Communism. In addition to the previously described speeches at the Eighth Party Congress, there were some major addresses at the National People's Congress of 1956, and in the editorial columns of major newspapers. Huang Shao-Lung, former Minister of Interior, made a strong public demand for the early publication of a complete criminal code at the People's Congress in Peking. He stated that:

> All those we talked to [at the Congress] including judges and others in judicial administration and laymen were in favour of this proposal [to publish a complete criminal code] (NCNA, 27th June, 1956, *in* SCMP No. 1321)

Huang was upset at the "lack of dignity" in the People's Courts and he argued that more formal procedures and a complete criminal code might tidy up the loose courtroom behaviour (which was a carry-over from popular justice) (NCNA, 27th June, 1956, *in* SCMP No. 1321, 1956). A leading Supreme Court Justice, Ma Hsi Wu, also criticized lower judges for their violations of legal procedures in People's Court trials (Ma Hsi Wu, CFYC, No. 1, 1956, *in* Leng, 1967, p.44).

Invitation to conflict: the second phase (1957)

In the winter of 1957 the national Party leadership raised the stakes of One Hundred Flowers by asking the non-Party intellectuals to help lead a "Rectification" movement against Party elitism. Along with lesser Party figures, Mao repeatedly confirmed this new political role for intellectuals as follows

> Now the Central Committee of the Communist Party has decided on another rectification within the party to be started this year. Non-Party people may take part in it or need not if they do not wish to. The main thing in this rectification campaign is to criticize the following three errors in one's way of thinking and style of work—subjectivism, bureaucracy and sectarianism (Mao Tse-tung, 1957, p.178)

Additional remarks by Mao and by other Party leaders flushed out the meaning of these "three errors" in Party leadership. Bureaucracy was described as "armchair leadership which suppresses the opinions of subordinates and pays little attention to the life of the masses". Subjectivism and sectarianism were defined as political narrow mindedness and dogmatism insensitive to local variations (Mao Tse-tung, 1957, pp.181-2 and pp.156-7). In short, Mao and the radicals hoped the intellectuals would serve as a counter force against the bureaucratic elite within the Party.

After several more months of official encouragement the intellectuals at last began to speak out on political matters, but they did not prove to be new allies for the mass line and the Maoists were to be bitterly disappointed. Before discussing the criticisms advanced in this second phase of the Hundred Flowers-Rectification period it would seem valuable to explore the reasons behind the decision to bring the intellectuals into political action. Bringing these non-Party people into conflict with the Party was clearly a conscious and deliberate act confirmed in scores of speeches and essays by Mao and other top Party officials.

The new prosperity of the intellectual class

The intellectuals had traditionally been a special elite group in China with recognized social prestige and, until the twentieth century, considerable political influence. Few intellectuals had actively supported the Communists in the Civil War, however, and there were few scholars in the ranks of the Party at the 1949 movement of liberation.

This began to change with the start of the Five-year Plan in 1953. The Communists recruited large numbers of intellectuals to serve as technical advisers for industrialization and economic planning and these advisers received generous salaries, and high social privileges. So long as centralized politics and the development of heavy industry were top priorities, the intellectuals could expect even more in the way of salary increases, comforts and prestige. With prestige and influence on planning boards inevitably came rising expectations of political power. The Party, to maintain the needed assistance of the learned experts, felt obliged to widen their political sphere and hear more criticism from the intellectuals.

Events in Eastern Europe also contributed indirectly to the good fortunes of the Chinese intellectuals. The Chinese, tied to Soviet aid and Soviet political leadership, felt obliged to condemn the 1956 uprisings in Hungary and Poland as "bourgeois counter-revolutions aided by imperialist interests". But the revolts still prompted some sober thoughts and hard political reflections in the Chinese Party (Mao Tse-tung, 1957, pp.120-22; Radvanyi, 1970, pp.122-5).

The Party careerists had consciously modelled their bureaucracy and political ideology on those of the Soviets, and some of the final costs of the Soviet system were revealed in the streets of Budapest. The Russian rule by a close party bureaucracy had largely excluded both the general public and the intellectuals from positions of influence, and the intellectuals had responded by helping to organize the rebellions in Eastern Europe.

The Chinese Communists were determined to ensure the support of their own intellectual class and the Party leadership prepared to make more adjustments to the needs of the learned few. It is likely that disenchantment with Soviet Communism increased as the Chinese noted fundamental differences between mass line politics and Soviet rule. The Maoist leadership became more concerned with preserving mass support and was more ready to hear intellectual criticism of narrowness and bureaucratic abuse among the Party.

Maoist dialectics versus Stalinist party discipline

Another source of the decision to turn One Hundred Flowers into a political struggle may be found in Mao's concept of political dialectics. The idea of progress through conflict has been accepted by nearly all Communists as essential to understanding history *before* Communism, but few have joined Mao in extending dialectical analysis to the interpretation of socialist development after the revolutionary victory over the old regime.

Certainly Stalin was ready to announce the end of dialectic struggle and the successful establishment of the "dictatorship of the proletariat" once the Russian Civil War was ended and the Party had begun its campaign of lightning industrialization. Stalin argued that the success of socialism after the Revolution would depend upon the maintenance of an "iron discipline" within the Communist Party. Like Liu Shao chi, Stalin drew a sharp moral and political line between the Party and the general public. Communists were, he said, "made of special stuff", and the Party is the "rallying centre of the finest elements of the working class". He demanded that Party members keep differences silent and submit without reservation to the orders of the Party leadership (Stalin, 1970, pp.103-5). Stalin denounced those who called for a more flexible, open-to-criticism Party as follows:

> . . . the principle of directing Party work from the centre not infrequently gives rise to attacks on the Party of the wavering elements, to accusations of 'bureaucracy,' 'formalism,' etc . . . (Stalin, 1970, p.108)

It is worth noting that Stalin wrote these words in 1953, at a time when Mao and the Chinese leadership were locked in a heated Three Antis-Judicial Reform struggle against "bureaucratic" Party officials who ignored the mass line and held themselves above the common people. The obvious contradiction here was for a time officially ignored while China accepted Soviet loans, technical advice and machinery. Russia remained the undisputed leader of the socialist camp, but at the same time the Maoist leadership was increasingly aware of differences between the mass line and the style of Communism in the Soviet Union.

While the recent era of centralized politics and industrialization had weakened mass organizations, the new ideology was still on the lips, if not in the hearts of Chinese Communists. Even conservatives like Liu Shao chi argued for the mass politics, although he wanted to harness mass power rather than obey it. The fundamental contradiction between mass line and centralized bureaucratic structure was only beginning to show.

Mao and especially the radical Communists were determined that the mass line should prevail in China, even at the cost of some Party discipline. The 1957 Rectification-One Hundred Flowers action showed that the Maoists were quite willing to expose the Party to pressure even from those outside the Party ranks. It was hoped that the intellectuals might contribute to the dialectic development of the Party by criticizing bureaucratic violations of the mass line.

The second blooms: criticisms by the intellectuals and the bureaucratic elite

Unfortunately it turned out that the intellectuals did not generally regard themselves as representatives of the masses. Instead they looked upon Rectification as a springboard to greater power and luxuries for themselves. Rather than criticize the Party for its bureaucratic elitism, most of the intellectuals asked only that the bureaucratic elite move over and share more of their special privileges with them. The scholars did not call for a resurgence of mass political participation and did not criticize policies like the use of material incentives which created larger wage gaps between the educated and the unskilled.

Intellectuals and bureaucrats in the making of professional justice

In the realm of justice the scholars speaking in the Hundred Flowers-Rectification campaign generally backed up the Party conservatives, as both groups called for tighter legal codes, greater bureaucratic independence (from Party or mass political pressure) and strict limitations on mass action and popular justice. The legal "experts" sought to rope off justice as their own domain and declared that law was a "special science" understood only by such experts (WLP, 8th May, 1957, in Leng, 1967, p.57). Many intellectuals felt more comfortable with pre-revolutionary KMT laws than with popular justice action, and they asserted that the People's Republic could profit by re-examining the KMT legal codes. Law professors talked a great deal about the "continuity of law" and some argued that many KMT laws could be dusted off and added to the rather sparse collection of Communist laws (KMJP, 1st, 23rd, 29th April, 1957, in CNA No. 203, 1957).

Many of the "blooming and contending" intellectuals also criticized the Party for its failure to develop a "legal consciousness". The Party, they said, had not created enough legal codes and had too often interfered with the procedures of the legal agencies (Shi Huang, KMJP, 17th May, 1957, in CNA No. 184, 1957; Rickett and Rickett, 1964). Scholars noted that the Five Antis trials of the capitalists in Canton were marked by procedural irregularities, and the intellectuals scolded the Canton courts for extorting money from the wealthy defendants at those trials (Lo Lung-chi, in Chen, T., 1960, p.143). They played down class conflicts and criticized other mass campaigns, such as the 1954-55 suppression action and Judicial Reform for their "irregularity and their excesses" (Lo Lung chi, Chang Po-chun, KMJP, 22nd May, 1957, in SCMP No. 846, 1957; Chang Nai chi JMJP, 2nd June, 1957, in Chen, J. T., 1970, p.152).

Not surprisingly, the demand for a more "objective" judicial system was accompanied by a call for more specialized legal training and higher "professional standards" (Rickett and Rickett, 1964). Three prominent legal scholars, including the President of Peking University, urged the establishment of a national legal research institute which might provide scholars and government officials with the scientific foundation for the study of jurisprudence.

All of these arguments and proposed "reforms" essentially denied the "political relativity" of law and the scholars consistently played down the role of law in class conflict. Like the conservative bureaucratic elite in the Party, the intellectuals hoped to shut out the era of class conflict and would rely on the law and bureaucratic rule to protect their own rising status from future mass actions and social reshufflings (JMJP, 13th September, 1957, *in* CNA No. 203).

The One Hundred Flowers critics often complained that too many university graduates were asked to do manual labour and that the salaries and prestige granted them were still not enough for an elite group, although recent wage increases and preferential housing treatment had already widened the gap between the learned minority and the less privileged peasants and workers (JMJP, Arch.23, 1957, *in* Snow, 1964, p.382; Leng, 1967, p.58). The Dean of Law at Wuhan University complained that the low wages of legal scholars lessened the prestige of the law in the eyes of the general public (Han Te-p'ei, KMJP, 12th June, 1957, *in* CNA No. 203). The Vice-Chairman of the intellectuals' Democratic League Party, Lo Lung-chi, warned the Communists that the scholars were "proud people" whose slogan was

> If I am treated as a scholar of the state, I respond as a scholar of the state; if I am treated as a commoner I respond as a commoner (Lo Lung chi, *in* Chen, T., 1960, p.148)

The Chinese Political Science and Law Association organized a series of forums in Peking which summarized and publicized the Rectification criticism. The Association strongly recommended broadening and enlarging law school programmes to further the development of legal professionalism, rapid codification of the law and greater political independence for the justice bureaucracies. Finally, the Association demanded an end to the mass movements of popular justice which usurped the authority of the regular People's Courts (JMJP, 5th June, 1957, *in* URI, 1958, p.41; Yang Yu ch'ing, JMJP, 5th June, 1957, *in* Chen, T., 1960, pp.167-168).

The conservative bureaucratic elite in the Party was emboldened by the intellectuals support and its spokesmen joined in calling for more professionalism, legalism and social discipline. The Assistant Procurator General of the Transportation Procurate complained about Party interference in professional matters of the Procurate (KMJP, 20th December, 1957, *in* URI, 1958, p.77). The President and Vice-President of the Supreme People's Court criticized the Party radicals for interference in justice and stated that:

> . . . the Party should render leadership over the court only at the time of codifying laws, and should not interfere with the actual trial . . . (JMJP, 12th December, 1957, *in* URI, Vol. I, 1958, p.77)

Like the intellectuals, these two judges denied the "political relativity" of law and hoped to run a tighter bureaucratic ship by barring politics from judicial matters. The two chief justices stated:

Politics is politics, and law is law; our job is to enforce the law and not politics (JMJP, 12th December, 1957, *in* URI, Vol. I, 1958, p.77)

Overall, One Hundred Flowers-Rectification did little to help a resurgence of the mass line within the Party. There were some challenges from students who resented the favouritism shown to children of Party officials (KMJP, 23rd January, 1957, *in* CNA No.168; Goldman, R., 1962, pp.142-8). There were also a number of faculty gripes about Party control of curriculum and publishing houses, and artists complained that the "social realism" prescribed by Party did not encourage creative expression. These criticisms, especially those of the students, did attack narrow-minded elitism in the Party, but most of established intellectual leaders who questioned Party policies did not speak on these matters and when they spoke of "academic freedom" they meant academic *influence* and academic *privilege*. The senior scholars spoke not as public representatives, but as members of a self-consciously elite group. The Maoists had evidently made a serious miscalculation and One Hundred Flowers-Rectification only strengthened the hand of the developing bureaucratic-technological elite.

Nearly everyone in the Party had been anxious to bring the scholars into the counsels of industry (as technical advisers) and this eagerness goes some way toward explaining the miscalculations of One Hundred Flowers. After the "intellectual reform" campaigns of 1951 and 1954 the Party happily and quickly accepted the statements of "reformed" scholars who claimed to have discarded their arrogant ways and special needs (Johnson, 1959, pp.56-68). It was clear after One Hundred Flowers that the Communists, and perhaps even the intellectuals themselves, had been deluded in thinking old attitudes were so easily changed.

Looking over history's shoulder one can see three very important lessons in One Hundred Flowers-Rectification. Firstly, the decision to call non-Party people in to criticize and reform the Party was a clear departure from Soviet Communist tradition and it demonstrated the commitment of the Maoist leadership to mass line politics and dialectic struggle. Their willingness to expose the Party and the government to attack did not work out well on this occasion, but the precedent was established for more powerful actions such as the 1967 Cultural Revolution. The Communist Party of China was not going to wear a divine mantle of authority, not even a red one.

Secondly, some important political tensions were revealed, not only between Party bureaucrats and the intellectual elite, but between the bureaucrats and an activist and courageous national student body. Western (i.e. anti-Communist) observers have generally described One Hundred Flowers as a struggle over "academic freedom" or "intellectual expression", but that analysis comes lose to being correctly only when applied to the student activists of 1956-57 rather than the established scholars. The young people were angered by favouritism shown to the children of Party members, and they resented the privileges of the hand-picked members of the Party's Youth League. Although committed to socialism, the students were determined that the Chinese version be mass-oriented with equal opportunities for all loyal citizens. In most respects the students' demands at places such as Peking University came closest to Mao's hopes for renewed support of the mass line in the One Hundred Flowers action. Criticism from the students was overshadowed by the more prominent and very different complaints voiced by the established intellectual leadership, but the growing tension between the youth and the bureaucratic conservatives was to be released later in the Cultural Revolution.

Thirdly, the attacks from the established intellectual leadership shocked the Party leadership and forced a quick and decisive reaction. In the closing weeks of June 1957 several scholars even called for the assassination and overthrow of the Communist Party and the elimination of socialism; but many more urged a complete freezing up of the revolution within a tight system of law and bureau-cracies. The latter proposals were more threatening since they were echoed by leading members of the Party and government bureaucracy and were warmly greeted by the Soviet Union. The swing to political consolidation and social discipline prompted by the need to industrialize had come so far as to threaten the very character of the revolution. By the end of June the Maoist Party leadership had begun to move against the critics and spokesmen for elite rule.

The forces of "constitutional consolidation" were to be driven back by this counter-action and one result would be a resurgence of popular justice. Most importantly, the renewed support for the mass line would be backed by a new sort of economic game plan, emphasizing popular participation in a vast decentralized industrialization effort.

7 The Great Leap Forward and Back

The Party leadership listened to the "Blooming Flowers" in stunned silence. For weeks no attempt was made to silence or censor critics, not even those few intellectuals who called for the overthrow of socialism and the death of the Communist Party (JMJP, 8th June, 1957, *in* CV, 1958, pp.49-53). Ultimately the Maoists had to react since the combined force of the conservative bureaucrats and the elitist intellectuals presented a serious threat to the mass line ideology. Western observers have generally stressed the Communist "repression" of the intellectuals, but the main force of the counter-attack did fall not on the intellectuals but on conservative Party members and government officials who had forgotten the mass line and had deserted popular politics for elite privileges and the new bureaucratic code of professionalism.

The reaction began in late June 1957 as the radicals started printing rebuttals alongside the continuing attacks from the One Hundred Flowers critics. The conservative intellectual and bureaucratic critics were collectively described as "rightists", and that label carried the weight of a political-legal judgement in the action which followed. The Party leadership began a national "Anti-Rightist" campaign and regained the political initiative.

The Anti-Rightist Movement

The Anti-Rightist campaign, like the One Hundred Flowers, was not primarily a popular justice matter. The general public certainly watched both of these public events and the masses were to participate in a much diluted form of both movements later in 1958-59; but the critical conflicts of 1957-58 were pretty much restricted to the middle and top political levels. The Maoist leadership led the radicals of Party, government and university in a sweeping counter-attack against the One Hundred Flowers "rightists". As a result of the new movement, the conservatives were drawn back from their One Hundred Flowers positions and with them went the defeated banners of professionalism, bureaucratic "consolidation", legalism and "due process". Popular justice sprang into the open ground, abandoned by the retreating professionals, and within the regular justice agencies the young radicals took leadership authority away from the older law-trained bureaucrats.

The Anti-Rightist counter-attack concentrated on three fronts. Students who stormed Party and government offices in Hangyang or demonstrated against Party elitism at Peking University faced serious criticism (and occasionally expulsion) once order had been restored (JMJP, 16th July, 1957, *in* CNA No.193, 1957; NCNA, 5th August, 1957, *in* CNA No.194, 1957; Goldman, R., 1962, p.153). But the other and more important reactions were directed against more established conservative elites in academic and political circles.

The weeding of intellectual flowers

Senior faculty critics and the leadership of the older intellectual parties, such as the China Democratic League, were debated, heckled, criticized and publicly humbled for their arrogance and their anti-Party posture during the One Hundred Flowers. As in the case of the Five Antis, Three Antis, Judicial Reform and the 1954-55 suppression campaigns, the Anti-Rightist action emphasized public education, criticism and reform, rather than punishment or physical violence. Students and faculty colleagues formed study-criticism groups which examined and "struggled" with fellow intellectuals who sought "special status" or voiced anti-socialist sentiments. Large open demonstrations featured self-criticism by former One Hundred Flowers critics. At one such event several hundred senior scholars marched through the streets of Peking to a public gathering where they "gave their hearts to the Party" in a loyalty ceremony (URI, 1957, Vol. I, p.81).

In August 1957 the Minister of Public Order presented a quickly written directive "Decision on the Problem of Labour Training" (Lo Jui ching, JMJP, 2nd August, 1957, *in* CNA No.194, 1957). This new act provided for a new sort of punitive labour and education sanction which could be applied to Flowers rightists. In an official *People's Daily* editorial, a Party spokesman remarked that:

> The rightist elements attack us, alleging that labour training is unconstitutional . . . [but the] decision clearly applies to all those who complain without reason (JMJP, 2nd August, 1957, *in* CNA No.194, 1957)

Despite the stern sound of this warning, the records indicate that very few rightists were actually sent to the labour training camps, and those for only about one year. Most of the accused and criticized rightists remained at the university under the watchful eye of Party members and more leftist intellectuals. When the universities re-opened in the fall of 1958, new courses in "Socialist Ideological Education" had been added to the required curriculum. The rather legalistic 1957 law text "Lectures on the Principles of Criminal Justice" was still printed on time, but with a hasty preface noting rightist errors (Goldman, R., 1962, p.153; Snow, 1964, pp.390-91).

Liu Shao chi, who still spoke as a leftist, called upon the intellectuals to abandon professionalism and elitism and to reject:

> . . . the so-called slogan of 'specialist first and red second', [a slogan] that could only serve as a call to escape politics (Liu Shao chi, 1958, *in* Jacobs and Baerwald, 1963, pp.88-89)

The Department of Public Order (police), as the least specialized and most mass-oriented of the justice agencies, was least disturbed by the events of 1957-58; but the courts, procurates and the Ministry of Control were convulsed by criticism and reorganizations. Many officials from those three agencies were transferred, dismissed or even sent to labour re-education projects. The lawyers' collectives, as leading supporters of professionalism and strict legal procedures, were sharply criticized and few law school graduates remained in the justice agencies (Cohen, 1965, pp.11-12).

One of the first individual targets of the Anti-Rightist action was Chia Ch'ien, a Party member serving as Chief Justice in the Criminal Division of the Supreme People's Court. During One Hundred Flowers he had argued for more "judicial independence", legal professionalism and tighter judicial procedures. Chia stated that the Constitution and the new legal codes should serve to separate politics from justice, and he felt that continued Party involvement in legal affairs was "insulting to the judiciary" (Chia Ch'ien, PJC, Vol. I, 1958, *in* Cohen, 1968a, p.992; Hsia, Tao-Tai, 1967, p.16). His remarks were printed along with heated replies prepared by the Department of Law at the People's University of Peking. Radical legal spokesmen attacked Chia for his "loose ignorant talk and bourgeois thinking" and they criticized the judge for his view that "those outside the [legal] profession cannot lead those inside the profession" (PJC, Vol. I, 1958, *in* Cohen, 1968a, p.992). In September 1957 the judge was labelled a rightist and was removed from both the Communist Party rolls and the Supreme Court (URI, 1957, Vol. I, p.43).

Other court officials who had called for greater legal professionalism faced much the same experience. The legal adviser to the Supreme Court was attacked as an elitist and a rightist after his remarks during One Hundred Flowers. He had complained that many ex-KMT lawyers and judges were working as coolies and he also belittled the new citizen-judges for their ignorance of legal procedure and professional standards. In August 1957 he was criticized and later dismissed (JMJP, 28th August, 1957, in CNA No.203; JMJP, 12th December, 1957, in CNA No.311, 1957).

These were not isolated instances since scores of judges, legal research experts and procurators were dismissed or criticized in the course of the Anti-Rightist action. More important than the campaign's impact on individual political careers, however, was its broader effect on judicial policy and budget allocations to justice agencies. The de-emphasis on legal procedure and the adversary system of "professional" justice prompted a reduction in the already tiny staffs of People's lawyers. Trial procedures were also shortened, simplified and loosened up for greater public participation in the courtroom (KMJP, 28th August, 1957, in CNA No.203, 1957; URI, 1957, Vol. I, p.43; Cohen, 1968a, p.990).

The Procurate was sharply criticized for neglecting class struggle in dealing with all cases in a ritual bureaucratic fashion and not distinguishing between the people and counter-revolutionaries. Fully 15% of the national Procurate staff were dismissed during the Anti-Rightist action, and most of these people were legally trained specialists appointed during the recent constitutional period (Lubman, 1970, pp.38-40). One Party spokesman complained that:

> In the Procurate organs, rightist ideology is chiefly manifested in the failure to prosecute cases which should have been prosecuted, and in the laxity in supervision over adjudication work. Such laxity in fact means toleration of criminals and cruelty among the people (Hsieh Fei, FH No.2, 16th February, 1958, in SCMM, No.135, 1958)

The judges and procurators were roundly scolded for their general failure to include the masses in their work and for their preoccupation with legal procedures and their failure to work political education and class perspective into a politically relative judicial system (Cohen, 1965, p.10). The Party leadership also grew impatient over the professionals' lukewarm involvement in mass campaigns, and one radical pointedly asked:

> How is it that these people have a mistaken conception of the political situation in the country, of the class relationships and the class struggle? They generally hold that in our society large-scale class struggle has been basically concluded, that the socialist transformation of capitalist industry and commerce has been completed, so there are no more counter-revolutionaries and bad elements . . . But the facts are entirely different. Even after the conclusion of socialist transformation, class struggle will continue for a long period to come (Hsieh Fei, FH No.2, 12th February, 1958, in SCMM, No.135, 1958)

The Ministry of Control was perhaps the most seriously scrambled of all the judicial agencies. It was closely identified with the new legalism of the mid-1950s and its job was to see that Party and government bodies behaved according to written law (WKCFYC No.1, 1955, *in* Hsia Tao-Tai, 1967, p.38). Given the weak tradition of written law in China and the Communist preference for directly involving the people in political action, it is not surprising that the Ministry had a short and difficult career. During the Anti-Rightist movement the Control officials received a more than equal share of criticism.

Wang Han, member of the Central Control Committee of the Republic and P'eng Ta, Vice Chief of the Second Ministry of Control were both criticized for their bureaucratic arrogance and both were expelled from the Party and removed from office. These and a number of lesser Control officials were said to "despise mass politics" and the entire Ministry was informed that bureaucratic consolidation would not be permitted to eliminate public participation in government (URI, 1957, Vol. I, p.42; Schurmann, 1966b, pp.353-59). The Party continued to lead the people in periodic attacks on government abuse, and the bureaucratic checks of the Control Ministry did not replace the political check of direct popular justice action.

The overall political meaning of the Anti-Rightist episode was unmistakable. The Party leadership and the radicals within the regular justice agencies ended for some time the talk about "stabilizing the revolution" and professionalizing justice. They insisted that the era of class conflict and social contradictions was not past and pointed to the existence and dangerousness of the rightists as proof of that argument (Rickett and Rickett, 1964; Li Shao-Sheng, CFYC No.3, 30th June, 1958, *in* SCMM No.140, 1959). The radicals were not willing to retire popular justice or to subordinate it entirely to an elite-controlled professional justice. The regular agencies themselves henceforth reflected the principles of mass line more closely and their procedures resembled more nearly the informal open procedures of popular justice. Popular support and public participation in judicial processes was thought more important than a set of "professional standards" and correct legal procedures. The movement toward a Soviet-style legal bureaucracy was stunned almost stone-dead, and it never really recovered.

The first months of heated conflict passed and the Hundred Flowers-Anti-Rightist movements passed into a quieter stage of general public action. Peasants and workers were encouraged to "bloom and contend", examine and criticize shortcomings of government officials and Party members attached to each local factory, collective farm or city district. The Party leadership felt it important to hear public gripes and develop better mass-cadre relationships in preparation for the co-operative effort of the Great Leap Forward (JMJP, 27th June, 1956, *in* SCMP No.1326; Chou en Lai, 26th June, 1957, *in* CFIA 1971, pp.322-24; Teng Hsiao Peng, 23rd September, 1957, *in* CFIA, 1971, pp.349-50). In the realm of justice, policemen and judges were urged to work more closely with mass organizations and avoid the arrogant self-righteous traditions of

pre-Communist governments (Cohen, 1968a, p.489; Leng, 1967, pp.64-66).
Local investigation teams were formed to hear citizens' complaints and public
accusation meetings were called to criticize abusive or lazy officials and to apply
the social pressure of popular justice towards the reform of elitist cadres (Teng
Hsiao Peng, 23rd September, 1957, *in* CFIA, 1971, pp.349-50; Hughes and
Luard, 1959, pp.155-56). So it was the political message of the Anti-Rightist
reaction trickled down to the villages and neighbourhoods.

Handling Contradictions through Continuous Revolution: Strategy of the Great Leap

After the One Hundred Flowers-Anti-Rightist campaigns it was clear to
everyone that there were some serious tensions in China. Differences between
intellectuals and political leaders and between conservatives and radicals within
the Party and the government poked a dozen holes through what had before
seemed a smooth fabric of unified national Communism. The need for the rapid
expansion of government and industry had prompted the central leadership to
overlook many of these differences until 1957; and indeed the leadership's
economic programme had caused the widening of several important social
contradictions. The wages of industrial workers had increased much faster than
the peasants' earnings and mass-leadership co-operation had broken down as
bureaucracies grew larger and more concerned with production schedules than
with the involvement of the masses in political decisions.

The Great Leap strategy developed from the conscious recognition of these
social gaps and political problems. In the winter of 1957 Mao prepared a crucial
essay entitled "On the Correct Handling of Contradictions among the People"
and described some of the major conflicts within China. These he identified as
either "antagonistic" or "non-antagonistic" contradictions, and the two
categories required two sorts of solutions. Antagonistic conflicts included the
historic struggle with landlords and capitalists, as well as with the new "right-
hand men" of the reactionary classes: the revisionists. These revisionists, Mao
said, "are attacking the quintessence of Marxism", and they "oppose or try to
weaken socialist transformation". The revisionists were to be "resolutely
opposed" and stripped of political power (Mao Tse-tung, 1957, *in* FLP, 1967,
p.154). It is clear that these revisionists and the bureaucratic-technological
rightists were one and the same enemy.

The essay also considered the case of non-antagonistic contradictions such as
the differencs in rural and urban living standards or the still unequal position of
women in the society. The Chairman urged that these conflicts "among the
people" be resolved through "criticism, persuasion and education" and in a far
gentler manner than might be used to handle antagonistic contradictions.

In many ways this two-category division of social conflicts recalls the private versus official justice categories of Imperial or Republican China. The essential difference here, of course, is the application of socialist ideology to the resolution of both sorts of conflicts, and the larger fact that the official world was not insulated from the popular world by wealth, prestige, or power. In summary, the "Handling Contradictions" treatise must be regarded as a pivotal document in the evolution of Communist justice, since it re-asserted the importance of class conflict ("contradictions") and restated the political relativity of law (which was to provide two sorts of justice for two sorts of contradictions) (Mao Tse-tung, 1957, *in* FLP, 1967, pp.115-40).

The idea of "continuous revolution" appeared again in 1958 as a second political beacon for the Great Leap Forward. This concept is a fundamental and original element of Maoist Thought, equalled in importance only by the "mass line". It represents a significant extension of historical dialectics beyond the limits of Leninist, Stalinist, or even Marxist thought, and this philosophical advance would carry China far past the "example" of Soviet Communism (Johnson, 1969, pp.51-52). In "Handling Contradictions" Mao hinted that new developments in knowledge and production would lead to new social conflicts, even after the establishment of socialism or even Communism (Mao Tse-tung, 1957, *in* FLP, 1967, pp.149-51). Later in his "Sixty Articles on Work Methods" the Chairman fleshed out this social philosophy and called for "Permanent Revolution" as follows:

> Our revolutions follow each other, one after another. Beginning with the seizure of power on a nation-wide scale in 1949, there followed first anti-feudal land reform; as soon as land reform was completed, agricultural co-operativization was begun . . . The three great socialist transformations were basically completed in 1956. Following this we carried out last year (1957) the socialist revolution on the political and ideological fronts. This revolution can be basically complete by July 1st of this year. *But the problem is still not resolved and for a fairly long period to come, the method of arising of views and rectification must be used every year to solve the problems in this field* [my italics]. Every mutation or leap is a revolution and they must all go through struggle. The theory of no classes is metaphysical (Mao Tse-tung, 1965, *in* Schram, 1971a, pp.226-7)

The theory of "continuous revolution" did little to calm career bureaucrats already threatened and uneasy from Anti-Rightist and earlier rectifications of Three Antis, Judicial Reform and the 1954-55 Suppression action. Mao's promise to use "rectification every year" was picked up by the Party radicals, and the conservatives hopes for a "consolidation" of government were dashed. Those officials who sought to link power to privilege and security would continue to face "struggle meetings", rectification movements and (in some instances) People's Tribunals. The bureaucratic elite, weakened by Anti-Rightist dismissals, faced the prospects of a permanent mass line ideology and long-term pressure from an active and strong popular justice.

The revolution did not end with the establishment of state control over production. The Maoist leadership called for a deepening of social consciousness in all citizens and a broadening of public involvement in the development of an industrialized but still popular political economy. The mass organizations would not be politically disarmed as long as the Maoist leadership counted popular support as its first resource and mass mobilization as its first political-economic strategy.

The continuous revolution ideology line and the mass line springs from a deep faith in the wisdom, power and basic goodness of the common people. The achievements of mass line politics before and after liberation reinforced this confidence in the people as progressive force; while the dangers of bureaucratic rule became more obvious in both the Hungarian uprising and the rightist elitism of One Hundred Flowers. The public mobilization strategy of the Great Leap reflected a renewed faith in popular politics and a readiness on the part of the leadership to sacrifice the secure "efficiency" of centralized control in order to open opportunities for grassroots action.

The Great Leap programme called for mass action in a social revolution designed to eliminate some of the more serious "contradictions", such as the city-country wage gap, prestige differences in mental versus manual labour, the restrictions of male versus female economic and political roles, and the alienation of government and Party from the people (occurring as a result of bureaucratic isolation and elitism). These sweeping changes were to be accomplished by decentralizing government and the industrial economy, and by integrating education, technology and political leadership with the needs and desires of the public in each local area.

The radicals not only believed that these great social changes were necessary to maintain and deepen popular support, but also expected that the re-arrangements would release tremendous new productive energies and speed up China's industrial development (Chang Chien CHCC, 9th May, 1958, *in* SCMM No.135, 1958; Ch'en Po-ta, *Hung Ch'i*, 1st July, 1958, *in* CFIA, 1971, pp.452-3). Like post-war reconstruction, this was an ambitious programme and as in the past, the Party leadership counted on a total mass mobilization to make the Great Leap. Public support was to be channelled through a new set of mass organizations: the communes (*Hung Ch'i*, 1st September, 1958, *in* CFIA, 1971, pp.457-59). The communes amounted to a radical escalation of mass line politics, since they would unite production and political action for the first time within a single set of community associations (CC-CCP, 29th August, 1958, *in* CFIA, 1971, pp.455-56). Within the new commune structures in city and country-side, popular justice was to grow in strength and professional justice become increasingly popular in procedures and working ideology.

Big City Chauvinism and the Rural Communes

Before the Leap even the most pro-Communist peasants knew that the city folks were getting the best deal from the Chinese revolution. Though famines, epidemics, female slavery and landlords had been ended by the new government, the farmers' wages did not match those of the urban workers and the gap widened throughout the First Five-year Plan (1952-57) (Schram, 1963, p.22). At first the government tried to minimize this widening gap, but the peasants continued to grumble. By 1957 the available figures showed a wide difference in living standards, as measured by consumption and reported as follows:

Per Capita Consumption of Basic Goods in 1956 (TCYC, No.1, 23rd January, 1958, *in* Schram, 1963, p.13)

	Urban	Rural
Food grains	200 kg	216 kg
Oil	6·4 kg	1·9 kg
Sugar	7·0 kg	3·8 kg
Cloth	20·6 metres	6·6 metres

While these differences are remarkable, the most serious gaps in living standards were either unreported or statistically unmeasurable. Reports appearing in the Chinese press and travellers' accounts indicate that the country folk were eating enough in food bulk, but were not getting nearly as much meat, high-quality grains and diet supplements as the city workers (Hughes and Luard, 1959, p.157). The farmers watched most of the best crops disappear down the road to the cities.

Even more important than the setting of the peasants' tables were the differences in career opportunities available to inhabitants of city and country. While the Communist Party was still predominantly made up of peasants, the recruitment was increasingly concentrated in the cities and especially among the intellectual class (Townsend, 1968, pp.30-36). The schools provided for the peasant children, though vastly better than ever before, were not the equal of city schools. Peasant youngsters lucky enough to reach university did not easily pass the "objective" examinations which have always plagued the poor and under-educated in every country.

Even more aggravating were the government's assertions that these differences were "natural" because farmers' work was simpler and less valuable than industrial work. This type of economic chauvinism is obvious in the following statement by the Statistical Research Bureau:

Is the material discrepancy in the amounts of consumption between [urban] labour force and the peasants appropriate. We hold that it is appropriate basically. It should be realized that at the present, this difference . . . is due to the fact that the levels of production in agriculture and industry are different and formed by historical conditions. On the other hand the degree of complexity of labor of the (urban) labor force and the peasants are also different. This means also that under the present economic conditions in our country, it is necessary and desirable to preserve a certain discrepancy between the consumption of labor force and peasants (TCYC, No.1, 13th January, 1958, *in* Schram, 1963, p.13; *see also* JMJP, 17th April, 1957, *in* Hughes and Luard, 1959, p.188)

In fairness to the People's Government, it should be remembered that the Communists did not invent the city–country gap. It had existed decades before the Revolution of 1911. The peasants were, however, growing impatient and it was clear that a Soviet-style industrial concentration in the cities would not bring the peasants up to the levels of the city workers. The Great Leap programme attempted to counter this problem by bringing industrialization to the countryside and by increasing the production power of the peasantry through the social re-organization of the commune system.

The collectivization of agriculture in 1955–56 had pooled tools and resources and made farming a more efficient business, but it had left the rural social structure pretty much unchanged. The Mutual Aid Teams and the Agricultural Producers Co-operatives generally followed the old lines of large and small villages. Though the clan organizations and the feudal marriage customs had been abolished, farming was still mainly a man's occupation, with the women staying inside performing household chores and handicrafts. The countryside was almost exclusively devoted to farming and industrial technology remained a mystery to the peasant.

The Great Leap began by merging the thousands of farming co-operatives into hundreds of larger communes (each with several thousand families). By 1st January, 1959 it was reported that over 99% of the peasant population had been organized into the new communes (Hughes and Luard, 1959, p.157). In addition to farming, each commune had responsibility for setting up and operating dozens of small industrial plants, such as the famous "back-yard steel furnaces". While the larger plants were still to be "the backbone of production", the Party leadership encouraged the communes to "go in for industry in a big way". These small-scale plants were regarded as important since they could be set up quickly and at far less cost than the large urban industries. The commune steel mills, parts factories and textile mills were usually tiny affairs employing only a few dozen commune members (CC-CCP, 10th December, 1958, *in* Jacobs and Baerwald, 1963, p.121).

There were also a number of "service centres" which provided for the child-care, laundry, cooking and household repair needs of the commune families.

As of 1956 over 120 million women were still confined to household chores and the service centres were expressly designed to free women for production and political work (Crook and Crook, 1966, pp.244-46, 511-566; Waller, 1971, pp.144-7). The success of the commune industries and indeed of the whole Great Leap effort was to depend very much on the efforts of women brought into the labour force as coequal workers.

Higher education followed industry into the communes of the countryside, and both the peasants and the educational system were deeply affected by the experience of the Great Leap. The Maoists were determined that the schools and colleges be free from the intellectual arrogance and elitism so noticeable among the One Hundred Flowers scholars. Rather than simply transfer the old educational system, the Leap programme established scores of "Red and Expert" schools and universities in the communes. Thousands of students and teachers from the old universities went into the countryside to help the communes set up the new schools and thousands of peasants and workers enrolled as full- or part-time students (Goldman, R., 1961, pp.104-6; Hsu, 1964, pp.150-51; Lewis, 1966, p.17). Peasant children were also given special preference in entrance exams for the regular universities (CKCN No.13, 1st July, 1958, in SCMM No.144, 1958; Lu Ting yi, Hung Ch'i, 1st July, 1958, in CFIA, 1971, pp.439-449).

The "Red and Expert" schools were built along the principles of the mass line, and were designed to unite intellectual expertise with local practical needs and socialist ideology. The "expert" was expected to pass knowledge on to the people and the new schools concentrated research and teaching on the needs of local industry or agriculture. Academic language was avoided and the intellectuals were expected to take part in manual labour as members of commune production teams (JMCY, No.6, 16th May, 1958, in SCMM No.158, 1958; Crook and Crook, 1966, pp.180-81; Mao Tse-tung, 1965, in Schram, 1971a, p.227).

The older, more established universities in the cities were drawn into similar efforts, where students and teachers left the classroom for regular work shifts in large industrial plants or in small factories built by and operated entirely by the university community. Students criticized older professors who advised them to remain in classrooms and confine their practical experiments to laboratories. The idea behind both the "Red and Expert" schools and the new work-study programme at the older universities was to unite the intellectual class with the workers and peasants and, in the process, to pierce the "mystique" of professional specialization and so make knowledge more the collective property of the whole people.

The political management of the countryside, like the industrial and educational systems, became more decentralized during the Great Leap. The ideals of the mass line and continuous revolution were behind the decision to close down many county and city governments and to place local government directly in the hands of the communes and the local Party committees (Schurmann, 1966a, p.5).

The Anti-Rightist attack on bureaucratic elitism continued on the local level and peasant criticisms of arrogant or isolated officials wre given wide publicity and coverage in the press. This popular justice phase of the Anti-Rightist Rectification consisted of hundreds of "fact finding meetings" where the masses interrogated officials to discover responsibility for mistakes and shortcomings. Officials were often called to come forward to "speak themselves white" (i.e. confess their faults), and they were pressurized to follow the new suggestions of the masses. The size of the government payrolls was cut considerably as the communes began to control their own industries, schools and construction projects (Kau, 1969, pp.49-57). Many of the remaining bureaucrats also left their offices to work among the workers and peasants of the communes (Hughes and Luard, 1959, pp.155-56; Crook and Crook, 1966, pp.61-64; Dutt, 1967, pp.96-97).

In 1957 the Party leadership ordered government bureaux to send many more of their staff to the rural communes. In this national "hsia fang" campaign thousands of officials worked alongside the farmers in the hope that they would, as a result, better understand the problems of the country folk. In 1959 the Mayor of Peking called for 30-50% of the city officials to "go down" and work in fields and factories (CT, 1st October, 1957, in SCMM No.114, 1957). Though most of these stayed for only a few weeks or months, the campaign still made an impression on the officials, particularly since the difference between being "sent down" to the countryside for a few weeks for "labour retraining" and remaining there for months or years as a commune farmer was largely a matter of political discretion. Manual labour is officially regarded as an opportunity and a patriotic duty but there is no doubt, however, that the bureaucrats usually preferred office work to the fields, and liked the city better than the more humdrum rural commune life.

As a result of office cut-backs, the hsia fang campaign and the general pressures of the Great Leap, the remaining bureaucrats became acutely aware of their own political vulnerability and they streamlined office procedures to meet the needs of the public (Kau, 1969, pp.57-59). The Party leadership kept continuous pressure on the bureaucracy and also cautioned the new officials of the communes that:

> . . . leading functionaries of all levels in the communes must put the mass
> line thoroughly into practice . . . They must look upon themselves as
> ordinary working people and treat the commune members in a comradely
> way. Kuomintang and bourgeois styles of work are strictly forbidden
> (CC-CCP, 10th December, 1958, in Jacobs and Baerwald, 1963, p.130)

The communes were designed as a radical step and indeed they left the ancient systems of private governments far behind. As promised, the communes did promote "radical changes in human relations", as lines of specialization were broken down, old village class and family arrangements were discarded and social energies were concentrated on the extraordinarily ambitious production goals set by the membership of the rural communes. During the first year of the Leap, it seemed that the rural social revolution provided enough human energy to make up for the lack of money and machinery still being concentrated on urban industrial growth.

The Urban Communes and the Struggle with Materialism

Throughout the years of reconstruction and the First Five-year Plan, the Communists had used a system of material incentives to spur industrial production in the cities. By 1957 there were eight wage grades for workers and 18 for university graduates. The salaries of professors, technicians, workers, engineers and ranking government employees far outstripped all others (Ch'eng-chih Shih, 1962, pp.142-43; Hoffman, 1969, pp.68-70). The bureaucratic-technological elite, though not yet a dominant political force, was certainly distinguishable in terms of high wages and living standards . These social gaps and material differences weakened the sense of community identity on the part of city dwellers whose loyalties still centred around their individual families and careers.

The Great Leap also called for the narrowing of these urban wage gaps, but the Communist strategy for the cities was far more conservative than the massive social revolution in the countryside. Urban communes were created in many cities but the Party leadership was cautious lest it unduly upset industrial production only recently established under the First Five-year Plan. Some key industrial areas, such as Shanghai, had virtually no urban commune organizations and most urban communes were restricted in size and power (CFJP, 29th March, 1958, *in* Ch'eng-chih Shih, 1962, pp.54-56). Nevertheless, it was hoped that the urban communes would both increase production and equalize incomes. This more moderate revolution in the cities involved both social change and intensive political education. As in the countryside, the urban communes set up thousands of small industrial plants and service centres, and women provided much of the new productive energy needed to run both the political organization of the commune and its industries (Tang and Maloney, 1970; Salaff, 1967, pp.98-101). The commune de-emphasized material incentives and counted on political education and the collective spirit of the residents to push production (Waller, 1971, p.151; King, H. H., 1968, pp.194-5). The old system of piece-rate wages was attacked as contributing to "jealousy, poor quality of products and improper equipment maintenance (JMJP, 13th October, 1958, *in* Newton, 1959, p.22; Hughes and Luard, 1959, p.121). The official Party newspaper, the *People's Daily*, declared that:

> We have over-emphasized the importance of material incentives, while neg-
> lecting our political and ideological work . . . This failure was responsible for
> the growth of individualism, egoism . . . (JMJP, 21st November, 1957, *in*
> Hoffman, 1969, p.100)

In the opening months of 1958 urban communes were formed rapidly in many of China's large and medium-sized cities. By the beginning of 1960, communes had been established in Peking, Tientsin, Chungking, Harbin, Sian and numerous other cities and totalled 20 million in population (or about 35% of the Chinese urban population) (PACL, 1960, p.11). The mostly female commune labour force in 43 cities operated over 44,000 (mostly small) industrial units (PACL, 1960, p.24). Communes were basically of three types organized around large factories, residential areas, or schools and government bureaux. (Cheng-chih Shih, 1962: 41-50; Li Chieh-po, NCNA, 8th April, 1960).

The communes assumed many of the duties of urban government and govern-ment officials left their offices to live and work among the commune members (Cheng-chih Shih, 1962, pp.41-42). The residents' committees and street offices were incorporated under the commune organizations and these older associations helped mobilize public support for production and political action (Townsend, 1969, p.161). New "Red and Expert" schools were set up in the factories and neighbourhoods and, as in the rural communes, education was tailored to meet the immediate needs of the city residents (Salaff, 1967, pp.103-5).

The urban social changes begun by the commune movement were impressive, as were the figures released by the government which showed huge amounts of steel, cotton goods, spare parts and food stuffs produced by the communes. For a time it seemed that the communes of town and country would indeed carry China quickly past under-development and up to the level of a modern industrial power. The whole of Chinese society had lurched ahead and the judicial system was inevitably transformed by the changes of the Great Leap.

Professional Justice under the Great Leap

The radicals within the professional justice agencies had read Mao's essay on "handling contradictions" with great interest. The call for renewed class and ideological struggle clearly supported the radical view that law should be politically relative and that justice should be primarily an educational rather than a legal process (Cohen, 1968b, p.494). The members of the Department of Law at the People's University of China (the official

Party university), reviewed Mao's statements and related them to justice as follows:

> . . . the spearheads of the People's democratic legal system, being a fierce weapon for solving the central contradiction between ourselves and the enemy, should be pointed toward the enemy . . .

> [Political-legal officials] should clearly recognize the internal contradictions among the people and should not point the spearhead of the legal system toward the people (JMMFC, *in* Hsia Tao-Tai, 1967, p.19)

Justice was charged with two entirely different tasks and officials were cautioned to use different sorts of reform and control measures for the two types of contradictions. The first task of police and judges in the Great Leap, as in the Civil War and liberation periods, was the capture, reform and control of political and class "enemies" and the second mission entailed the resolution of conflicts among the people. These two sorts of justice call for a separate analysis.

Repression and reform for "antagonistic contradictions"

The "enemy" was said to consist of five main social groups; namely, some former landlords, counter-revolutionaries, some rich peasants, rightists and other "bad elements". These "elements" were said to be organizing gambling, political conspiracy, riots and sabotage. The Party leadership believed two-thirds of the former landlords and rich peasants had successfully remoulded themselves, but the remaining "reactionary and stubborn minority" was to face intense public criticism, loss of civic rights, or even labour reform or imprisonment (Teng Hsiao Peng, 1958, *in* CFIA, 1971, pp.343-44). Another leading justice official described the enemy as "those who seriously threaten and disrupt the urban and rural social order, including gangsters, hooligans, robbers, murderers, rapists, swindlers, corrupt officials and other criminals who undermine public order and seriously break the law" (Teng Hsiao Peng, 20th June, 1958, CFYC, *in* SCMM No.139, 1958).

The Minister of Public Order outlined police practices with regard to the "enemy" as follows:

> The counter-revolution is being rapidly weakened, and is more and more isolated from the masses. The internal disintegration of the counter-revolution and the revolutionary classes are continuing to become aggravated.

> Our task is to make the fullest use of these favourable conditions . . . adopt correct methods in the continuation and intensification of the struggle against the enemy . . .

We must strive to disarm them as soon as they reach out their hands. The various weapons at the disposal of our dictatorship for punishment, including the most severe punishment, should be concentrated for dealing with these counter-revolutionary saboteurs.

Of course . . . as long as they give themselves up, or contribute meritorious service in remission for their offenses, they must be given magnanimous treatment in accordance with the concrete facts of their cases . . . (Lo Jui ching, HH, 18th June, 1958, *in* SCMM No.139, 1958)

"Gentle breeze and light rain" for
"non-antagonistic contradictions"

The other side of justice "among the people" was a far gentler sort of persuasion, and Mao related his "handling contradictions" philosophy to this side of law as follows:

. . . the method employed [for resolving social conflicts among the people] is not forcible repression but persuasion.

It is only in dealing with those law breakers who seriously disrupt the normal social order that this political power [the justice system] adopts temporary, and in varying degrees, repressive methods as a supplement to persuasion.

It is only toward serious counter-revolutionaries and saboteurs that we adopt the method of repression (Mao Tse-tung, 1965, *in* Schram, 1971a, p.228)

The chief of the national police force, Lo Jui ching, adopted Mao's advice in his recommendations on police work as follows:

The relations between the police and the masses of the people are of course relations among the people . . . but here are also certain contradictions of an internal nature . . . public order organs and personnel for the protection of normal social production and normal social life . . . come into contradiction with a small number of the masses of the people whose acts are not in keeping with administrative orders, such as certain acts which violate the police regulations, and certain acts which undermine public order or violate public morals. Such contradictions, generally speaking, fall within the scope of discipline and freedom, the scope of centralism and democracy. The correct method of handling them is persuasion, and not suppression (Lo Jui ching, HH, 18th June, 1958, *in* SCMM No. 139, 1958)

It is evident, however, that judges and policemen had some difficulty in separating out the different sorts of contradictions, especially since for almost its entire history, the regular justice system had concentrated its energies against "enemies" involved in "antagonistic" contradictions. There was little professional justice experience of conflicts among the people, which had usually been resolved by the popular justice arrangements. The national police chief also noted in this 1958 article:

> . . . we have won a gigantic victory in the struggle against the enemy. However, we must admit that with reference to the important ideology of the correct handling of contradictions among the people, our understanding has not yet been thorough, and both in our ideological self-awakening and in our action in the thorough implementation of the ideology, there is still room for improvement (Lo Jui ching, HH, 18th June, 1958, *in* SCMM No.139, 1958)

Process and organization of Great Leap justice

The re-emphasis of "class perspective" and political-legal relativity led to a downgrading of formal legal procedures which would handle all cases according to uniform bureaucratic routines (a standard which China never reached even before One Hundred Flowers-Anti-Rightist). Judges and police were encouraged to spend more time in the educational and reform aspects of justice as courtrooms again became schools for ideology and socialist morality.

The renewed emphasis on the political role of law also meant that the Communist Party would have greater influence in judicial matters. Judges and policemen began to work more closely with members of local Party committees in a range of cases. The National Conference of Political-Legal Officials in May 1959 was addressed by a number of Party officials who spoke on this very issue of Party influence and the role of political ideology in justice. The delegates concluded the conference with a resolution encouraging all justice professionals to "put politics in command" of justice and to seek Party advice in all important decisions (Cohen, 1965, p.17).

The increased Party prominence did not, however, mean that control of justice was to pass from the hands of the bureaucratic-technological elite into the hands of an equally isolated Party elite. Along with the wider Party role the Great Leap programme called for closer Party-mass contact and for strong popular justice organizations capable of supervising and assisting the local Party committees. The public was to participate more directly in the business of justice through the justice organizations of the communes. The Party members, like the police and judges, were strongly encouraged to work more closely with the mass representatives, and the pressure of possible popular justice sanctions (as in accusation meetings or mass campaigns of rectification) loomed behind these encouragements (Leng, 1967, pp.64-65).

The People's supervisory committees were granted new powers and were once again able to conduct independent investigations and prepare charges against abusive officials. The practice of "mass supervision" had become largely an empty ritual while local supervisory committees were under the tight central control of the Ministry of Control; but the Ministry of Control was abolished in 1959 and the local supervisory committees grew stronger and more independent within the new commune organizations (Waller, 1971, p.107).

The expanded public role as political watchdog replaced many of the bureaucratic checks and balances set up during the constitutional period. The inter-agency pressures between police, courts and Procurates dropped off and officials from the three bureaux formed combined "justice teams" which toured the fields and factories of the communes to handle cases on the spot and work more closely with the local masses (Cohen, 1968b, pp.489-90; Cohen, 1968a, p.995; Waller, 1971, pp.110-111). Centralized bureaucratic control was sacrificed to encourage popular participation and the weakened Ministry of Justice, with less and less effective influence over local judges, police and procurators, was eventually abolished in 1959. The end of the central Ministry of Justice, like the decline of the Ministry of Control, was a serious blow to conservative professionals remaining in political-legal agencies, since the Ministry of Justice had sponsored professional training, legal research and the recruitment of legal specialists (Wu Chien Lu, CFYC No.3, 1959, in Hsia Tao-Tai, 1967, p.28).

The Procurate and courts, already shaken by Anti-Rightist Rectification, continued to lose personnel and power, while the police and the mass organizations assumed greater influence under the provisions of the 1957 Security and Punishment Act which re-organized professional justice (Cohen, 1968a). Few of the ordinary cases reached the courts and the judges were increasingly facing only the most serious sort of political offenders. Trials of such class or political enemies were widely publicized and used for political education and heightening of the public's class consciousness. One Communist jurist wrote in 1958 that most of the cases before the People's Courts "involved contradictions between the enemy and the people" (Ma Jung Kuang, FH No.7, 1958, in Hsia Tao-Tai, 1967, p.21). The procurators were in the weakest position and they were unwilling to challenge police recommendations and thus risk charges of "bureaucratic legalism" or even be labelled "rightists" (CFYC No.3, 1958, in Cohen, 1965, pp.10, 27-29).

Social pressure, political education and productive labour on the "justice slide"

The "continuous revolution" philosophy prompted a new emphasis on educational reform rather than legal process in handling offenders. Under Great Leap justice, procedural lines between the various penal reform sanctions were blurred, and the fate of the accused became increasingly tied to his individual progress in social-political reform. The 1957 Security Administration and Punishment Act granted the police (working with local Party committees and mass organizations) wide discretion in investigation and sanctioning of offenders. The new act gave the police authority to impose "administrative sanctions" in serious criminal cases, which is to say that the police, in concert with mass organizations, could assign an offender to a three-year period in any of several reform programmes without a formal court trial and without Procurate approval (Cohen, 1968a). The most common and most important of these "administrative sanctions" included the following (listed in order of seriousness):

Labour Reform: Those sent to Labour Reform Brigades were generally assigned the roughest work in the countryside, such as dam building or land-clearing. (This more punitive sanction was generally reserved for the more serious violent criminals, for the more dangerous class enemies such as 'stubborn and reactionary' ex-landlords and corrupt or unbendingly arrogant Communist officials.)

Labour Re-education: Those assigned were usually sent from cities into countryside where they worked alongside the peasants of the communes in regular production tasks. (Most frequently reserved for 'rightists' and other government or Party officials singled out for criticism during mass campaigns.)

Mass Control: Under which the offender was not generally permitted to leave the local area and was required to submit weekly or monthly reports of his/her productive work and progress in social ideological reform. (Often used for those guilty of street crimes, such as theft, and especially applied to class enemies from the pre-liberation era, such as ex-landlords and ex-rich peasants.) (Cohen, 1965, pp.18, 24-27)

Fines, executions and imprisonment behind walls were deliberately avoided as these sanctions were regarded as strictly punitive and without educational or productive value. Labour is regarded as the central human activity in most Communist systems and the Chinese judicial and correction arrangements are no exception. The Minister of Public Order, the man ultimately responsible for the management of labour reform, labour re-education and mass control described the central importance of productive labour in social-political reform as follows:

. . . we must, on a nationwide scope, develop on a large scale and in a planned manner reform work with the combination of productive labour and political education, among all counter-revolutionary elements and reactionary class enemies who are capable of abandoning their reactionary stand (Lo Jui ching, HH No.12, 18th June, 1958, *in* SCMM No.139, 1958)

The Minister, like many other justice officials, was confident that all but the most stubborn "enemies" could be reformed and usually re-classified as citizens in good standing as he noted in 1958:

> Through production labour and political education, they must as much as possible be transformed into good labourers who live on their toil. They must be changed from passive factors into active factors in socialist construction . . . with the exception of the determined counter-revolutionary elements . . . we must adopt chiefly the method of transformation (Lo Jui ching, HH No.12, 18th June, 1958, *in* SCMM No.139, 1958)

In addition to the above most serious sanctions, the mass organizations relied on directed social pressure techniques all designed to educate and reform socially irresponsible commune members and so resolve "contradictions among the people" *before* they became so serious as to warrant formal "administrative sanctions" by the police (Cohen, 1965, p.17). These community sanctions were really the guts of the Great Leap judicial system and they will be discussed in some detail in the next section on popular justice.

The various justice sanctions were not designed as legal categories permanently assigned to offenders after some fateful weighing of "guilt" and "innocence". Instead, all of the sanctions, including both "administrative sanctions" of the police and the informal social pressure techniques of mass organizations form a sort of *justice slide*, with the various sanctions arranged as points on a continuum between social isolation and acceptance. Under the provisions of the SAPA act the police, in consultation with the local mass organizations of the offender's community, could keep the offender on the slide for three or, in some cases, six years (Li, 1973).

Whether a person stayed at one point, moved on to a more punitive reform sanction, or moved off the slide to regain his former position and status was determined by that individual's reform progress, as decided by the police officials and by those who worked alongside the offender. Except in the case of the very few confined to walled prisons and some of the Labour Reform Brigades, the offender's co-workers included both other sanctioned individuals and ordinary working members of the communes. In any case, the entire national labour force (of offenders and ordinary citizens) was periodically involved in intensive criticism, self-criticism, and political education sessions. Only a minority of offenders are socially isolated or morally condemned in a permanent labelling process of courts and prisons. Instead he/she is subjected to intense social pressure by co-workers. Within the Labour Reform Brigades this pressure is controlled and manipulated by the police, but the communes supervise the far more numerous offenders assigned to "mass control" or "labour re-education" (Li, 1973; Snow, 1964, pp.351-56).

Throughout the Great Leap, professional justice became more class conscious, decentralized and community-oriented. Bureaucratic procedures and legal professionalism were sacrificed as justice became increasingly a matter of social re-education and community pressure in which "scientific" legal procedures and set criminal categories were cumbersome and irelevant. The number of professional legal publications decreased markedly, as did activity and enrolments in the specialized legal research institutes. Training in justice at the Red and Expert schools concentrated on political ideology and practical police problems (TKCK, Vol. 45, Nos 8, 9, *in* URI, 1963, Vol. I, p.123).

The public played a central role in this educational reform process and the Maoist leadership also counted on the mass organizations of the communes to keep officials honest and close to the mass line. The public powers of discretion and initiative in matters of justice and politics reflected the renewed confidence in the people which was the watchword of the Great Leap. The Soviet-style judicial system of regular procedures, legal professionalism and bureaucratic checks and balances were replaced by a system of supervised police and community organizations.

The abandonment of the legal process model in favour of the education–reform model of justice was further evidence of the Great Leap confidence in the common man. This confidence extended to offenders and criminals of all sorts whom the government was confident could be recovered and reformed by participating in labour and social-political education. As might be expected, while the professional agencies became less centralized and more community-oriented, the public communities developed larger and more powerful popular justice institutions.

The Revival of Popular Justice

Though the movement toward a professional justice stalled in the face of Anti-Rightist rectification, popular justice did not really begin its national comeback until the onset of the Great Leap. The new communes of city and country re-established the sense of community identity and deepened the public's political self-confidence, and made possible popular justice institutions. Mediation committees, commune security teams and commune People's supervisory committees grew in size and power as the commune citizens became more active in both the control of crime and the control of local government bureaucrats.

The constitutional restrictions on mediation were cast aside by the communes and arbitration with a strong dose of political education and social pressure was prescribed for a wide variety of social conflicts, including most minor criminal offences. People's "Conciliation and Handling Committees" were set up across the country in 1958. The local Party branch in each commune influenced nominations and the public elected three to nine volunteers to these more powerful versions of the earlier mediation committees (Myrdal, 1965, pp.370-71; SHJP, 8th May, 1958, *in* Hsia Tao-Tai, 1967, pp.8-9). The People's Courts now shared control over the mediation groups with the communes.

The actual extent of court control was rather unclear, as popular justice advanced deep into the political turf only briefly held by the justice professionals (Hsia Tao-Tai, 1967, pp.7-8; CFYC No.4, 1864, *in* URI, 1964, Vol. I, p.165). Legal spokesmen in China noted that the new 1958 "Tentative Regulations of Mediation Committees" granted mediators more power as follows:

> In the past the lower level committees had no way to deal with such persons (more serious offenders). Now they have great powers and will certainly do well this work in the future (CFYC No.6, *in* URI, 1964, Vol. I, p.165)

The mediation teams were especially important in the cities both because crime had always been concentrated in cities and because the formation of the urban communes involved some social relocation. People moving into their commune areas were suddenly dealing with new neighbours and (especially for the women) whole new social roles and conflicts were naturally sparked by the friction of the Leap's social change. The number of criminal and civil cases handled out of court increased markedly across the country. In Hanan province alone there were 8080 mediation teams by 1958, as compared with only 139 People's Courts (TK, *in* URI, 1969, Vol. I, p.65; CFYC No.2, 1960, *in* Hsia Tao-Tai, 1967, p.7).

Within the urban communes, the Conciliation and Handling Committees were one of three core organizations set up by commune counsels to protect the new system. New committees were also organized in factories, schools and other production units (URI, 1964, Vol. I, pp.164-5). Mediation work was recognized by the central Party leadership as an essential method of resolving contradictions among the people. Teng Hsiao Peng, a member of the Central Committee, included a discussion of mediation in his "Report on the Rectification Movement". He encouraged mediation work and described it as:

> . . . a kind of mass self-education, self-supervision and self-restraint. It is an important method for the restriction of individualism by socialism, for the transformation of old customs and habits, and for the evolution of new customs and habits (Teng Hsiao Peng, 1958, *in* URI, 1962, Vol. I, p.64)

Citizen-policemen in the communes

Both rural and urban communes organized local security patrols which worked alongside the regular police (of the Department of Public Order). In the city this volunteer work was often done by the Dormitory Management Committee (when residents lived in dormitories). In other cases the people formed "Civil Security Departments" which guarded the factories and streets and provided all adult citizens with arms and militia training. In the countryside the communes organized "security committees", and the production brigades of each commune also elected one security representative. These rural patrols helped protect crops and machinery (JMJP, 22nd October, 1957, *in* CNA No.183, 1957; *Hung ch'i*, 16th October, 1958, *in* Cheng-chih Shih, 1962, pp.41–46; Snow, 1964, pp.344–45).

The social thought of Mao's landmark "Handling Contradictions" essay was to be closely applied to community justice. The Party leadership urged the communes to reserve repression for only class enemies and the most serious criminals, but to rely on persuasion and education (rather than repression and legal processes) in handling conflicts "among the people". An example of the Party's position on "contradictions among the people" may be found in the following excerpt from the official Party newspaper. The editorial was entitled "Talking of Unruly Clerks and Workers" and it asked:

> What should be done when the masses get out of hand? Obviously a mere prohibition is not the correct answer: it only makes matters worse. The disorder itself should be used as an occasion for overhauling the [government] bureaucracy and educating the people (JMJP, 8th, 13th May, 1957, *in* CNA No.183, 1957)

Professional justice was largely concerned with "antagonistic contradictions" and quite frequently the regular police turned less serious offenders over to the communes. There the security committees might assign them extra work or ask them to complete additional social-political education courses. These security teams and the local commune committees were also empowered to arrest and detain offenders. This jail sanction was limited to 15 or 30 days and regained police approval, but nonetheless amounted to an increase in the powers of local popular justice bodies. These informal sanctions and "scrapes" with the local authorities were not recorded, but the effectiveness of community sanctions goes a long way toward explaining the extraordinary low crime rate in China (Barnett, 1966, p.32; Li, 1969b, pp.18–19; Snow, 1964, pp.344–48).

The importance of community social pressure in the reform of class enemies and the most serious criminal offenders has been mentioned previously in this chapter. The general public was involved to a greater or lesser degree in the three main professional police sanctions: labour reform, labour re-education and mass control. Mass control was, of these three, the most commonly used reform sanction and it involved the public most closely. The local commune security committees were directly responsible for surveillance of all "bad elements" working under mass control in the area. The volunteer police regularly submitted progress reports regarding both production work and changes in political and social attitudes among these "elements". Those who made progress could have "their hats taken off" (be restored to good standing) upon the recommendation of the local security committees and the regular police (Barnett, 1966, pp.32-35).

In guiding commune police work the Party spokesmen often pointed out that reactionary views and personal shortcomings were not in themselves regarded as grounds for arrest or repression. Such "ideological" contradictions were to be dealt with by education, criticism and persuasion. Legal action was permissible only when a person (especially if a "bad element") engaged in illegal political activity. However, the line between "ideological" contradictions and "crime" was at times rather fine and considerable discretion was granted the community security workers. Again, the assumption here was that the local citizens were best qualified to know who and what was a serious social or political threat to the community (JMJP, 4th September, 1958, in Chen, C. S., 1969, p.244).

Another principle of security work demanded that police (both professional and volunteer) work closely with the local residents. The security staff was "not to create an air of mystery" about their work, and divisions between the people and their police were considered a dangerous carry-over from the old KMT regime. Public co-operation and participation in peace-keeping was considered essential to successful police work (Crook and Crook, 1966, p.187).

As noted previously, the commune organizations were active in supervising the work of government bureaux and often called out the cadres of Party or government for extended investigation and criticism meetings. This aspect of popular justice was co-ordinated by the volunteer supervisory committees organized in the communes of city and country, and other mass organizations (such as the trade unions). According to the 1958 "Tentative Regulations for People's Communes", supervisory committees were elected by the Commune Congress, but the commune congresses met rather infrequently and the supervisory committees were probably often appointed by the commune management committees (Chen, T., 1967, p.87; Chou en Lai, 22nd March, 1962, in Jacobs and Baerwald, 1963, pp.226-7).

The supervisory workers collected complaints from all commune members and prepared both criticism and formal charges against abusive officials. The Central Ministry of Control had been much weakened by Anti-Rightist rectification and its final elimination in 1959 left the commune supervisory committees pretty much on their own, responsible only to the commune and the local Party committee.

People's supervision grew stronger and, along with other aspects of community justice, found new political life in the mass line atmosphere of the Great Leap. Popular justice surged ahead, growing in importance both as a peace-keeping force and as a political counter against bureaucratic elitism at the local level; but the new prosperity of popular justice was intimately bound to the economic success of the communes and the Great Leap programme, and the national economy which had advanced so confidently throughout 1958 was beginning to sputter and drift as floods and crop failures struck China in 1959.

The First Failures and the Maoist Reaction

China in 1959-60 was a farmer's nightmare. The longest drought in decades was followed by the worst floods in a century. The hundreds of dams built during the Great Leap water conservation campaign of 1957-58 were not enough and by the start of 1960 the chairman of the national State Planning Commission reported that 600 million acres or fully one-third of the country's farmland was unusable (Li Fu ch'un, PR, 26th January, 1960). Failures were not limited to the country-side. The steel smelted in the small rural and urban commune furnaces turned out so badly as to be almost worthless and machinery breakdowns slowed production in the larger factories. These problems were compounded because local officials, not wishing to dampen Leap enthusiasm, had falsely reported bumper crops and record industrial outputs, so for a time the national leadership was not fully aware of the crises at hand (King, H. H., 1968, pp.188-189).

Bad weather was not the only cause of the recession that began in 1959. As it turned out, massed commune labour and independent commune production goals had some real limitations as economic strategies. The rural communes had freed millions of women for production labour but their labour was not always used in the most rational way, and many of the peasants were unable to handle the accounting and administration tasks assigned them by the newly independent communes.

The "vast armies" of commune farmers were ideal for such work as building dams or farm buildings, but the armies were rather unwieldy for some of the equally important smaller tasks. For example, the lack of drainage ditches and smaller canals prevented the peasants from fully using the large new dams in flood prevention and irrigation (Dutt, 1963, p.132). Many small patches of land were ignored since they could not be profitably farmed by the massed commune labour. The Communists actually cultivated less acreage in 1958-60 than before the Leap because so much farm labour was diverted to industry and because they were confident that much higher yields per acre would come with massed labour and revolutionary farming methods (Hughes and Luard, 1959, pp.176-77).

The urban communes were plagued with some of the basic problems which caused the rural crises. There was a great deal of moving about as individual families, mass organizations and government offices were relocated within the new commune areas. A tremendous number of women were added to the labour force by the commune service centres, but this also meant some new difficulties with so many untrained workers on the job and so many more small industries to manage and supply. Finally the tremendous pressure to produce more often resulted in products of marginal quality, and machines broke down from the production speed ups and the lack of time devoted to maintenance work (Wang Shao-tao, JMJP, 26th May, 1961, *in* Schurmann, 1961, pp.5-6).

The struggle with materialism also presented some especially difficult problems in the social re-organization of the cities. The labour force there was far more stratified in terms of wages, working conditions and life styles than were the peasants. A major conflict soon developed within the trade unions since some unionists continued to see wage demands as the first duty of a workers' mass organization. Not a few union officials were dubious about the commune programmes for equalizing wages, pooling resources and crossing lines of labour specialities (Harper, 1969, JMJP, 9th May, 1957, *in* CNA No.183, 1957; Cheng-chih Shih, 1962, p.68; URI, 1969, Vol. I, pp.46, 58). Political education of the workers and the criticism or even (in a few cases) the removal of some union officers, did not fully resolve this problem, which would still trouble the Party radicals in 1967.

The intellectuals and a number of government careerists were also worried about some of the personal effects of the commune re-organization. The ex-capitalists were uneasy lest the communes move to stop their monthly interest checks, paid by the central government for the nationalization of former private enterprises. A number of intellectuals, party and government cadres, were afraid that their bank accounts or household possessions might be confiscated (PACL, 1960, p.3; Cheng-chih Shih, 1962, p.68).

Overall it is apparent that the sense of community identity and the socialist commitment in the cities was not yet strong enough to soothe the doubts, frustrations and administrative mix-ups which were almost inevitable in such a vast social experiment. One observer, who touted the Chungking communes, noted that:

> There was animosity and sharp contradictions among the people of Chungking at the time of re-organizing their economic life there . . .

> . . . there are many among us who are worried in the midst of the people's commune movement, especially over the formation of communes in the cities. Some have even had doubts and conflicts (Wang Yung sun, 1960, *in* PACL, 1960, p.35)

Shortening the Leap: modification of 1959–60

In response to the crises in the national economy the Party called a meeting of the Central Committee in December 1958. There the leadership assessed the situation and decided to conduct a national shakedown of local Party cadres and to cut back on some of the more radical social changes of the Great Leap. The urban communes had always been regarded as an "experiment" and the Central Committee's "Resolution on Some Questions Concerning the People's Communes" announced a more cautious and shorter Leap in the cities, as follows:

> People's Communes have now become the general rule in all rural areas inhabited by our people . . . Some experiments have also begun in the cities . . . There are, however, certain differences between the city and the country-side.
>
> Firstly, city conditions are more complex than in the countryside.
>
> Secondly, Socialist ownership by the whole people is already the main form of ownership in the cities, and the factories, public institutions and schools, under the leadership of the working class have become highly organized.
>
> Thirdly, bourgeois ideology is still fairly prevalent among many of the capitalists and intellectuals in the cities; they still have misgivings about the establishment of communes — so we should wait a bit for them.
>
> Consequently, we should continue to make experiments and generally should not be in a hurry to set up people's communes in the cities. Parti-cularly in the big cities, this work should be postponed except for the necessary preparatory measures. People's communes should be established on a large scale in the cities only after rich experience has been gained and when the sceptics and doubters have been convinced (CC-CCP, 10th December, 1958, *in* CFIA, 1971, p.491)

Little more was heard about the urban communes after the 1960 "postponement", and while some of the small factories and child care centres remained, the larger commune organizations were almost certainly disbanded.

Though the radicals were prepared in 1959 to step back from the urban commune "experiment", they were unwilling to discard the basic Great Leap ideas of the mass line and continuous revolution. They remained confident that massed labour, national socialist spirit and new social changes could carry China quickly past "backward nation" status. More concretely, Mao and the still dominant Party radicals would not abandon the central Leap programmes of combining industry and agriculture in the rural communes.

Nevertheless, some minor modifications were made in the rural arrangements and the Party leadership did caution local cadres and local populations against thinking that "we have reached Communism". A larger portion of the national cash reserves and more of the new industry was to be applied toward the improvement of the crops in 1960-61 and the leadership did note that some farm tasks were better done by smaller teams and so emphasized more the role of the production brigades (there were usually 10-20 of these per commune) (CC-CCP, 10th December, 1958, *in* CFIA, 1971, pp.492-3, pp.497-8; Dutt, 1963, pp.128-9; Ahn Byung-joon, 1971, pp.1-5).

The second Anti-Rightist campaign

The Party leadership felt that many of the setbacks in 1959 were caused not by weaknesses in the basic commune idea but by the failure of many lower level cadres to implement fully the mass line in their organizational work among the commune farmers. The radicals were angry over what they regarded as hesitant and conservative attitudes among these basic level officials, and so launched a second Anti-Rightist campaign in 1959. This was not a popular justice campaign but was generally confined to long study and criticism sessions inside local Party and government offices. It did not involve such heated "struggle meetings" and public demonstrations as the earlier Anti-Rightist rectification of the 1957-58 Anti-Rightist action; but the 1959 movement was important since it did reach higher into the top political circles than any previous movement since the Civil War.

The slogans and directives of the campaign called for a closer mass-cadre relationship and another hsia fang programme was to send officials down from their offices to work alongside the production brigades. Party members who "exaggerated certain difficulties" encountered in work were criticized as "rightist-inclined" and were occasionally demoted or transferred for their failure to inspire confidence among the local citizens (Cheng-chih Shih, 1962, p.85; Ahn Byung-joon, 1971, pp.3-5; Dutt, 1963, p.114).

The most dramatic events, however, did not take place on the rural communes, but in the General Staff of the People's Liberation Army. The Chief of Staff, P'eng Teh-huai, had become increasingly disgruntled over the instability which followed the Great Leap. During the course of rectification he was said to have described the Leap as a "left tendency caused by petty bourgeois fanaticism" (Ahn Byung-joon, 1971, pp.5-6). P'eng was never known to be an especially tactful general and his timing was very poor since there was already evidence of some tension between the radicals and the Chief of Staff. P'eng had always been close to the Soviet advisers, and he had come to accept their ideas for a conventional Chinese army, armed with sophisticated weapons and led by a specialized, highly paid officer corps. This sort of army would be organized and equipped expressly for the specialized needs of defence against other modern armies (Siamonds, 1969, p.122; Waller, 1971, pp.118-19).

The Party radicals still expected the army to be a political-military guerrilla force and to play an active part in farming, construction, public education and industry. They saw no reason why the mass line should not extend to the military, and were irritated by the increasing specialization and the wide status and wage gaps which were opening between officers and men. The conflict deepened throughout the Leap as the general was slow to commit troops to the fields and factories (Charles, 1961, pp.65-70).

Mao finally demanded a showdown at the 1959 Central Committee meeting of 1959 and with tears in his eyes warned that: "If the army should follow P'eng, I will fight a guerrilla war". Mao's prestige was so great that, despite the initial setbacks of the Leap, his demands were met and P'eng was removed from his post by the Central Committee. Those who followed the ethics of professionalism and stabilized bureaucratic rule had suffered another setback, but the fact that Mao had to intervene directly with such an ominous threat indicates just how serious was this latest challenge to mass line politics (Mao Tse-tung, 1959, *in* Ahn Byung-joon, 1971, p.6; CC-CCP, 12th August, 1959, *in* Chai, 1969, pp.352-8).

P'eng was replaced by Lo Jui ching, who had served as the Minister of Public Order since liberation. Assisting Lo would be Lin Piao, a general hand-picked by Mao for his loyalty to radical Communism. Lin and his deputies almost immediately began a great Socialist Education campaign to re-establish mass line in the organizations and social relations of the army. The study of Mao's social thought was a central part of that campaign and the modern "cult of Mao" was very much formed in this PLA movement. Along with political education, the radicals instituted some structural reforms; the elevated status and higher wages of officers were reduced and the army was fully involved in production work alongside the civilians (Charles, 1961, pp.67-71; Powell, 1968, pp.44-48; Ahn Byung-joon, 1971, pp.13-15).

The overall aim of Lin Piao's campaign was to make the PLA into an ideological and organizational example of Maoist practice, and the campaign did certainly help assure Mao of army support in later conflicts such as the 1966-67 Cultural Revolution. The army reforms will be discussed in more detail in the next chapter, but the whole P'eng-Mao-PLA affair was most important in 1959-60 as an indication of the extent of conservative opposition which began to surface in the wake of the Great Leap economic failures.

Continuing Crises and the New Conservatism

The minor adjustments of 1959 did not prevent more crop failures in 1960-61 after another series of droughts and floods. By 1961-62 the national production schedules had been wrecked, even in the industrial sectors where industry could not even match the output of 1956. The agricultural collapse had crippled the transport system and had caused shortages of the raw materials and foodstuffs needed by the factories and the city workers (Chou Ming Li, 1964, pp.10-11; King,

The neglect of agriculture in favour of industry, the mismanagement of massed labour, and the social dislocations resulting from the lightning formation of the communes, made for a disastrous combination. These basic problems could not be covered by the belated 1959 attempt to mechanize farming. Likewise, the 1959 Anti-Rightist movement did not help economic matters much, though it did at least involve the Party more deeply in commune work and thus make the leadership more aware of the serious rural problems.

After three straight years of failure (1958-61), the Party radicals no longer spoke so confidently about "great national advances". Mao himself admitted to "serious mistakes in planning and organization" and accepted a loss in political prestige and influence. He gave up his position as Chairman of the Republic in 1962 (but remained as Chairman of the Communist Party). Although he had made this decision in 1958 at the height of his power, the actual resignation in 1962 seemed to many observers to mark the decline of Maoist influence in the central decision-making bodies. Certainly political and press references to the Party Chairman dropped off sharply and the new Chairman of the Republic, Liu Shao chi received wider mention in both the national and the international press (Townsend, 1968, pp.28-30).

Liu represented a new kind of conservative bureaucratic communism, and was described by the admiring Soviets as "the organization man". The 1962 re-issue of his book "On How to Be a Good Communist" was a major event accompanied by a national campaign of Liu Shao chi study. His book and his policies as Chairman in 1962-65 showed the deepest concern for economic security and social discipline which seriously challenged the mass line. The failures of the Leap had seriously shaken the Maoist ranks and behind Liu gathered thousands of cadres disillusioned with the mass line and these formed a new sort of conservative elite in China.

This new conservative faction included veterans of the Civil War and many who sat in the highest posts of political leadership. They were convinced that China needed a more centralized government and for this reason many observers have called them the "planners". That seems to be a fair label since it helps distinguish their brand of bureaucratic Communism from the "rightist" conservatism of 1953-57 (Yomiuri Shimbum, 1968, p.47; Dernberger, 1970, pp.103-108; Gray, 1970, pp.127-30).

Mao and the radicals were still a real and present power, and the planners never dared openly attack either the Chairman or the official mass line philosophy. The Party leftists remained in control of foreign policy and it was the radicals who forced the open break with the USSR in 1960-62. Political initiative in domestic matters had, however, clearly passed over to the conservatives. The society was to become more centralized, bureaucratic and disciplined as the spread-eagled and exhausted political economy was prized loose from the too hastily designed social structures of the Great Leap.

The old "rightists" of the constitutional era were rather pleased by the changes in political leadership. They had been sceptical of the Great Leap from the first, but did not have the power to challenge the Maoists. The conservative professionals of university and bureaucratic circles gained new prominence and privilege under the socialism of the planners which emphasized material incentives, central control and social discipline as the means to a quietly efficient economy. Though the "rightists" were politically "covered" as important advisers for the planned economy, however, they were never able to lead the new conservative politics or reassert their One Hundred Flowers positions (Townsend, 1963, p.149; NFJP, 14th November, 1960, *in* Goldman, 1969, pp.54-60; KMJP, 5th January, 1961, *in* SCMP No. 2430, 1961).

The planners wanted to correct the mass line excesses of the Leap, but they did not share the rightist desire for a fully professionalized legal system and a government regulated by tight legal codes. The planners wanted to bring the intellectuals and specialists into economic planning councils, but they still wanted the Party to exercise broad political and social leadership, unhampered by laws and unchallenged by the intellectuals. Some tension continued between old and new conservatives. The rightists, in order to escape the mass line pressure of the radicals, had to accept a very junior partnership under the planners. There was, nonetheless, a considerable recovery of rightist fortunes in 1961-64 as the planners became increasingly powerful in the Central Committee of the Party and especially at the middle levels of government in the provincial capitals and large bureaux.

The first priority in the planners' programme was a reversal of the most radical Great Leap social and economic changes. The central bureaucracy was increased as officials were recalled from the communes and offices were reopened. The planners moved quickly to restrict the independence of the communes, and the farmers were ordered to cut back on the unprofitable rural industries and concentrate on growing the crops.

Many of the rather sudden Leap reorganizations were reversed as commune social functions were reduced and the planners emphasized the smaller "production brigades" which were similar to the old village social arrangements. Not a few women returned to the home fires as commune mess halls and some "service centres" for laundry, household repair, and child care were closed down (JMJP, 23rd January, 1961, *in* SCMP No.2430, 1961; NFJP, 19th November, 1960, *in* SCMP No.2430, 1960). Finally the planners organized a number of rural "trade fairs" which allowed for individuals or groups of farmers and workers to sell excess crops and handicrafts for a profit (Hoffman, 1969, pp.106-8; Dutt and Dutt, 1970, pp.9-10). This, together with the reintroduction of the piecework pay system in factories and the return of large wage differences, amounted to a rejection of the Leap idea that political and community commitment was the strongest stimulus for production (JMJP, 25th November, 1960, *in* SCMP No.2393, 1960; NFJP, 13th November, 1960, *in* SCMP No.2400, 1960; *Hung Ch'i*, 16th September, 1961, *in* SCMM No.282, 1961).

The rightists made their biggest gains in education since the planners agreed with them that "expert" was more important than "redness". They quietly applauded as the planners called it "wasteful" to encourage students or other intellectuals to participate in extensive manual labour or to devote long hours to political study (Li Cho Pao, *Hung Ch'i* No.24, *in* SCMM No.295, 1960; Goldman, 1969, p.36). The Red and Expert schools were curtailed, and "academic standards" and "objective" examinations returned to alienate politically and practically minded lower class students at the universities (KMJP, 24th September, 1960, *in* SCMP No.2405, 1960; Hou Wai-I, *Hung Ch'i*, 1st October, 1960, *in* SCMM No.284, 1960).

The Maoist educational ideas were repudiated in no uncertain terms by leading officials across the country. The Vice-Premier and Foreign Minister, Ch'en Yi, opened a Peking commencement address by praising the "shining example" Mao Tse-tung, but then he spoke in the new language of planner conservatism saying that not everyone can be both "red" and "expert" and emphasized specialized professional training as follows:

> During the early period of liberation, it was necessary for the Party and the government to stress political training in education. Today it is necessry to emphasize specialized training so as to cultivate large numbers of specialists to transform our country into a great socialist state, with a modern industry, a modern agriculture, and a modern scientific culture . . . This is our great political mission . . . It is the political mission of the student to master his specialized studies, and it is the political mission of the schools to educate large numbers of specialists (Ch'en Yi, *in* Hsu, 1964, p.155)

Another Vice-Premier, Nieh Jung-cheng advised students that:

> If you do not unite work with study, but squander away your time on all kinds of activities, you may seem to be giving a good deal of attention to "redness", whereas in fact you are neglecting your primary duty in socialist construction (Nieh Jung-cheng, *in* Hsu, 1964, p.156)

Lesser figures echoed these sentiments in venturing even further from the mass line (Townsend, 1968, p.100). The Party Secretary at Yunnan University discouraged students from working part-time alongside the workers in city factories saying it was important to "preserve the students' health". Instead, he argued for more concentration on laboratory work and on technical education, saying that: "A school is after all a school" (JMJP, 14th April, 1961, *in* SCMP No.218, 1961).

Justice under the planners: bureaucratic control and social discipline

The planners, as mentioned previously, made no attempt to rebuild the courts, Procurates, or other aspects of the professional legal system demolished in 1957-58. They did reduce the pressure on the rightists by removing the "rightist element" classification and thus restoring the old conservatives to the status of citizens in good standing. Liu Shao chi announced that 260 "rightists" had been reformed and reclassified in 1960; later that number was raised to 19,000 as virtually all of those denounced in 1957-58 were now once more considered part of "the people" (NCNA, 24th November, 1960, *in* SCMP No.2387, 1960).

The police had become increasingly important under the Great Leap, and the planners felt no need to curtail the wide discretionary powers granted police under the SAPA act. However, a number of changes were made in hopes of bringing the police under tighter, more centralized Party control. New officials were appointed to all levels of the Public Order Department often chosen directly from the Party ranks, and the careers loyalty of these new police was first to the Party and only second to the Department. In addition, the Party expanded the Staff Office designed to keep the Party informed as to the activities at each of the various police substations. The Party cadres who worked in the staff offices reported directly to the local Party organization, from which they also received their instructions (Li, 1970, pp.52-54).

The planners' concern for centralized political control led them to establish and, in 1962, greatly strengthen the Central Control Commission. In many ways this new bureaucracy continued the work of the defunct Ministry of Control, but the Control Commissions were entirely staffed by Party members and Party appointees. The Central Commission counted on a network of local Party control commissions each of which worked directly with the local Party committee in this area. There was no place for popular involvement as on the old people's supervisory committees which reported to the Ministry of Control (Waller, 1971, pp.106-7). The great importance attached to the Control Commissions was evident when the Party brought in its top legal specialist, Tung Pi Wu, to head the Central Commission. Tung has been the President of the Supreme People's Court but the courts under the planners, as under the Leap, had little power or influence in judicial matters, and the best that Tung could do was to tackle more important work in the Control Commission (Waller, 1971, p.107; Lubman, 1970, pp.50-51).

The public role in justice, as in politics, steadily diminished in the years after the Leap. The police increasingly regarded the Party as their major source of criticism and suggestion. The public, represented by residents' committees, street offices and the rural communes, were largely restricted to a passive role as auxilliaries and information bearers (Salaff, 1967, pp.14-20). People's supervision ended for all practical purposes since government watching was now entirely in the hands of the Party committees and the Party control commissions. The conservative-led Party continued to encourage public participation as assessors in the relatively powerless People's Courts and still favoured mediation, which was emphasized as a technique of "people's self control" (JMJP, 1st January, 1965, in Hsia Tao-Tai, 1967, p.10). The police did announce a national "love the people month" in which they heard public suggestions and "did good deeds", but such public relations work was hardly a substitute for strong popular justice institutions and mass rectification campaigns (JMJP, 6th February, 1961, in SCMP No.2440, 1961; KMJP, 20th February, 1963, in URI, 1963, Vol. I, p.121).

The mass organizations of city and country deteriorated within the narrow area left under the conservative regime. In the face of the Party emphasis on material incentives, the trade unions became even more concerned with wage demands, rather than political participation or social change (SSST, 21st October, 1962, in SCMM No.344, 1962; NFJP, 23rd, 25th, 28th October, 1960, in SCMP No.2401, 1960). Popular participation in the residential committees and street offices dropped off and the students at the university were forced more and more into the restrictive academic culture of competitive examinations and tight specialized subjects. Rural communes lost a great deal of their political and economic independence. The planners specified crop quotas and production schedules, and sent professional accountants and other Party experts to manage and control the economy of the communes (JMJP, 6th November, 1960, in SCMP No.2385, 1960; Hung Ch'i, 12th July, 1st October, 1961, in SCMM No.282, 284, 1961).

The economy responded well to this tighter management and a number of Leap mistakes were erased, but the cost in 1960-64 was dear in terms of popular justice and popular politics. The radicals of Party and government grew increasingly uneasy as the social reforms of the Leap were sacrificed in favour of discipline and production. The government slipped further from the control of the people and the wage gaps and social contradictions so deliberately attacked in the Leap again widened to divide the intellectual from the labourer, the worker from the peasant, the student from the teacher, and the leadership from the led.

Mao and the leftists had counted on a strong popular justice to replace the bureaucratic checks of procurators, courts and the Control Ministry. The conservatives effectively crushed the popular justice check and after 1961-62 the police and other government officials were answerable only to the Party apparatus. The police became increasingly a conservative force, committed to order and social discipline, but little concerned with social change, educational reform and mass line politics. The Party conservatives depended upon the police and the law to secure their powers and privileges in the face of the inequalities produced by their political and economic policies.

Social inequalities and the new class

At the top of the increasingly unequal Chinese society were the new bureaucratic conservatives who controlled government at the lower and middle levels and who were gaining strength at the top. The "planners" had brought back the system of material incentives and had reserved for themselves the fattest salaries and the softest jobs. Their economic and political policies implicitly rejected the "continuous revolution" and the Great Leap faith in the common man, even while they falsely declared their loyalty to the mass line. The elevation of Party officials drove a wedge into social relationships, with China divided into the cadres ("we") and the masses ("they") (Malden, 1965, pp.84–88).

Mao and the Party radicals watched these developments with great concern and their attacks on the Soviet Party's "elitist revisionism" were increasingly relevant to China as well. A book written by the former Vice President of Yugoslavia, Milovan Djilas, also prompted Maoist worries about the decay of mass line politics.

Djilas had described the development of the Party-mass line split in Soviet Communism and, like Mao, he believed in extending Marxist analysis even to societies which claimed to be Marxist states. He noted that the bureaucratic-technological elite ran the Communist Parties in Eastern Europe and observed that this elite enjoyed an elevated standard of living, unquestioned social prestige and unchecked political power. Moreover, this elite controlled industrial and agricultural production and was politically insulated from the people and protected by the military, the police and the legal system, all of which upheld the unequal Soviet status quo. These special powers and privileges are, according to Marxist theory, the definition of a ruling class. Djilas, therefore, had excellent factual and theoretical support for his argument that official talk of the "advance to a classless society" was a myth, and that the Soviet Revolution was frozen dead with society firmly in the grasp of a new exploiting elite. That bureaucratic-technological elite Djilas called "The New Class" (Djilas, 1957, pp.37–59; Johnson, 1969, pp.53–55).

A quick glance back at the domestic politics of China after the Leap revealed that the Party conservatives were indeed building up the privileges and powers necessary to rule as a New Class, free of popular politics and the need to push social reforms. Mao and the radicals did not think China's revolution was lost, but the dangers outlined by Djilas haunted them. The advance of China's New Class behind production successes was a far greater threat to popular revolution than the "rightist" forces of 1956-57 had ever been, and the radicals began to sense an inevitable struggle.

8   Cultural Revolution and the Limits of Populism

The planners and conservative bureaucrats of the rising New Class continued enlarging their influence over domestic policy through the 1960-64 post-Leap recovery. Politics and justice were increasingly controlled by tightly disciplined Party members working in specialized and centralized bureaux. In many areas of political life, the mass line was traded for the bureaucratic leash, as the New Class hoped to make popular politics the docile beast of burden for their conservative policies.

Conservative gains and radical strengths

Industry and agriculture more closely followed the Soviet model with material incentives opening greater wage gaps between workers, peasants and bureaucrats. Economic co-ordination between communes and industries was demanded and enforced by the Party authorities and bureaucratic "experts" were despatched to plan and control the work of the communes. Education once again concentrated more on "academic" subjects with "objective" examinations which favoured the well-prepared children of bureaucrats over those of peasants and workers. Justice agencies, like other bureaucracies, became almost entirely occupied with maintaining public discipline on the job and in the streets and they reduced public involvement in the enlarged and more specialized police force. These and other conservative moves to stabilize the political economy consistently sacrificed social reforms, local independence and popular political initiative powers which were the basic stuff of the Great Leap Forward.

While each of these "adjustments" demonstrated the strength of the New Class conservatives, they also provoked sharp conflicts with radicals resentful of the retreats from the Leap. Soon there was grumbling about a "restoration of capitalism" and there were complaints about the arrogance of conservative cadres who bossed the masses while reserving fat salaries and soft jobs for themselves. Though the radicals were outnumbered in the provincial organizations and in many other middle- and upper-level bureaux, they remained strong in several key areas.

Many of the red and expert schools survived in the countryside, and though conservatism and academic administration had returned to the universities, a large number of worker and peasant children had enrolled there and these students were yet loyal to the educational reforms of the Leap. The lower class students resented the advantages and "pull" of the New Class offspring. The Party leftists were sensitive to the tension between the lower class students and the still lingering elitism of the academic world. The radicals were strong enough to keep the pressure on the old-style academics, and lower class students were encouraged to criticize teachers or classmates who showed signs of arrogance and elitism.

A second major source of strength was the army. Things there had been moving in a leftish direction since the Soviet-inspired Minister of Defence, P'eng The-haui, was fired in 1959. The new Army Chief, Lin Piao, was devoted to the thought and person of Mao, and he worked to put mass line politics "in command" of the army. Enlisted men were recruited into new Party committees and relations between officers and men were improved by more active mutual criticism within army units.

The commune movement of the city and country (especially the countryside) had, for all its economic problems, been successful as an introductory course in popular politics. A vast number of farmers and housewives gained experience and confidence through their work in the political management of the communes. Most of these local activists were unpaid and outside the official bureaucracy, and they resented the arrogant intrusion of many Party experts sent down to manage commune production and supervise commune politics. They resented also the cadres' frequent habit of skimming off surplus commune income and adding public funds to their already generous salaries. These desk-bound accountants and production experts lived in comparative luxury and were known as "empty sleeves" from their habit of draping their work jackets over their shoulders while supervising farmwork from the sidelines. The tension between Party experts and local farmers, as well as the political strength of the local unpaid peasant activists, was a third element in the Maoist comeback strength.

Fourthly, there was the prestige and charisma of Mao himself. So powerful was the popular support for the Chairman that the conservatives, even at the height of their power in 1961-63, never dared openly criticize Mao or the mass line ideology. Indeed they felt it necessary to support nearly all of their major proposals with quotations from Mao. The Chairman's philosophy had evolved considerably over 30 odd years and the conservatives simply avoided his recent works on "continuous revolution" and quoted mostly from Civil War essays when (like the conservatives of 1960-64) Mao was much concerned about expanding Party influence and centralizing political control. This selective re-reading of Mao was bitterly criticized during the Cultural Revolution; but in the 1960-64 period the radicals replied by quoting Mao's most recent work. They moved beyond quotation to make intensive study and thorough discussion of Mao's thoughts a national project involving the entire people. Mao's thought was elevated beyond the authority of laws or even Party directives and so was prepared as a sort of ideological measuring rod for the Party rectification which was to come.

Socialist Education and the Renewal of Popular Politics

The radicals, counting heavily on the strength of the above four elements, made their move in 1962 with the announcement of a new mass campaign: the Socialist Education Movement. The movement, not surprisingly, sprang from Lin Piao's earlier Mao study campaign (within the PLA), and was closely related to the "Learn from the PLA" campaign which urged the nation to model itself after the organization and social practice of the army.

Socialist Education began late in 1962 and was to involve the entire country (especially the rural areas) in a re-examination of both official behaviour and cadre-mass relationships. That Mao and the Party radicals chose to call in the general public rather than try a behind-the-scenes Party shakedown is not surprising, given their long tradition of relying directly on popular action in times of crises. The new movement went through several phases and consisted of both intra-Party struggles and the investigation and criticism of Party or government officials by local mass organizations (especially in the rural communes).

The opening phase: intra-Party reform at the local level

The first rumblings of the campaign were heard in communiques prepared at the Tenth Meeting of the Central Committee in September 1962. The radical attack on Soviet revisionism was at last being applied to Chinese domestic politics, as the Maoists began moving out of the foreign policy niche allotted them in the 1960-61 division of powers. The Central Committee, prodded by the radicals, spoke out strongly against certain weaknesses in the work of Party cadres as follows:

> It should be pointed out that some of our work is not well done. For instance, because of the incompetence of leading cadres, some production teams, some factories and some business establishments have produced less or become unwelcome to the masses (PR No.39, 1962)

A number of Party directives were prepared and these began to circulate down to Party organizations in the provinces and rural communes. Local Party branches called special meetings to read and discuss these directives outlining the aims and methods of the campaign. These "unhealthy tendencies" among both the people and the Party were said to have arisen from the neglect of political education work and the de-emphasis on collective ownership, both of which were conservative adjustments made after the Leap. It was stated that:

> Everyone knows that during the 10 years following liberation . . . a great effort was made in education. There was a similar effort in 1958 [rectification], and there have also been such things as education for co-operativization. These things have been done well, conditions were very good. In recent years, we encountered difficulties [the Leap] and some shortcomings in our work . . . we slackened in our socialist education for cadres and for the masses. Now capitalist and feudalist thinking has again reared its head among some people. If we fail to take a firm grasp of ideological work and pay attention only to production, it will not do (CCP, 1962, *in* Baum and Tiewes, 1968, pp.56-7)

The struggle with Soviet revisionism was applied to China as the radicals warned that a "restoration of capitalism" lurked behind the profit-making devices of private plots and rural trade fairs (Fan, 1968, pp.51-52). The remedy for this revisionist danger was to be more education emphasizing the importance of collective ownership and community response as follows:

> If we do not do well the things that we mentioned [political education] will we become a capitalist country? There are facts with regard to this. Everyone knows that originally Yugoslavia was a socialist country; now capitalism has been restored, land can be bought and sold freely, there are a great number of rich peasants, and more than 90% of the land is worked individually. We have to think about China and we have to think of ways to prevent it from becoming like that (CCP, 1962, *in* Baum and Tiewes, 1968, p.53)

It was also pointed out that local party cadres had contributed to this "restoration of capitalist thought" by their own materialism, extravagant habits and their failures to follow the mass line principles of living like the people and seeking out the people's advice in political leadership. Party officials were criticized for just going through the motions of Socialist Education, without any real attempt to correct their own errors or the materialistic ideas and practices which had developed among the people around them. It was said that:

> Some people carrying on by themselves and engaging in speculation are
> lying low. They are waiting for the movement to be over so that they can
> again take up their practices (CCP, 1962, *in* Baum and Tiewes, 1968,
> pp.56-57)

The radicals were angered by the conservatives' resistance and by their
materialistic tendencies. Socialist Education was expanded to involve a new class
struggle in the countryside, closely tied to the struggle with Soviet revisionism as
follows:

> There is one important thing we should understand. That is whether we
> recognize it or not, classes exist and there is class struggle. To fear the class
> struggle and not to engage in it resolutely, to coexist peacefully, to have a
> peaceful transition to communism and not to fight, these things constitute
> revisionism (CCP, 1962, *in* Baum and Tiewes, 1968, p.55)

Something new was brewing here. Everyone in the Party spoke often about the
importance of class struggle (at least since the 1958 rectification). But when Liu
Shao chi and the conservatives spoke of class struggle they referred to a mop-up
operation against ex-landlords, ex-rich peasants, and ex-capitalists and other
former supporters of the KMT. Socialist Education pointed to a new set of
opponents, including peasants who had become rich peasants through speculation and profits made at the rural trade fairs and the "expert" cadres who
encouraged peasant capitalism while living high on commune money.

The exact status of these new opponents was unclear in 1962-63. They were
not explicitly described as "class enemies", but the methods used to pressure
them would increasingly resemble those used against the old "reactionary
classes". In the early phase of Socialist Education (1962-63) the struggle with
capitalist-revisionist tendencies still sounded much like the pattern of earlier
Party rectifications. The Party directive quoted above advised:

> We must combat capitalism, feudalism and the political degenerates, but
> when we say struggle, we refer to ideological struggle as the most important.
> This means using all forms and methods of fighting. Naturally some people
> will have to be dealt with according to law, while others will have to be
> handled differently.

> The extremely bad elements should be dealt with according to law, but this
> will involve only extreme cases whose number will be very small. The others
> should be handled by ideological struggle, but ideological struggle should
> also be applied to those who have to be dealt with according to the law (CCP,
> 1962, *in* Baum and Tiewes, 1968, pp.56-57)

Throughout the first years of the movement, socialist education remained an
internal Party matter. Investigations were conducted by leading Party officials
often from the county offices, probing the affairs of subordinates and a great

many criticism/self-criticism sessions were held in local Party offices of communes across the nation. The middle-level Party offices also formed "work teams" of cadres selected for their poor peasant class backgrounds and these teams conducted on-the-spot investigations of local officials at the commune level. Along with investigation and political education, all cadres from the county level down were directed to devote at least one-third of their time to physical labour as farmers alongside the commune members. Overall, the results were not particularly earth-shaking. Some local officials were demoted or scolded but few were dismissed or purged from the Party and public involvement was minimal (*Hung Ch'i*, 10th July, 1963, *in* CFIA-EARC, 1971, p.41).

Despite initial claims of success, it was soon apparent that the work teams of "Party justice" were not serious enough about Socialist Education to cause any real change in the affairs of the countryside. This is hardly surprising given the fact that the planners and their conservative philosophy was strongest at the middle levels of government and Party where the work teams were recruited. The half-hearted house-cleaning efforts of the work teams and the middle-level officials was sharply criticized in a second Party directive released late in 1964. The directive noted that:

> During the . . . [Socialist Education] movement, because of fear of 'hurting the cadres' feelings', or of [adversely] affecting the unity of the cadres, or of the cadres quitting work, the work teams in some places assumed a tolerant attitude toward cadres who had committed even serious mistakes. They were afraid to criticize, to engage in struggle and especially to mobilize the masses to solve their problems. They thought by these means they had achieved unity. Yet the result was that they were seriously divorced from the masses and achieved only a superficial, temporary and false consolidation of the masses (CCP-Fukien Province, 1962, *in* Baum and Tiewes, 1968, p.112)

The second phase: popular justice and class struggle

A second period of the movement began in 1964, and this time the radicals were stronger and they called for popular participation in the investigation, accusation, punishment and reform of the high-living Party experts. Socialist Education at this point became a major popular justice action which established many patterns for the coming Cultural Revolution.

The radicals in the Party leadership moved to strengthen the mass organizations of peasants and draw them into active participation in Socialist Education. The peasant organizations were re-built with the Maoist concerns about class struggle and the "restoration of capitalism" in mind. The 1964 "Organizational Rules of the Poor and Lower Middle Peasant Associations" specifically excluded wealthy farmers from the organization and the organization was charged with "supervising and reforming landlords, rich peasants, counter-revolutionaries and bad elements" (CCP-Fukien Province, 1963, *in* Baum and Tiewes, 1968, p.96).

The peasant associations directed political education campaigns and concentrated social pressure against those farmers who sought to turn high profits from the private sale of crops and so raise their fortunes above those of the commune communities. The associations stressed the greater economic and social advantages of collective ownership and actively opposed any "restoration of capitalism in the countryside". There was, however, no move by either the Party leadership or the peasant associations to eliminate the small private plots cultivated by farmers in their spare time, and there was no confiscation of private property. The movement remained one of social pressure and political education, and did not call for a return to the completely collectivized ownership established briefly under the Leap.

The peasant associations were also asked to supervise the work of Party and government officials attached to the local communes and were encouraged to send representatives to the officials' meetings. In order to prevent the association officers from following the elitist and corrupt practices of Party cadres, the "Organizational Rules" specified that local association officers would not receive special work point subsidies (like the cadres did), but would instead be paid only for their labour as common farmers (CCP-Fukien Province, 1963, *in* Baum and Tiewes, 1968, pp.96-7).

The associations assumed a leadership role in criticizing and investigating local officials. Local associations formed financial supervisory groups which snatched commune records out of the cadres' hands and inspected documents for any sign of corruption. The peasants reported numerous cases of "nepotistic favouritism", "bribery', "falsification of records" and misappropriation of funds. Cadres were publicly accused and criticized in commune rallies and several lost their jobs (Bridgham, 1968, pp.65-66; JMJP, 11th December, 1964, *in* Baum and Tiewes, 1968, p.32). Some tried to ward off popular justice probes by arguing that:

> . . . if the masses criticize the cadres, the cadres will not be able to lead them at all. It's all right for higher level cadres (such as the work teams) to criticize cadres, but if the masses do it, things will become chaotic (Radio Tientsin, 19th December, 1964, *in* Baum and Tiewes, 1968, p.33)

Such arguments were dismissed by the top Party leadership and cadres were advised not to try to stop or slow the work of the peasant supervisory committees.

More important than the sanctions of popular justice and the sacrifice of some Party discipline to mass politics was the new definition of class struggle which accompanied this second phase of Socialist Education. Official corruption and the conflict between peasants and cadres were, after 1964, being openly described as an "antagonistic contradiction" which demanded the most serious sort of "class struggle". Those elitist or corrupt officials who elevated themselves above the rural masses were called "anti-socialist" and "anti-Party" enemies (Malden, 1965, p.83; NFJP, 26th December, 1964, *in* Baum and Tiewes, 1968, p.34). Speaking before the National People's Congress in late 1964, Chou en Lai hinted at the escalation in political conflict when he referred to Socialist Education as a movement of "revolutionary and historic significance". Chou is certainly not a Party leftist, but he was sensitive to the radical forces behind the new developments in Socialist Education and he voiced his concern about the restoration of capitalism and the revisionist influence in the Party as follows:

> . . . new bourgeois elements, new bourgeois interests and other exploiters will be ceaselessly generated in Party and government organizations, in economic organizations and in cultural and educational departments.

> From 1959 to 1962 . . . the class enemies at home launched renewed attacks on socialism . . . In the domestic field quite a few people advocated the extension of plots for private use and free markets, and the increase of small [capitalist] enterprises (Chou en Lai, 22nd December, 1964, *in* Malden, 1965, pp.83-85)

An Tzu-wen, another member of the Central Committee, indicated that a serious struggle was in the making when he stated that there was a faction of senior Party leaders no longer suited for leadership. This faction, he observed, included ranking officials

> . . . who have fallen behind the march of time during the new Socialist Education stage of revolution, because of their failure to prepare themselves ideologically and to reform themselves conscientiously for the socialist revolution; [they] should no longer be regarded as good cadres and good successors if they do not strengthen their ideological reform . . . (An Tzu-wen, *Hung Ch'i*, 22nd September, 1964, *in* Malden, 1965, pp.85-86)

The Central Committee made a strong collective statement on the impending struggle at their January 1965 meeting, as follows:

> In our cities and villages alike, there exists serious, acute class struggle. After the socialist reform of the ownership system was basically completed, the class enemies who oppose socialism attempted to use the form of 'peaceful evolution' to restore capitalism. This situation of class struggle is necessarily reflected within the Party. The leadership of certain communes, brigades, enterprises, and [PLA] units has either been corrupted or usurped (CC-CCP, 1964, *in* Baum and Tiewes, 1968, p.119)

The conservative code of specialized professionalism and the privileges and power of the rising New Class came under increasing fire from both the peasant associations and the radical wing of the top Party counsels. Socialist Education had grown from closed criticism meetings at local Party branches to a national mass campaign of popular justice and class struggle. The line between the people and the enemy had been moved, once again demonstrating the political relativity of Maoist justice. Before examining the third and final stage of Social Education, it would be worthwhile to glance at developments in legal theory during these last years before the Cultural Revolution.

Legal theory and the new class struggle

Radical politics showed clearly in a number of 1964-65 legal treatises as Socialist Education lit up political conflicts and social inequalities. Spokesmen in justice agencies and political-legal institutes produced works which attacked the conservatives' "legal revisionism" and called for a return to mass line politics in the judicial system. One such spokesman, Hsiang Shih, wrote in a leading legal journal that:

> The modern revisionists have completely negated Marxist-Leninist concepts of the state and the law, denied that classes and class struggles exist in a socialist society, denied the irreconcilable nature of class struggle, and loudly proclaim the theories of 'reconciliation' and 'harmony' of contradictions . . . they have invented the false notion of the 'state of all the people' and simultaneously cooked up the basic notion of 'the law of all the people'.

> . . . we must firmly and thoroughly criticize the utter falseness of the so-called 'rule of law', which the bourgeois legalists so strongly advocate; and we must firmly criticize statements which, under any pretext whatsoever, place the laws of a socialist system in opposition to and above the dictatorship of the proletariat (Hsiang Shih, CFYC No.3, *in* CLG, Vol. I, No. 3, pp.4-5)

Chen P'u, writing at about the same time, linked the struggle with legal revisionism to the earlier legal conservatism of the rightists and agreed that mass campaigns and class struggle were a continuing necessity, saying:

> The problems of the legal system has always been one of the sharpest and most concentrated aspects of class struggle. It is therefore only natural that in order to realize the restoration of capitalism, bourgeoisie rightists would, in their assault on the Party and on socialism, focus even more firepower on the question of the legal system.

We must recognize, however, that the struggle in thought and ideology cannot be resolved ultimately and thoroughly by one or two movements . . . As long as there are still classes and class struggle in society, it cannot be said that the remnants of the old legal views have been finally irradicated, or that the task of criticizing the old legal views has been accomplished once and for all (Cheng P'u, CFYC, *in* CLG, Vol. I, no.3, pp.74-75)

Another observer focused on the corruption and elitism of the New Class which he explained as follows:

. . . while engaged in activities for the restoration of capitalism, the enemy class is bound to do its best to disseminate ideological poison . . . Consequently, a violent struggle on the political and ideological level becomes inevitable. In this struggle there are bound to be persons among the ranks of the working class and cadres of state organs whose will is not firm and who are fraught with individualism . . . Their lives gradually degenerate . . . When they have been trapped by the bourgeoisie mode of living, they usually engage in such activities as graft, theft, speculation, and profiteering . . . this is an important source for the emergence of new counter-revolutionary elements (Tzu tan Tsao, CFYC, *in* CLG, Vol. I, No.3, pp.88-89)

The radicals in justice demanded that the professional agencies (meaning primarily the police) work as agents of revolutionary social change, rather than stand behind legal codes as the flat-footed guardians of the status quo. Justice should not, they asserted, ignore the still present unequalities and class interests among the people; nor should officials divorce themselves from the people through corruption and the arrogant abuse of authority. The radicals applauded the new mass campaigns for political education and popular justice which they felt were necessary in the face of new and old class conflicts and the conservative isolation of many justice professionals. Throughout 1964-65 the radicals continued to attack the revisionists for their attempt to "stabilize" the revolution with an order-oriented "rule by law". Though these initial criticisms were confined to abstract arguments about the role of justice in China, the implications for conservatives in the police force and other justice departments were darkly threatening.

Socialist Education, final phase: the creation of the "Mao cult"

While radical legal scholars and officials continued their attack on revisionist justice, the Socialist Education Movement entered into a last phase of increased political conflict and nationwide study of Maoist thought. Previously the campaign had mobilized the masses to criticize individual officials for corruption or elitist behaviour. The turn to Mao-study involved a deliberate confrontation with the professional ethics of the New Class as a whole. The radicals pumped mass line politics into the press and other media, declaring that high production levels were not an excuse for "Mandarin-style" behaviour on the part of Party or government cadres.

These general ideological criticisms were backed up by co-ordinated action against New Class conservatives in government. Socialist Education advanced another political notch in 1964-65, moving from the peasant investigations of local basic-level cadres, to criticisms of county and even provincial leaders. Bureaucrats working in county offices were prodded to leave their desks and to take part in manual labour alongside farmers and factory workers; all this in hopes that they would better understand the problems and needs of the citizens. The Maoist dissatisfaction with elitism among middle-level officials became increasingly obvious and it is noteworthy that 57 provincial Party secretaries were not re-elected at the National People's Congress of 1964 (Malden, 1965, p.87).

Along with the attack on bureaucratic privileges and professionalism came a renewed emphasis on the ideology of the mass line. Throughout 1965 cadres and citizens were drawn into study and discussion of Mao's writings, especially his essays on the importance of the mass line in political leadership (Wing Ping-yen, CKCN, No.3, 1964, and CKCN No.2, 1964, in SCMM Nos 414, 409, 1964). The Chairman's personal prestige had long been unmatched in the public mind, but the Mao-study campaign was designed to make Mao's political philosophy an intimate part of the mass culture (T'ang Ao Ching, Hung Ch'i, 1st October, 1965, in SCMM No.406).

There is, to be sure, a fair amount of cult and hero-worship in Mao-study; but the movement was much more than that. The Party conservatives often demonstrated that they were quite willing to enshrine Mao as the national hero, if only the hero would remain inside the shrine. Socialist Education was politically threatening precisely because Mao-study moved beyond ritual glorification into the business of political education (Townsend, 1968, pp.13-15).

The national Mao-study campaign centred on a few of the most explosive ideas in Mao's writings: that socialist political leaders must share the concerns and life style of the commoners, and that the masses are a progressive political force of unmatched revolutionary importance (Ku Ta-chun, Hung Ch'i, No.1, 1964, in CFIA, 1971, p.55). The re-assertion of mass line, mass political action and continuous revolution was pointed directly at the New Class conservatives. The conservatives were, however, still unwilling to confront the Chairman openly and so the mass education movement grew and Maoist thought became the political bread of China. The campaign was crucial to the course of later events since it strengthened the radicals' hand in two important ways. Firstly, it deepened the public's self-confidence in mass politics and encouraged those who complained that government was becoming bureaucratic and elitist. Secondly, the campaign opened a direct channel between Mao and the masses and re-established Mao and Maoist thought as a political power independent of the Party or the Party line.

Socialist Education had begun in the army and, as might be expected, the first revolutionary reforms of the movement appeared in the PLA. Political lectures concentrated on the importance of human factors in warfare, such as courage and unity among soldiers and civilians (CKCN, No.10, 1964, *in* SCMM No.427, 1964). Lin Piao ordered a number of major changes to put socialist education into practice and army personnel moved into villages and towns to work as farmers, factory hands, school teachers and health officers (King, V., 1966, pp.18-21; Dutt and Dutt, 1970, pp.63-64).

The most radical changes occurred within the ranks. New Party committees were established in PLA units and these committees were granted political powers which paralleled the military chain of command. Enlisted men were encouraged to join the Party and frequently they became the leaders of the new committees. Soon officers were challenged on political grounds by their military subordinates. Those professionally minded officers who had been preoccupied with sophisticated weapons and military specialization were sharply criticized for their neglect of political education and their arrogant isolation from both enlisted men and civilian workers (*Hung Ch'i*, 1st August, 1966, *in* CFIA, 1971, p.249).

Army affairs became increasingly influenced by the Party left and in May 1966 Lin Piao appointed Mao's very radical wife, Chiang Ching, to lead political-cultural work at an even more militant pace. Chiang prepared for a long and serious struggle with the New Class professionals who remained among the PLA officers. In one of her first addresses to the PLA she stated that:

> We have been under the direction of a black anti-Party and anti-socialist line which is diametrically opposed to Chairman Mao's thought . . . the struggle between the two roads in the front of literature is bound to be reflected in the armed forces (Chiang Ching, 6th February, 1966, *in* Fan, 1968, p.102)

The army conservatives rolled with the punches and the radicals pushed new reforms which further committed the army to Mao's leadership and the mass line ideology. Salary differences between officers and men were cut back and officers (including generals and field marshals) were required to spend one month a year as privates. In May 1965 all ranks were formally abolished, and though ex-officers continued to give most of the orders, discipline and social relations moved still closer to the mass line ideal. The entire nation was urged to study and emulate the advanced socialist practice of the PLA.

Cultural Revolution: the Seizure of Power

Mao was well pleased by the progress of Socialist Education in the army and in the countryside where local conservative cadres were under the continuing pressure of popular justice criticism. Assured of these important supports he drew up general plans for a Cultural Revolution to begin in 1965. As planned this movement was to consist of more mass line education and a wider Party rectification directed against the Party conservatives. Mao counted especially on the massed energies of soldiers, peasants and students to challenge the leaders of the New Class. The students had not been as deeply involved in Socialist Education as the other two groups, but Mao was sensitive to certain basic tensions within the schools which might contribute to the radical forces.

Student revolts and a divided party leadership

During One Hundred Flowers several hundred students had moved beyond the bounds of acceptable "blooming and contending" to storm local Party head-quarters. A similar set of events occurred during Socialist Education in 1965 when students at Peking University began open demonstrations against the Party-appointed University President and students at Tsinghua University also later denounced a number of teachers and administration officials.

Throughout these local revolts the students restated their unanswered 1957 complaints; namely, that the academic curriculum was archaic and irrelevant to both the needs of the Chinese people and their own future careers, that teachers and Party officials treated students with contempt and rudeness, and that children of Party members, along with members of the Party Youth League, were given special privileges and preference (Hinton, 1972a, pp.44-90). Many of the 1965-66 students were recruited from peasant and worker families during the Great Leap and, as mentioned before, they were tripped up by academic subjects and objective exams which were beyond their preparation in the schools of communes and factory districts. After a period of police repression, threats and counter-threats, the local authorities agreed to a number of limited university reforms, provided that students kept their criticisms and challenges confined to local university politics (Dutt and Dutt, 1970, pp.63-64; CKCN No.4, 1964, *in* SCMM No.411, 1964; PR No.26, 24th June, 1966).

A compromise was also worked out a few months earlier on the larger question of Mao's proposed Cultural Revolution. The divided Central Committee would not endorse the Chairman's idea for a sweeping national rectification and the Party conservatives protected themselves by limiting the Cultural Revolution to academic debates over the good and bad aspects of China's literary and artistic traditions. Shortly afterwards the students began a rather boisterous and destructive national "re-examination" of classic Chinese culture and feudal moral ethics (NCNA, 25th August, 1966, *in* Fan, 1968, p.62; Peking Red Guards, 1966, *in* Fan, 1968, pp.185-88). This kind of intellectual "revolution" was not what Mao had in mind, and he left Peking to consolidate his forces elsewhere.

Neither compromise survived for long. During 1966 the revolt against Party favouritism, academic irrelevance and class discrimination spread across the country and high school and college students began attacking not only "feudal ideas" but local conservatives in charge of schools and universities and even some city officials. These mostly lower class students were forming a new sort of mass organization which did not fit the submissive role allowed by the New Class conservatives; they called themselves the Red Guards. The conservatives had some success in dividing or co-opting their young opponents, but in general they could not offer serious reforms without endangering their own political and economic advantages (URI, 1966, Vol. 45, No.2, p.17; Fan, 1968, pp.115-29).

The pressure from the student rebels continued and the Party conservatives, led by Liu Shao chi, increasingly turned to methods of intimidation and repression. They branded radical student leaders as "anti-Party" or "counter-revolutionary class enemies". The conservatives also organized their own "Red Guard" units, made up mostly of Party offspring and members of the Party Youth League. The rival guard groups criticized, debated, arrested and assaulted one another and there was much violence and a few deaths. The police generally favoured the conservatives, but did not often directly intervene in these struggles. The army was also ordered to stand clear of the campus battles and the Party itself took up the task of control and investigation (Hinton, 1972a, pp.70-90).

The Peking municipal government, controlled by Liu and the conservatives, sent in a series of "Party work teams" whose responsibility it was to hear complaints, investigate crimes and restore order. Though the teams were officially described as "revolutionary organs" it soon became apparent that they were mostly concerned with protecting the status quo and breaking the back of the student dissent. The most radical of the student rebels, despite threats and tremendous political-legal pressure from these teams, refused to confess their mistakes. Instead Red Guard criticisms became more militant and radicals added the work teams to their list of targets.

The "Sixteen Points" and popular justice action against New Class revisionism

Mao returned to Peking in the summer of 1966 to force a showdown in the Party and especially the Central Committee. Last ditch conservative attempts to keep the lid on the schools failed, and Red Guards packed the Eleventh Plenum meeting of the Central Commiteee to demand new educational reforms and wide ranging political powers. The Party organization was overwhelmed by combined student-army pressure and the Committee passed the "Decision on the Great Cultural Revolution" authorizing a nationwide escalation of the movement. The Cultural Revolution had passed beyond the schools and beyond the bounds of earlier rectification movements; it became a national power struggle and truly a revolution in both political and cultural terms.

The Central Committee's decision (better known as the "Sixteen Points" communique) carried all the weight of codified law and throughout the Cultural Revolution it was cited along with Chairman Mao's own directives as the legal basis for popular justice action by Red Guards and conservatives alike. The constitution and most other Party or government legislation was discarded and the revolutionaries worked from a very brief legal "script".

Like the articles selected for Mao-study, the "Sixteen Points" emphasized the political power of the masses, recognized the correctness of Red Guard revolts and called for popular political action in the new class struggle with New Class revisionism in Party and government. The continuous revolution ideas of the Leap were re-asserted as was the need to distinguish between antagonistic and non-antagonistic contradictions which might confront the revolutionary forces.

The "Sixteen Points" also moved beyond restatement of Maoist themes to set specific outlines for popular justice action in this greatest of China's mass campaigns. The Red Guards were ordered to

> . . . struggle against and overthrow those persons in authority who are taking the capitalist road, to criticize and to repudiate the reactionary bourgeois academic 'authorities', and the ideology of the bourgeoisie and all other exploiting classes (CC-CCP *Hung Ch'i* No.10, 1966, *in* Fan, 1968, p.163)

Party members were to be investigated and closely scrutinized to determine whether they had "taken the capitalist road" seeking special privileges in violation of the mass line. The revolutionaries were urged to continue their demonstrations against such anti-socialist authorities, by means of wall posters, great debates and street actions. Cadres were to be classified as good, comparatively good, seriously mistaken but not anti-socialist and the "small number of anti-socialist, anti-Party rightists". The categories were defined in relative political terms in a manner much like the classification of the Chinese capitalists during the 1951 Five Antis campaign.

The Central Committee bowed to leftist pressure in passing several educational reform measures and in recognizing the renewed class struggle and the legitimacy of the Red Guard organizations. School terms were to be shortened and education was to be more closely tied to production and the needs of the masses. New elections were called to form the Cultural Revolution Committees then being organized in schools and Party organizations.

At the same time the Central Committee also laid out some general limitations on revolutionary activity, though urging the leftists to "put daring above everything else, boldly arouse the masses". Criticisms were to be concentrated on broad ideological positions (as in the Socialist Education campaign), and Party individuals were to be criticized by name only after the approval of the local Party committee. Scientists and technicians were to be entirely exempted from censure and militant revolutionary activities. Both the Central Committee and Chou en Lai ordered the students not to enter the factories or communes where the more manageable Socialist Education movement was to continue without interference (JMJP, 7th, 15th September, 1966, *in* SCMP No.3785, 1966). Violence was condemned as an unacceptable tactic, and even "active counter-revolutionaries" guilty of such crimes as "murder, arson, poisoning and sabotage" were to be "handled in accordance with the law" (CC-CCP, *Hung Ch'i* No.10, 1966, *in* Fan, 1968, p.168). The police and courts which determined the "law" were still, at this time, firmly in the hands of the conservative Party authorities.

Overall, the "Sixteen Points" reflected the divisions and political indecisiveness of the Central Committee in 1966. While some important reforms were implemented and some legitimacy was granted to student radicals, the limitations imposed by the Central Committee would have cooled much of the unrest and could have confined the Cultural Revolution to a few heated Party rectification actions. The key point in the "Sixteen Points", as it turned out, was the authorizations of the Cultural Revolution Committees which began to seize power and initiative from the weakened and divided Party organizations.

The Cultural Revolution Committees were elected by the student groups and various other mass organizations; the educational and political work of the committees was led and co-ordinated by the national Cultural Revolution Group. That Group virtually replaced the authority of the Central Committee and it was dominated by Party radicals like Chiang Ching and Lin Piao. Red Guards continued to pour into Peking; millions of them attending eight great rallies and cheered as Mao Tse-tung put a Red Guard insignia on his own arm. Directed by the radical Cultural Revolution Group, legally empowered by the "Sixteen Points", and backed by the army and the supreme political-legal authority of the Chairman, the Red Guards were, by August 1966, an awesome new power.

The attack on revisionists in the central government

The Mayor of Peking and a number of University presidents were removed from office for their attempts to repress the student revolt in its earlier phases, and in the late summer and autumn of 1966, Mao led the Red Guards in an attack on Liu Shao chi and his conservative followers in the Central Committee. The Minister of Defence and former national police chief, Lo Jui ching, was also tumbled from office by Mao and the army radicals after a series of demonstrations and sharp criticisms in the press. The charges made against all of these top conservative leaders in the central government were much the same. They were accused of revisionism, careerism and elitist professionalism.

Liu's fall was probably inevitable once the Central Committee had endorsed the Revolution in August. Press articles began to urge a concerted struggle against "the number one Party person in authority taking the capitalist road". It was soon public knowledge that that "person" was none other than the Chairman of the Republic, Liu Shao chi. In the autumn his name was openly used and he was attacked in the press, in Red Guard wall posters and in Peking street demonstrations. Despite the pressure against him, Liu refused to accept the radical criticism and would not appear for a public self-criticism.

The Red Guard accusations became increasingly bitter and the established press joined in denouncing Liu's entire political career. His recently republished book "On How to Be A Good Communist" was described as revisionist "poison" that encouraged passive obedience and stifled the people's revolutionary will. Liu's frequent statements about the masses becoming the Party's "docile tool" were thrown back in his face, and he was compared to Confucius for his view that Party members should be morally and politically elevated above the general public (NCNA, 7th April, 1967, *in* SCMP No.3916; JMJP, 6th April, 1967, *in* SCMP No.3920).

The long history of conflicts between Liu and the Party leftists was dramatically recited and Liu was attacked for his consistent violations of the mass line and his exclusive concern with expertise and professionalism (KMJP, 4th, 7th April, 1967, *in* SCMP Nos 3920, 3923, 1967). In the area of political–legal work Liu was criticized for his insistence that the era of class struggle was past and his strong support of the rightists during the 1954–57 attempt to stabilize the society behind a "comprehensive legal system" (NCNA, 4th April, 1967, *in* SCMP No.3916; *Hung Ch'i*, 8th May, 1967, *in* Fan, 1968, p.284). He was said to oppose mass campaigns for popular justice and was criticized for his post-Leap emphasis on the professional supervision of the Procurate and his aversion to people's supervisory work (CKS-JP, 15th March, 1967, *in* URI, 1968b, Vol. 47, pp.46-48; HPT, 10th February, 1967, *in* SCMP No.3916).

Finally Liu was denounced for his post-Leap economic policies which emphasized material incentives and social stability at the expense of social reforms and the development of a unified public community (JMJP, 9th February, 1967, *in* CNA No.654, 1967). The Red Guards were especially angered by the privileges Liu provided for the New Class bureaucrats, such as high salaries, and government subsidies for their children's schools. After making three humiliating self-criticisms before the Peking citizens, Liu was sent off to a Labour Reform Brigade (CKS-JP, 18th April, 1967, *in* JPRS No.41884, 1967, pp.1-3; NCNA, 27th July, 1968, *in* SCMP No.4230, 1968).

Lo Jui ching was attacked for his performance as National Police Chief and his work as Defence Minister. Under his administration the public role in justice through such organizations as the People's supervisory committees had been much curtailed and the police became almost solely influenced by the central Party apparatus and the Public Order bureaucracy. Police and army profession-alism was stressed, which meant the inevitable sacrifice of political education work and close army-community and police-community relations. Lo was sharply criticized for all of these revisionist developments and was accused of turning the police into an "independent kingdom" removed from the people and obedient only to bureaucratic authority (Lubman, 1970, pp.11-12; NCNA, 12th August, 1968, *in* SCMP No.4241, 1968). Red Guards were also especially bitter about Lo's role in the earlier police repression of the student revolts. After weeks of press criticisms and increased mass line propaganda work in the army, Lo was removed (Dutt and Dutt, 1970, p.32). The Red Guards' "supervisory group" at Peking College of Aviation arrested Lo and shortly afterward he was reported to have committed suicide (HPT, *in* Fan, 1968, pp.135-6, 153).

Peking and the central government were almost entirely under radical control by November 1966 and Mao ordered increasing numbers of Red Guard to attack centres of conservative power in other cities and in the provinces. The main strength of the New Class had always been in the provinces and Red Guard moves there were stoutly contested.

Class struggle in the provinces:
Red Guards, royalists and vigilante justice

The threatened Party authorities countered the attacks of the Red Guard by organizing their own Mao-quoting "revolutionary" units. These organizations were called "royalist guards" by their student enemies because of their loyalty to local Party chieftains. The royalist units included petty bureaucrats anxious to protect their jobs, and off-duty policemen determined to maintain law and order but prevented from officially moving against the Red Guard by Mao's orders. In addition, there were those citizens who had benefited from the material incentive policies of the Party conservatives and who wished to stay near the top of the developing class system. Those peasants who had most profited from the small-scale capitalism of the rural trade fairs were worried that the Red Guard might call for a redistribution of land and a return to the Great Leap emphasis on collective wealth.

The trade unions also furnished recruits for the royalist forces. Liu Shao chi was a former union organizer and his strongest mass support was in the unions. The conservative Party faction had generally favoured the skilled industrial workers, and they were content to watch the urban-rural gap widen in favour of the city workers. Among the primary accusations levelled at Liu was the charge that he had "furiously opposed the Party's leadership in the trade unions in a vain attempt to turn the working class into his anti-Party tools". The conservatives pushed the graduated wage scale and other material incentives, and Liu was bitterly attacked by the radicals for his policies of giving "priority to money, welfare, production, expertise and technique" over mass action for social reform and collective economic progress (Harper, 1969, pp.114-6).

Liu's success in winning at least the top union leadership may be deduced from the fact that during the course of the Cultural Revolution most of the officers in the All-China Federation of Trade Unions were dismissed and the national union newspaper was suspended. The national union leadership was heavily committed to material incentives, and wage demands, rather than mass politics, was the first concern of the union organizations in 1962-66. The union leadership and many of the more highly paid wórkers were loathe to accept a new revolution which might reduce their advantages. As a favoured economic group they were directly threatened by any "renewal of class struggle" or any re-emphasis of Great Leap collectivism (JMJP, 12th February, 1967; NFJP, 7th February, 1967, in CNA No.37, 38; Baum, 1970; URI, 1968, Vol. 46, p.220).

In contrast to the prospering classes which opposed the Cultural Revolution, were the far larger rural and urban masses who had not fared so well under the planners' incentives programme. The poorer peasants and the unskilled or semi-skilled workers were at the bottom of the steep wage scales, and there was for them little chance of improvement in an individualist urban-centred economy. These people had very little to lose in a return to collectivism, provided of course that another Leap could be better managed than before. They were potential recruits for the new Revolution and were, as shown in the Socialist Education movement, a powerful force for mass action and popular justice if ordered into action by Mao and allied with the Red Guards (Baum, 1970; Central Radio, 30th January, 1967, in Fan, 1968, p.242).

The Red Guards were given very little chance to exhort these people in 1966. The local authorities often tried to turn back student radicals arriving at the train station. Failing there, the conservatives attempted to sidetrack the radicals with special "celebration" feasts and plush accommodations, but such efforts at co-optation often served to heighten the Red Guards' suspicions. Later the local powers turned to less subtle forms of political defence. The conservatives solemnly pronounced the radicals "counter-revolutionaries" and extended this political-legal judgement to any peasants or workers who had joined them, thus preparing the way for the violent suppression of the radical "elements" in accordance with the law (Hung Ch'i, 30th March, 1967, in Fan, 1968, p.247; Dinucci, 1967, in JPRS No.42525, 1976).

The royalist organizations were usually given the main task of suppression and they were often aided by the passive or active support of the regular police. However, official orders to "support the left" cramped the police somewhat, and so much of their suppression work was done out of uniform. Suppression was, nevertheless, quite effective. Those whose jobs and material advantages were threatened were only too eager to crack heads, arrest, surround, evict or even kill the youths who invaded their pitch calling for social reform and class struggle.

Party conservatives also sent armed peasant militia units into the cities to help local authorities there in the struggle against the Revolution. Interestingly, at no time did the royalists openly declare their opposition to the Revolution and they still claimed to act in Mao's name. The students were still under orders to act alone and at any rate were so hard pressed as to make recruiting work extremely difficult. The royalists were older, better armed, better organized and more numerous than the high school and college radicals who faced them, and not surprisingly the students took a terrible beating (URI, 1968, Vol. 47, pp.182-5).

Mao reacted to the unexpectedly tough conservative resistance by expanding the Revolution and raising new allies for the Red Guards. New "Revolutionary Rebel" organizations of poorer workers and peasants were formed, and the Red Guards were at last authorized to spread the struggle far and wide. The radical Party leadership in Peking also denounced the conservatives at the top of the national unions and in the provincial Party organizations. The combined pressure of the Revolutionary Rebel workers and the hostility of Peking broke the strength of the All-China Federation of Trade Unions which split into many local organizations, fighting one another over the revolutionary question of material incentives versus social reform and collectivism (Dinucci, 1968, NU, *in* JPRS No.42525, 1968).

The conservative powers braced themselves for a second round of struggle in the winter of 1966-67. This time the radicals were powerful enough to attack not merely individual Party revisionists but also moved against the very structure of the Party and the government. High on the list of new targets were the professional justice agencies which had been directly or indirectly involved in the well-remembered repression of 1966. The police stations and courtrooms were besieged, denounced and, in many cases, overrun.

Popular justice versus the professionals: Red Guards, Rebels and the Police

The conservatives, with everything at stake, strengthened their royalist forces. The professional justice officials remained sympathetic toward the conservatives, and judges, procurators and police continued to enforce law and order at the rebels' expense. One such case of renewed police repression was described as follows:

The day before yesterday (28th January, 1967) the Shichingshan police bureau did something it should not have done. This deed was against the instructions of our great leader Chairman Mao. It despatched its policemen, not to support the leftists, but actually to help the rightists, whatever the circumstances. This was welcomed by the royalists. The leading officials of the bureau were first responsible, and then the policemen. In the future the policemen must support the leftists (Hsieh Fu-chih, 1st February, 1967, *in* JPRS No.1967, Vol. II)

This sort of police action infuriated the radical leadership, and prompted Chiang Ching to denounce a number of Procurate officials and the national police administration. In a winter speech before the Peking Red Guards she attacked the whole processional justice system as follows:

The Public Order units, the Investigation Department [a special political police section] and the Supreme People's Court were all introduced from bourgeois countries. They were all above the Party and the government and the Investigation Department investigates over our heads and censors our material. These are all bureaucratic organs which have opposed the thought of Mao Tse-tung for several years.

I suggest that the Public Order units be taken over [by the revolutionaries] except for the fire department (Chiang Ching, July, 1968, CLG, 1970, p.5)

The Red Guards moved against professional justice in cities across the country. Judges and procurators were criticized for their failure to support mass movements such as the Cultural Revolution, and for their conservative and bureaucratic views of justice as a matter of legal process. Red Guards disarmed the "inspection teams" who had acted as conservative political gendarmes, and the PLA disarmed the political police section of the Public Order Bureau (HWPP No.15, 22nd December, 1966, *in* JPRS No.40234, 1967; Kashin, 1968, p.15).

Most of the Peking municipal judges were removed from office, as were many magistrates elsewhere (CFIA, 1971, pp.116-17). The Peking judges were brought before a hostile public rally and, after mass accusations and criticisms, the Chief Justice of the High People's Court and most of his fellow judges were paraded through the streets wearing dunce's caps. Citizens cursed them and spat at judges who had offended or mistreated them in the past. The humiliations of these popular justice street sanctions were evidently too much for the Chief Justice and after returning home he shot himself (Tai Sung an, 1972, p.27).

The Courts were stormed and occupied by Red Guards, and Peking Law students for a time replaced the discharged professionals. One Red Guard newspaper described the seizure as follows:

In the pitched battle of the entire country's proletariat to seize power from the representatives of the bourgeoisie, we the People's University Political Science and Law Rebel Corps of the Political Science and Law Commune, have taken over all powers of the Peking Municipal High People's Court and the Peking Municipal Middle People's Court.

. . . for a long time the Peking Municipal High and Middle People's Courts have been under the control of the black accomplices [of Liu Shao chi], P'eng [Mayor of Peking], Lo [Minister of Public Order] . . . and their Party adherents . . . They have stubbornly opposed the proletarian revolutionary line of Chairman Mao and have carried out a completely revisionist line.

They suppressed the masses [especially the Red Guards] and concealed the present capitalist power holders in the Party (Rev.Law Commune, 1967, JPRS, 1967b, Vol. II, pp.1-2)

Mao was also angry at the police and he again ordered the Bureau of Public Order to support the revolutionaries. Moreover, the entire Bureau was to be reorganized under a new Minister. Hsieh Fu-chih, who was brought in from the PLA to replace Lo Jui ching (Lubman, 1970, pp.10-12). The new Minister was certainly no radical, but he started off by apologizing for the mistakes committed by policemen and promised to "support the left" in the future. He declared his sympathy with the Revolution and agreed that it was essential to

. . . completely revolutionize the Public Order, Procurate, and Judiciary Departments so that the revisionist influence of P'eng [Chen] and Lo [Jui-ching] may be rooted out completely (Hsieh Fu-chih, 1st February, 1967, *in* JPRS, 1967b, Vol. II)

Despite Hsieh's assurances, the power seizures and attacks on professional justice continued. Many of the radicals were still unsatisfied with the police reforms and reorganizations, as were those who explained the occupation of the Peking police station in the following statement:

This Bureau, formerly under the rule of the black gang, did many bad things and that black line has not been totally swept away after the [police] reorganization. Under this situation the Political Science and Law Commune rebelled against the Bureau. The takeover was very fine indeed. We should applaud it.

In the future several rebel organizations will take over the bureau as a group and study its problems. A joint organization of the Peking People's Commune is contemplated. Comrades of the Public Order Bureau should take a rest (Rev.Law Commune, 1967, JPRS, 1967b, Vol. II, pp.1-3)

Throughout December and January of 1966-67, radical students and workers surrounded local government offices to demand the resignation of official "power holders". Shanghai was the most thoroughly revolutionized city and there a new Revolutionary Committee gained complete control of government bureaux and the unions after a bitter struggle. The radicals organized a "Triple Union" to challenge the conservatives and won widespread worker support for the Revolutionary Rebel organizations (WHP, 5th, 6th, 7th February, 1967, *in* CNA No.649, 1967; WHP, 1st, 8th February, 1967, *in* URI, 1967, Vol. 47, pp.211-12). The leftists criticized the steep wage scales and emphasized greater mass involvement in collective political and economic efforts that especially benefited the great masses of less-skilled workers (NCNA, 19th January, 1967, *in* URI, 1967b, Vol. 46, p.209; JMJP, 20th September, 1967, *in* CNA No.191, 1967; JFJP, 9th January, 1967, *in* Fan, 1968, p.77). In Shanghai tables were turned and the reorganized "Red revolutionary" police, procurators and judges worked alongside radical students and workers to crush the remaining royalists (WHP, 6th, 7th February, 1967, *in* CNA No.653, 1967; WHP, 7th February, 1967, *in* URI, 1967b, Vol. 47).

In Canton a Cultural Revolution Group was formed to direct the work of the municipal police department and over 200 policemen were subjected to intense mass criticism, forced to wear dunce's hats and paraded through the streets (Dinucci, 1967, NU, *in* CSocAnth, Vol. II, No.3, 1972; IEWCP, 9th June, 1967, *in* JPRS No.42558, 1967). Many police officials at the provincial or national levels were purged during this period, especially those closely associated with former police chief, Lo Jui ching and his ideas of specialized police professionalism (Rev. Law Commune, 9th January, 1967, *in* JPRS, 1967b, Vol. I).

The revolutionary success in Shanghai and Peking was not the general rule. The Red Guards, even with their peasant and worker allies, had tremendous problems elsewhere. The provincial authorities had organized more royal guards and deep splits within the radical ranks began to sap much of the left's strength.

The conservatives continued trying to isolate the Red Guards by forbidding local peasants and workers to talk to them. The local officials also distributed public funds and emergency food reserves in the hope of buying off those who were beginning to listen to the Red Guards. New work teams established by the provincial authorities claimed special political-legal authority, and through them the conservatives again sought to condemn the radicals as counter-revolutionaries and so prepare the way for suppression. The royalist forces acted as the main conservative weapon in attacking and debating the leftists (Baum, 1970, pp.9-10; PR, 12th March, 1968; Vogel, 1967a; Dutt and Dutt, 1970, pp.140-45).

The police had been utterly demoralized by purges of the Bureau's leadership and by the attacks of rebels in the cities. Consequently, they tried to avoid further official involvement in power struggles after the winter of 1967. Policemen watched with folded arms as their stations and jails were used by the various conservative and radical forces (TFH, 11th July, 1967, *in* CSocAnth

Vol. II, No.3, pp.211-14). Red Guards seized weapons from police arsenals and established their own (rather controversial) provost corps to arrest and control their enemies. The royalists also invaded the stations and used police jails to hold captured radicals. Neither side was even slightly concerned with the "civil rights" of their enemies. Those who were jailed were rarely charged with specific offences, much less formally tried or sentenced (Salaff, 1975; WHP, 25th July, 1968, *in* SCMP No.4245, 1968; Strong, 1968, *in* CFIA, 1971, p.444).

The justice created by royalists and conservatives during the 1967 power struggles was expressly designed as a political weapon. The Chinese tradition of political relativity in law was pushed to the limit as Red Guards and royalists arrested, jailed and even executed one another without warrants, trials, or formal charges. Legal process was virtually non-existent (THPP, 17th February, 1967, *in* JPRS No.42313, 1967; CCK, *in* JPRS, 1968, Vol. II). The educational reform process of Great Leap justice was also discarded. The only concern of this vigilante version of popular justice was the control and punishment of political enemies (JMJP, 1st June, 1966, *in* JPRS, 1968, Vol. II; HWPP, 11th May, 1967, *in* JPRS No.41889).

The police were thoroughly intimidated and politically paralysed as an official judicial body, but they would often continue to support the conservatives when out of uniform. Professional justice was, for the moment, a ghost power. Throughout the next two years justice was straight politics and politics was violent struggle.

Factional Conflicts, Royalist Resistance and Intervention by the Army

In most areas where the leftists were successful, internal factionalism destroyed any chance of political stability. Political stability was especially difficult because there was no clear line of authority between Peking and the rebels. Mao and members of the Cultural Revolution Group were of course recognized as the supreme political leaders, but their general pronouncements and national policies could not guide local revolutionary governments.

Violent battles broke out between armed Red Guards even before the struggle with Party conservatives was complete. There were many midnight raids, arrests and kidnappings as rival guards fought for power. Revolutionary governments were no sooner proclaimed than challenged by another set of Red Guards claiming to be "more genuinely" committed to Mao's thought (CCK, *in* JPRS, 1967b, Vol. II). Rebel governments followed one another at a maddening rate in most places, except for Shanghai and Peking (CPY, 1st February, 1967, *in* JPRS, 1967b, Vol. II; HWPP, 11th May, 1967, *in* JPRS No.41889, 1967; THPP, 17th February, 1967, *in* JPRS No.41313, 1967).

Mao and the leading Party radicals were deeply troubled both by the unexpectedly fierce resistance of the conservative forces in the provinces, and by the vicious in-fighting among Red Guard units. Despite numerous conferences with the Red Guards, Chiang Ching and the radical leadership were still unable to stop this factionalism which bordered on anarchy. The conservative resistance did not let up and indeed the attacks on Red Guards grew bolder and more violent at a number of points. Armed militia units joined the royalist guards in a continuing effort to block the Revolution in the countryside (JMJP, 20th February, 1967, *in* Baum, 1970).

The factional struggles and the resistance of conservatives plunged the country into almost complete chaos. Industrial production slowed in the cities and agriculture was threatened by the neglect of crops and the diversion of so many hands into rural "power seizures". Memories of the 1959-61 crop failures were very fresh and it was imperative that a reasonable degree of order be restored, even if it meant the postponement or sacrifice of some revolutionary goals. There was only one organization capable of quickly restoring order and production: the PLA. The top radical leadership reluctantly decided to play their last card and send in the army.

Three-in-one alliances and compromise politics

The PLA was given two rather contradictory jobs: restore order by making peace among the warring Red Guard units and "support the left" in its continuing attack on Party conservatives. The soldiers were under no circumstances allowed to fire on the Red Guards or suppress them in any way. Despite the army's general loyalty to Mao and Lin Piao, they, like the police, were inclined to concentrate on the most easily understood of these tasks: maintaining order. New "Military Control" headquarters took over the tasks of local government, but violent "attacks on power holders" and "class struggles" were kept to a minimum (Topping, 1971).

The rebels and soldiers were directed to form new "three-in-one alliances" including the army, local mass organizations (such as Red Guards or Revolutionary Rebels) and "revolutionary Party cadres". This new political structure would, therefore, make a place for "power holders", provided they were "loyal" to Mao and the Cultural Revolution. The Army, as the largest and most cohesive force in the country, was usually able to decide who and what was "loyal", except where individual "power holders" had acted so openly against the rebels as to make their inclusion unthinkable (Khan, 1972, pp.54-58; CC-CCP, 1967a, *in* Fan, 1968, p.86).

Needless to say, the decision to slow down the revolution and cool the attack on the conservatives provoked resentment and sharpened divisions within the radical ranks. Differences between the moderates, led by Chou en Lai, and the more radical members of the Cultural Revolution Group, headed by Chiang Ching, were marked by split votes and disagreement manageable only by Mao himself. Chou en Lai remarked that "seizure and control of everything . . . as had been done in Shanghai . . . was not good" (Chou, *in* Bridgham, 1968, p.108) and he vowed to oppose moves which might "wreck the social order and the process of production and thereby make us a laughing stock". Chou had called for an end to mass struggles and power seizures and reinstatement of the People's supervisory system, which had rusted away under the power of Liu Shao chi.

Chiang Ching and the radical leftists took exception to Chou's remarks and his pessimistic analysis of the Cultural Revolution's progress. The extreme leftist "May 16" Red Guards posted criticisms of Chou en Lai throughout Peking. It was, however, a time for caution and even Mao and the radicals made some more limited criticisms of Red Guard mistakes (Ch'i Pen Yu, 1967, *in* JPRS, 1967b, Vol. II; CCAS, 1971, p.95).

The rest of 1967 and 1968 was marked by periodic shifts of policy as the political pendulum swung back and forth while travelling in a more moderate direction. The reorganization of government included many of the once-condemned old Party hands and the emphasis was on reform rather than removal of such officials. The tension between rebels and local authorities continued and new tensions developed between the radical youths and the troops assigned to support their struggle while still maintaining order. The army assignment became increasingly difficult as factionalism among the Red Guards and combat between rebels and conservatives dragged on (Nelson, 1972, pp.451-52).

Order was easier to proclaim than establish and the press reported continuing pitched battles across the country. The Party leadership in Peking demanded an end to such violent struggles, stating:

> At present, an evil wind of struggle by violence, in the form of beating, smashing, looting, ransacking and arresting is prevalent in some districts. This is a serious breach of Chairman Mao's teachings . . . great debates and big character posters are the correct method of struggle (Jun Li hsin, JMJP, 12th July, *in* CNA No.181, 1967).

The continued violence called for more direct leadership and action from the central leadership. Peking despatched senior Party leaders to the provinces to mediate between radicals and conservatives and between feuding Red Guard factions. These negotiating teams were personally authorized by Mao to restore order and ensure that the leftists were not suppressed. The negotiators were empowered to call in array support, if necessary, to back up their recommendations and cease-fire arrangements.

Wuhan and the radical reaction:
internal struggle spreads to the army

In July 1967 the central leadership sent such a peace-making delegation to the industrial city of Wuhan, where strife between Red Guards-Rebels and conservative workers had seriously upset production and local order. The Wuhan authorities, under the very nose of the PLA, had been packing radicals off to labour reform camps, and had raised two very strong royalist organizations: the One Million Warriors and the Kung chien fa.

The Wuhan royalists were true to the conservative pattern elsewhere. The One Million Warriors contained highly paid skilled workers, government bureaucrats, employers and factory management personnel, while the Kung chien fa was made up mostly of off-duty judges, Procurate staff and policemen. In addition to those in the Kung chien fa, hundreds of other policemen were grouped in the "8201 Division" and placed under the command of a conservative PLA commander. This police division was the core of the conservatives' resistance at Wuhan (Robinson, 1971, pp.410-12). The favoured classes and the professional justice staff were, as usual, standing together in defence of wealth, privilege and law and order.

The seriousness of the situation was underscored by the fact that Hsieh Fu-chih, Minister of Public Order, led the Peking negotiating team sent to Wuhan. Hsieh's commission surveyed the situation and, not surprisingly, ordered the army to support the radicals, disband the armed royalist organizations and make public self-criticisms for their own errors in suppressing leftists.

The local PLA commanders were enraged by the delegation's recommendations, and they ordered the Peking delegation to be arrested and confined by their troops. This move directly challenged the central Party leadership but cohesion and unity in the PLA was essential, so Peking moved cautiously to dissolve army resistance in Wuhan. Lin Piao made threatening speeches against those commanders who might back the conservatives against the leftists and Chou en Lai was sent to release and bring back the captured delegation. Paratroops and naval forces were moved into the area to face the army dissidents, but they did not open fire or move into the city (S.S., 1967, pp.31-32; Robinson, 1971, pp.408-12).

The conservatives in the city were emboldened by local army backing, and began a bloody attack on outnumbered Red Guards besieged in schools and factories. About a dozen students were stoned to death in one such attack and others were injured. The royalists and the local army units refused to surrender to Chou en Lai when he arrived, and later, when paratroops from Peking arrived, the 8201 division and the other royalists barricaded the streets and prepared to fight. After several days of confrontation the loyal troops entered the city and disarmed most of the conservatives peacefully. However, the fighting continued in isolated pockets for several weeks as royalists staged factory strikes and fired on Peking troops and Red Guards (Robinson, 1971, pp.416-17).

Though the immediate reaction to Wuhan was another crackdown on "rightists" in army and government, in the long run it could not but strengthen the hand of "moderates" like Chou en Lai. The unity of the PLA was essential to the Maoist strategy, given the virtual destruction of the Party and the factionalism of the Red Guards. The PLA was the only strong national organization which could maintain order and ensure rule from the centre (Peking). Mao could not allow the PLA to be split apart by the action of the Red Guards and the tensions of the army's dual job—peacemakers and "supporters of the left". Once the dust from Wuhan had settled and the PLA had been purged of a few of the most blatantly conservative leaders, the leadership in Peking moved to slow down the Revolution and reduce the pressure on the army (Bridgham, 1968, p.18; Nelson, 1972, pp.455-57; STJP, 18th October, 1967, in CNA No.212, 1967).

Chiang Ching and the Cultural Revolution Group informed their radical followers that the Revolutionary Committees were to be left alone and the attacks on PLA units were to be stopped. She denounced "anarchy" and "ultra-leftist" Red Guard organizations. Violent struggle was condemned and Red Guards were ordered to disarm and "return to their original units [at the schools and universities] immediately". Those who persisted in revolutionary activity were criticized, arrested and, in a few cases, sent to labour reform. Mao announced that the mass organizations (including the Red Guards) would have to undergo rectification and political education, alongside army units and Party members (CC-CCP, 1967a, in Fan, 1968, pp.216-17; Khan, 1972, pp.545-46).

The emphasis was increasingly on "great unity" and reconciliation among former enemies. The PLA was assigned the central task of "guiding the revolutionary masses" and keeping the peace through this period of reorganization and consolidation. More Party members denounced by the radicals were to be given a second chance and a place in the "three way alliance" between the Party, mass organizations and the PLA. The moderates, led by Chou en Lai, were especially active in these compromise efforts. The years after 1967 were dominated by the moderates, and the radicals, such as Chiang Ching, were less prominent both in Peking and in the new Revolutionary Committees organized in the provinces (JFJP/JMJP, 30th March, 1968, in Chai, 1969, pp.441-46; CC-CCP, 1967a, in Fan, 1968, pp.216-17).

Tensions among both leaders and citizens were not fully relaxed, however, and in April 1968 when Mao was inactive (probably ill), Chiang Ching called out the Red Guards for a last round of struggle, this time against the compromise politics of Chou en Lai and the three-in-one Revolutionary Committees. The Red Guards challenged the "revolutionary standing" of many Party cadres appointed to the ruling committees, and Chiang Ching indicated her dissatisfaction with the course of Chou's policies.

Radical resurgence in 1968: Canton

The events which followed in Canton seem a fair example of this last leftist upsurge, since that city was neither as radical as Shanghai, nor as quietly conservative as the countryside. There radicals again attacked the forces of order and social control, including both the remaining Public Order patrolmen and also the army garrisons and the worker-peasant provost corps established by the Revolutionary Committees. In Yingte district near Canton there were bloody fights between Red Guards and the armed volunteer patrols of local communes. Trade union leaders led workers' provost units in street fighting with the reactivated student leftists (PHHP, 6th June, 1968, in SCMP No.4249, 1968; TFH, 30th June, 1968, in SCMP No.4231, 1967).

Action was not always so violent but the conflict between order and social change was much the same even where leftists limited themselves to verbal criticisms. One Canton radical newspaper tactfully called for the revolutionary reorganization of the "Worker Discipline Corps" (which had taken over some of the police responsibilities) in Canton. The radicals were disappointed by their poor ideological and personal representation in the new revolutionary police forces:

> The Workers Disciplinary Corps should be the backbone contingent for the purpose of bringing about the dictatorship of the masses. It in no way should supersede the workers' movement, let alone the Great Cultural Revolution, in Canton . . . After the formation of the Workers' Disciplinary Corps some results have been achieved in the maintenance of social security and order as well as in the normalization of communications. However, in the progress of forming the Workers' Disciplinary Corps no efforts have been made to rely on the left wing of the working class; therefore, organizationally the line followed is wrong (KCKKL, 28th June, 1968, in SCMP No.4250, 1968)

The old pattern of off-duty policemen suppressing the radicals was apparently still in effect even among the "revolutionary" police, and Canton rebels complained that,

> . . . some card carrying members of the Workers' Disciplinary Corps are privately engaged in reactionary activities, thereby disrupting (revolutionary activities), pointed the spearhead directly at the revolutionary masses, and impairing the reputation of the Workers' Disciplinary Corps.

> The broad revolutionary masses . . . should help the Corps overcome bourgeois factionalism and should promote its ideological reorganization, so that through the correct leadership of the Kuangtung Provincial Revolutionary Committee and the Canton Congress of Workers it will transform itself and become a detachment of mass dictatorship (KCKKL, 28th June, 1968, *in* SCMP No.4250, 1968)

The central role of the PLA as keepers of the peace had worn down the "great alliance" between the army and the leftists, and when the radicals attempted their comeback in 1968, there were sharp clashes between soldiers and rebels. The radicals again accused the military of repressing the Revolution (which was in some cases true). The army garrison in Canton was attacked by armed students and workers from the Canton Combat Corps and there were many casualties. The army defended itself and arrested a number of radical leaders. There was, however, no reported all-out counter-attack, and as usual the soldiers showed great self-restraint (TFH, 30th June, 1968, *in* SCMP No.4231, 1968; SCLWCP, 13th September, 1968, *in* SCMP No.4272, 1968).

The resurgence of radicalism brought another agonizing series of factional struggles between rebel guard units. Kwangsi province, near Canton, was the scene of a terrific battle between the "Combined Command of Kwangsi" and the "Grand Army", which caused the destruction of draught animals and supplies destined for the people of Vietnam in their struggle against American imperialism. In Canton's Kwangting Province, the Red Guards besieged, arrested, tortured and killed one another in battles that devastated university campuses there (HKK, 12th June, 1968, *in* SCMP No.4236, 1968). Fighting also broke out again in Shanghai where Red Guards continued shooting in the face of PLA appeals to cease fire. Not infrequently warring Guard factions across the country each attempted to draw the army in as allies and the PLA's role as peace-maker and arbitrator became exceedingly difficult (HHWP No.8, July, 1968, *in* SCMP No.4236, 1968; WHP, 31st July, 1968, *in* SCMP No.4246, 1968).

Mao acted quickly to pull the country back from the anarchy of violent factionalism and at last ordered the army to disarm and disband most of the Red Guard units. The Chairman met with Red Guard factional leaders and with tears in his eyes told them:

> You have let me down, and what is more you have disappointed the workers, peasants and soliders of China (CCAS, 1971, p.95)

The top national leadership was rearranged and, despite continued radical influence, the moderates' dominance was now assured. Students were ordered to return to the schools, which had been closed for nearly two years, or were sent to the countryside to work as farmers.

There was some grumbling about this quieter role for young radicals and the army acted with force to suppress some last revolutionary struggles and force the release of prisoners and surrender of Red Guard weapons. Generally speaking, however, serious resistance was confined to isolated incidents as China moved into a rebuilding period (TCP No.1, July, 1968, *in* SCMP No.42334; Kuangtung Rev. Comm., 1968, *in* SCMP No.4243, 1968; KYCLCCTWTLCC, 1968, July, *in* SCMP No.4235, 1968). The year-long struggle between moderates and radicals was decided. Economic and political reforms continued to develop, but in a slower more systematic manner (NCNA, 18th August, 1968, *in* SCMP No.4245, 1968; WHP, 17th July, 1968, *in* SCMP No.4231, 1968). The shock and fury of the Cultural Revolution was over.

Reform and Recovery in Government, Justice and Mass Organizations

The end of violent struggle and power seizures in 1968 did not signal the failure of the Cultural Revolution, nor did the Maoist leadership abandon the ideals and reform goals which had fired revolution for three years. It was obvious, however, that the factionalism and musical chair politics of endless Red Guard attacks would not create a strong new government with wide public support. The revolution of 1966-68 had successfully broken the momentum of the New Class conservatives; it remained to reunite the country behind the new Peking leadership and the Revolutionary Committees which had replaced the old authorities at local levels.

The plan followed in the decade after 1968 was largely a combination of political education and structural reforms, with the overall aim of opening government to the public and levelling out serious socio-economic inequalities. The *continuous political education* campaign, centred on Mao-study and the mass line, helped restore national unity while encouraging peaceful social change and the rehabilitation of those denounced as political offenders in 1966-67. The *structural reforms* also gave new mass organizations wider powers over local government. Many of the social and economic ideas of the Great Leap were recalled, but the new plans for economic reform in the early 1970s were far more modest and sensitive to problems of infra-structure rashly overlooked in the Leap. All of these developments touched on issues and institutions of Chinese justice; and justice, both popular and professional, was much changed in the years of recovery and reform: 1968-78.

Political education: unity, criticism, transformation

The justice line between antagonistic and non-antagonistic contradictions moved with the shift towards recovery politics. The revisionist "enemy" was no longer to be attacked, but was instead to be rehabilitated by the gentler methods of political education. Political education developed quickly after the Revolution as a national movement considerably affecting the entire population, but especially challenging the most fundamental political ethics of conservatives in Party and government. As in the Socialist Education campaign, Mao-study classes were organized across the country, this time including not only communes and schools, but also government bureaux, factories and schools. Frequently, such classes involved over 80 to 90% of the urban population and vast numbers of people in the countryside. The mass line was taught and discussed and related to local social and political questions affecting the people, such as family relations, production goals, or leadership methods. Pressure was especially concentrated on those local leaders who had been criticized for arrogance or elitism during the preceding crisis years (WKTH, 16th July, 1968, *in* SCMP No.4240, 1968; Salaff, 1975).

The problem of continuing factional conflicts among workers and students was also considered in the Mao-study classes. These conflicts, like those between elitist officials and the public, were treated as "contradictions among the people" to be handled gently and without repression. The official Party press noted that:

> Young people today are different. In the past some youngsters, poisoned by Liu Shao chi's revisionist line, were like 'little lambs', lacking in revolutionary spirit.
>
> . . . however . . . some young people have been subject to anarchist influences. This requires us to explain the truth clearly and explain to these young comrades that the proletarian spirit of organization and discipline is necessary . . . and that anarchism would demoralize the revolutionary ranks, destroy the wealth created by the people, and erode the revolutionary will of the young people (Lu Yung, *Hung Ch'i*, 28th February, 1970, SCMM No.121, 1970)

Reports of such internal struggles continued in the face of government pressure and advice (JMJP, 7th, 21st, 29th May, 25th August, 1969, *in* CNIP No.270, 272, 273, 286, 1969) and the leadership was obliged to observe:

> We must absolutely not confuse the line between [revisionist] slavishness and the [necessary] observance of revolutionary discipline (JMJP, 29th July, 1969, *in* CNIP No.282, 1969)

That such problems should persist after a period of lawless power struggles is hardly surprising. The general hostility of radicals toward virtually any authority was exemplified in their argument that,

> . . . all rules and regulations are used to bind the people's hands and feet and must be rebelled against (JMJP, 16th August, 1969, *in* CNIP No.285, 1969)

Obviously such a political philosophy could not but cause difficulties for the new Revolutionary Committees charged with governing the country. However, both the national leadership and the local committees continued to rely on persuasion and education to resolve and calm factional conflicts, while reassuring the radicals that there would be no "restoration of capitalism" under the new revolutionary order.

Finally, the educational campaign also included a second round of attacks on Liu Shao chi and the revisionist ideology. The long-deposed Liu was again universally maligned as a "big careerist" who "villified the masses" in his attempt to "restore capitalism" (JMJP, 12th, 15th, 25th July, 25th August, *in* CNIP Nos 279, 283, 285, 286, 1969; *Hung Ch'i*, No.9, 1969, *in* CNIP, No.287; NCNA, 27th July, 1969, *in* SCMP No.4230, 1969). All of these charges and general criticisms had, of course, been recounted many times before, but their cadenced restatement in 1968-70 served some useful purposes. Firstly, it reassured former Red Guards and Rebels that there would be no abandonment of revolutionary positions. Secondly, it sought to bring the country together in peacefully summarizing the experience of the revolution. The ritual of collective denunciation along with personal self-criticism, was a first step toward the reform and reacceptance of officials denounced for following Liu.

Reinstatement and reunification after a struggle like the Cultural Revolution, however, required much more than ritual denunciation, criticism sessions and participation in Mao-study classes. Factional quarrels still smouldered and more than a few revolutionary committee members were yet unwilling to welcome back former conservative "power holders". Those who had risked all to seize power in 1966-67 expected clear evidence of reform before accepting the declarations of loyalty from the deposed officials (HKK No.8, 30th July, 1968, *in* SCMP No.4236, 1968; WHP, 15th July, 1968, *in* SCMP No.4248; Salaff, 1975). Mao and the central leadership quite agreed, and post-revolutionary ideological reform was to be much more intense than previous Party rectification.

On 6th May, 1966 Mao advanced a directive that would later become the guideline for the new political rehabilitation programme (Mao Tse-tung, 1966, *in* Macciochi, 1972, pp.89-92). Nearly all of the disgraced revisionist cadres were to be restored to good standing but often only after their successful completion of a term in a special new work–study institution. Hundreds of these institutions were set up and they became known as "May 7th Schools". Cadres from all levels of Party and government were sent to these schools for "terms" of from six months to several years. The May 7th Schools were designed to "re-mould" those once attacked as "enemies", but the schools were most definitely not prisons.

They had no guards or cell blocks, and those sent there were not "sentenced" by courts or police, but were considered to be on "assignment" from their original office or Party branch. Frequently cadres remained on the rolls of their home organization and their families were still supported by the state. On the other hand, the schools *were* officially described as "rehabilitation centres" and those sent there (at least in 1967-72) were regarded as political offenders to be pressurized, challenged and re-educated. Officials were separated from their families except for brief visits. As with People's supervision or mediation teams, the May 7th Schools simply had no parallel in Western justice (Pfeffer, 1972).

Like most other post-revolutionary schools, the May 7th institutions involved students in both study and productive labour. Initially the curriculum hardly touched academic or professional topics, as both classes and work periods were designed to prompt self-examination. During the day each cadre, regardless of rank (or former rank) was called to manual labour, usually working on the schools' farmlands or tending to one of the small industries. Occasionally the former officials returned to their old bureaux in nearby towns or communes, and there were given the hardest and most menial tasks, such as cleaning floors or toilets. Evenings were set aside for political study and criticism sessions, where the emphasis was on mass line methods of leadership and the elimination of old ways of thinking and elitist habits. During the first years especially, the burden for showing progress was placed on the cadres who would resume their official careers only if they showed evidence of change in personal and political attitudes. Each school's own Revolutionary Committee, composed of trainees and elected by their peers, was also to have some voice in the local reform programme and in the reassignment of reformed cadres (Macciochi, 1972, pp.93-96; Pfeffer, 1972).

Reassignment to another official post did not, however, mean an end to the rehabilitation process. Those returning to the bureaucracy (often in a different region and at a lower rank) faced the continuing test of "mass supervision" and were (at least until 1975) the object of a continuing on-the-job remoulding process known as "open rectification". The various Revolutionary Committees generally created and maintained their own local political reform programme (Chang, 1973, pp.3334-3340; Macciochi, 1972, pp.96-99). This open rectification applied not only to those returning from May 7th Schools but also to the new "revolutionary" cadres. Open rectification was thus regarded as a permanent feature by the Maoist leadership. The workers, peasants and students were continually encouraged to discuss their gripes and complaints against administrators or executives in "heart-to-heart talks" held frequently in factories, schools and communes (JMJP, 11th April, 1969, *in* CNIP No.268; Bennett, G., 1970, pp.6-10).

The reshuffled Peking leadership also reinstituted the "hsia fang" idea of "sending cadres down" from their offices to farms in the countryside where they worked alongside the farmers (generally for only a few weeks or months). Those selected were to share the living standard of the peasant folk and in the evenings attend political study classes with the local people. This was not as intense a reform process as the May 7th Schools, since it did not segregate cadres into specialized institutions. Hsia fang did, however, break the routine of bureaucratic careers and many of those sent down were pointedly advised to rethink their attitudes if they desired to return to their former positions (JMJP, Arch. 17, 1968, *in* CNS No.458; Wuhan Radio, 17th February, 1968, *in* CNS No.458).

All of these various rectification processes evince both the Maoist emphasis on popular activism and the rather optimistic hope that through such means one might "cure the disease to save the patient". The country simply could not afford to dispense with the services of its administrative and technical specialists, nor could it await the training of a new more "revolutionary" generation of cadres. The infusion of some new blood at the lower levels of the Party and government, and limited structural changes within mass organizations and the loyal revolutionary committees were important aspects of the Maoist reform strategy in 1967-75. However, the most important task was the ideological transformation of those elites who were so bitterly attacked during the Cultural Revolution. The transformation process depended upon a delicate balance between prodding and recognition, reintegration and criticism. The process was made even more difficult by China's pressing need to get back to the business of full-scale production, education and efficient administration, and by the smouldering resentments and bitter memories of those who found themselves on opposite sides during the tumultuous years of 1966-68).

Given all these difficulties, it is surprising that the various rectification processes seemed to work as well as they did in the early 1970s. Visiting scholars and journalists from the West (Macciochi, 1972, pp.96-9; Pfeffer, 1972, pp.645-50; CCAS, 1971, pp.97-101) provided convincing accounts of genuine reflection and changes of heart among those sent to May 7th Schools or subjected to critical rectification at workplaces, schools and in local government or Party branches. However, as China turned increasingly to these same objects of reform from leadership in matters of production, administration and education, it was inevitable that the rectification process would lose a great deal of its force. Indeed the whole history of mass campaigns in the People's Republic suggests that it is difficult to sustain a prolonged and intense level of activism, particularly if conflicts, as in rectification, are part of the mass campaign agenda.

The May 7th Schools had, by 1975, become a routine part of professional training for virtually all "revolutionary cadres" (as all cadres were now described). The curriculum of Mao-study and criticism at the schools was considerably less pointed and more concerned with practical aspects of administration in the mid-1970s. The Revolutionary Committees at schools and workplaces and local government branches were increasingly dominated by returning bureaucrat or technical specialists whose skills and experiences lent them increased power. The programmes of Mao-study and criticism/self-criticism which comprised "ongoing rectification" became increasingly routine and ritualized as the social hierarchy reasserted itself despite reform efforts. It was perhaps inevitable, given the tight limits of the Chinese economy and the enormous gaps in education, that the anti-bureaucratic rectification effort would itself grow bureaucratic even as it became institutionalized.

Structural reforms: in education and mass organization

Along with the creation of Revolutionary Committees and the rectification process, the Maoist reform strategy emphasized the growth and further empowerment of the mass organization and democratization of higher education. Both of these reform efforts carried considerable momentum from the Cultural Revolution; but both were also confronted with increasingly difficult contradictions during the early 1970s.

Conflicts within higher education touched off the Cultural Revolution, of course, and the schools and universities were perhaps the most seriously affected of all social institutions by the reform initiatives of the following decade. Theoretical studies were deliberately tied to production needs, and manual labour was integrated into the curriculums wherever possible. Teachers were particularly singled out for rectification, with thousands sent to May 7th schools, hsia fang assignments or other forms of manual labour before returning to teaching posts and continuing Mao-study programmes there. The aim throughout was consciously to challenge intellectual elitism and professional narrowness (Bennett, 1972; HK students, 1972; *Hung Ch'i*, 1st January, 1970, 1st June, 1971, 1st October, 1972, *in* SCMM No.671, 708, 739).

The "red and expert" schools of the Leap also reappeared in a new set of part-time schools for workers and peasants. These schools offered technical and political courses and varied in length from occasional night classes to a two-year stay at regional technical institutes. The overall purpose was, once again, the fusion of work and study and the erosion of technological "mystiques" which inevitably seem to develop in a population marked by wide educational gaps (NCNA, 27th April, 1973, *in* CNS No.416; Canton Radio, 14th April, 1973, *in* CNS No.437). Finally, those wanting to take university entrance examinations in the decade 1967-76 were required to be nominated by their fellow workers, peasants, or soldiers. Each production or army unit was then allotted a certain quota of nominees. The nominees were to be chosen for both scholarship and demonstrated unselfishness and loyalty to the community (CCAS, 1971, pp.178-80, 202-8).

Despite these reforms and the continuing mass line fervour of the ex-Red Guard students, the intellectual world remained a source of tension and contradiction. China's need to be self-reliant meant that she had to have her own "experts" and develop specialized training and professional researchers. The post-Cultural Revolution leadership recognized this dilemma, of course, which explains their reluctance to reopen the universities until political re-education there was well established. Enrolment in certain specialized fields, including law and some of the social sciences, remained below the 1966 levels for over a decade.

Despite efforts at democratization, the universities' primary interest in specialized training continued to cause conflicts with the mass line ideology. A few years after 1967 lower class students were once more complaining about the discrimination of the so-called objective examinations, which were reinstated in the mid-1970s (JMJP, 11th September, 1972, *in* CNS No.437, 1972; *Hung Ch'i*, 1st January, 1970, JMJP 16th August, 1969, *in* CNIP No.285).

Mass organizations changed and prospered in the decade of reform from 1965-75. Mao-study emphasized the importance of mass political action and public organizations such as the trade unions, women's unions, peasant associations and residents' committees received more attention from the Party leadership. The Maoists had been distressed by conservatism in the national leadership of some mass organizations during the Cultural Revolution, and in the years immediately following 1967 the local organizations were encouraged to act more independently of their national headquarters (Pye, 1969, pp.16-22).

The former national officers of the All-China Federation of Trade Unions were part of the New Class coalition, and were sharply criticized for their isolation from the working class rank and file. Many top union leaders were sent to May 7th Schools and the national union headquarters has been relatively inactive over the past few years. The Party leadership in the period from 1969-75 ordered that the new decentralized unions more closely represent their membership and then ruled that at least 65% of all union delegates sent to provincial workers' congresses be line workers personally involved in production (HCNT No.2, July, 1968, *in* SCMP No.4241, 1968; Harper, 1969, pp.117-19). The local trade unions also sponsor local political study courses designed to combat "economism" and encourage collectivism among the working class community. Unions were of course intimately involved in the open rectification of industrial management and Party officials (NCNA, 8th June, 1973, *in* CNS No.471; JMJP, 24th April, 1973, *in* CNS No.464; Chengtu Radio, 29th March, 1973, *in* CNS No.462).

The Chinese Federation of Women gained new prominence after the Cultural Revolution and functioned as a steady if quiet advocate for sexual equality and other social reforms. The conservatives, by contrast, had done little to change the inferior status of women, since they were primarily concerned with discipline and social stability. The Revolutionary Committees made considerable efforts to recruit women for leadership positions and women also became increasingly active in the trade unions (NCNA, 23rd April, 8th June, 1973, *in* CNS No.464, 471, 1973). Chiang Ching served in part as the national women's spokesman and the Federation did grow somewhat in influence under her leadership (Hupeh Radio, 13th May, 1972, *in* CNS No.467; King, V., 1966, pp.10-11).

The peasant associations of the country had been reorganized and invigorated during the Socialist Education movement. At that time the Maoist leadership had directed the associations to include only the poor and lower middle class farmers, and that policy continued in the years after the Cultural Revolution. The associations gained increased prominence in a series of national conferences held after 1968 and they were encouraged to participate in the ongoing rectification and supervision of rural officials.

Despite some considerable pressure from the Red Guards and Revolutionary Rebels the top Party leadership decided not to shake up the communes by eliminating private plots and private profit making at the rural trade fairs. Instead, the Maoists counted on political education to check materialistic appetites among the middle class peasants. The poor and lower middle class peasant associations sponsored political study classes which taught rural commune residents the superiority of collective property and collective work. The Associations were thus designed as a political and educational hedge against capitalist tendencies which threatened the community cohesion and collective economy of the rural communes (Shensi Radio, 27th January, 1972, *in* CNS No.454, 1972).

Urban residents' committees had never been particularly strong mass organizations, and under the conservative regime of 1961-66 the committees had become totally impotent and almost solely concerned with neighbourhood gossip and petty jealousies. The Red Guards and Rebels spent many exasperating hours exhorting and haranguing housewives and homebodies without much result. The city stay-at-homes were too timid and politically inarticulate to act upon their grievances and the radicals found few allies here for their power seizures in 1966-67. Such a gaping hole in urban community organization was another type of threat to popular politics and popular justice, and the Maoist leadership was determined to close this urban gap in the years after the revolution.

A number of concrete reforms were instituted to break the pattern of local Party "boss rule" in the neighbourhoods. Elections had always been an empty ritual before 1968, with city dwellers almost always following local Party "recommendations" and rubber stamping the Party's slate of candidates for the local residents' committees. With the Party's power broken, the post-Revolution elections became matters for wide debate and real political contest among a number of candidates (Salaff, 1975).

The Revolutionary Committees emerged as the new national and local governing bodies, and were intended by the Maoists to be permanent. Committees gradually stepped free of the PLA support that had dominated government during the crises of 1967-68, and began supervising the rebuilding of the Communist Party. Army leaders still held down their third of the three-in-one alliances, but newly recruited citizen activists, revolutionary Party cadres and rehabilitated ex-conservative officials by 1976 held most political posts at all levels. This turn toward civilian control was especially noticeable at the middle and local levels of government where the PLA had largely withdrawn from leadership (CCAS, 1971, p.91).

Justice in the recovery period: people's supervision, police work and mediation

As might be expected, popular justice returned to prominence behind the leadership of the Maoists and the resurgence in mass organizations and mass line politics. The public contribution to political rehabilitation of conservative cadres in the open rehabilitation and hsia fang programmes has been discussed previously.

From 1968-75 People's supervision also became very decentralized and so varied greatly with local conditions. A number of factories and industrial districts established "Red Sentries", who were directly elected by the workers on a rotating basis. These sentries were active both in promoting the Mao-study campaign and in watching and reporting on all paid officials. In other areas, the workers or peasants elected new People's supervisory committees and these committees prepared reports and evaluations on cadres. Supervising workers were intensively educated in mass line ideology and instructed to be constantly alert for official elitism (NCNA, 9th December, 1969, *in* CNIP, No.301; JMJP, 19th March, 1969, *in* CNIP No.265, 1969).

Mediation work was also steadily encouraged during the decade after the Cultural Revolution as the preferred means of "handling contradictions among the people". Local residential organizations and unions were expected to maintain their own mediation committees which had considerable contact with the police, but seemed to be little influenced by the courts. Mediation was especially valued as an educational device and mediators were encouraged to discuss conflicts and disorders in the language of Maoist thought and social change.

The army retired from active involvement in police work during 1968-69, and by 1974 most of the soldiers had been replaced by Public Order patrolmen, sometimes newly returned from rehabilitation and nationwide reorganization. Special May 7th Schools were set up to retrain policemen and to combat selfishness, bureaucratism and professional isolation among the police. Many new patrolmen also joined the force to replace those police still considered politically unreliable, stubbornly arrogant, abusive and insensitive to public needs. Often the new patrolmen were recruited directly from the ranks of the PLA or from among activists prominent in the Cultural Revolution organizations (CCAS, 1971, pp.128-30; Macciochi, 1972, p.99).

The uniformed police were strongly assisted or even substituted by volunteer police from many local mass organizations. In the cities, especially Shanghai, members of the newly strengthened local militia often patrolled the streets in the early 1970s. Trade unions and peasant organizations (to a lesser degree) also created a network of volunteer provost guards. Gradually, however, the regular police of the Department of Public Order reasserted their clear primacy in the maintenance of order and law enforcement.

The People's Courts receded into the background during the early 1970s. A great many courts remained closed, and the diversion of so much court business to the informal dispute settlement procedures of mediation in the mass organizations significantly reduced their role. Judges remained in hsia fang assignments or May 7th Schools longer than did many other officials, and the law schools remained closed long after other university departments had reopened. Interviews with legal officials during this time (Ruge, 1974; Lamb, 1975) leave the consistent impression of slow and modest recovery and a deliberate de-emphasis on formal procedures and professionalism. The Procurate, as in the previous rectifications of 1957, suffered the most during the Cultural Revolution and made the slowest recovery in the decade afterwards. Indeed, there were some observers who, in the early 1970s, doubted that the Procurate would ever regain even a fraction of its always circumscribed power, let alone assume the greater roles allotted it in theory under the Constitution of 1964. It is noteworthy that the 1974 Constitution, which reflected the reform initiative of the early 1970s, made a special point of insisting on the incorporation of the "mass line" into the world of this, the most professional and formalized of the legal bureaux (FLP, 1974).

In sum, China's dual justice system became more integrated after the violent conflicts which raged around the police, courts and procurate during the Cultural Revolution. Popular justice institutions were considerably expanded and invigorated, both in the area of rectification and in more routine peace keeping, but the professional agencies, especially the police, had made long strides toward a recovery of their positions by 1975. Ultimately, of course, the path of this dialectic development was to be set by forces larger and more powerful than legal institutions. In retrospect, it is clear from the vantage of 1981 that the efforts to reform and reintegrate Chinese justice and the larger political economy during the reform decade of 1966-75 were simply not successful. The death of Mao Tse-tung in 1976 let loose a storm of conflict of astonishing violence and exposed serious weaknesses among the radical Maoists who had depended so heavily on the Chairman's support.

The Looming Problem of Succession:
Political Antagonists on the Eve of Mao Tse-tung's Death

Before considering in the final chapter of this book the explosive struggles of 1976-81 and the most recent developments in the Chinese legal system, it may be useful to sketch briefly the situation with respect to competing leadership groups and ideologies at the time of Mao's sudden death in 1976. Observers at the time recognized three distinct elites among the ruling circles in Peking, each with their own political agenda for foreign and domestic policy (Yomiuri Shimbum, 1968, p.63; Hinton, H., 1969). These may be briefly identified as the radicals, the moderates and the military chiefs (Chen, J., 1974, pp.208-11).

A number of *radicals* joined the Central Committee after the Cultural Revolution and they were expected to play a major role in the foreseeable future. Chiang Ching was ranked among the top five national leaders along with Wang Hung-wen. Chiang was, even in 1976, in very poor health, but Wang at the age of 40 was by far the youngest and healthiest member of the Central Committee. He was the former leader and organizer of the radical workers in Shanghai and did not hesitate to speak out for radical social reforms since his elevation to the highest political body. He was the first to oppose Lin Piao openly when that now-deposed leader attempted to consolidate too much personal power and deviated from the mass line course. Mao made a special point of supporting Wang and the other Party radicals and the leftists were able to count on support from Shanghai and from many students and lesser-skilled workers elsewhere (Chen, J., 1974, pp.209-15; Hinton, H., 1969, pp.40-4; Schram, 1971a, pp.243-4).

The military chiefs still figured prominently in the Central Committee and in regional and municipal branches of government in 1976. There had been conflicts between the military and the radicals when the PLA was called in to restore order in 1967, but on the other hand, no Chinese institution had been so thoroughly immersed in Mao-study and mass line reforms as had the army. Many Western observers were of the opinion in 1975 that the military would not insert itself into factional fighting after the death of Mao, as long as these struggles were manageable and did not involve disorder on the scale of 1966-68. Certainly, the PLA tradition has not been one of interference with political leadership by the Party (Ghosh, 1973, pp.18-26).

Those whom the Western press usually refers to as the "moderates" among the Chinese leadership were led by Chou en Lai until his death; and Chou was perhaps the only moderate who might have forged a workable compromise with the radicals. Chou, and also Teng Hsiao-ping in particular, were backed by the old guard of the Party and government apparatus, and by professionals and technocrats and skilled workers, all of whom had a material stake in the sort of pragmatic wage-incentive policies long favoured by the conservatives. Given the country's shortage of skilled administrators and technical experts, it is not surprising that even those most heartily denounced as revisionists continued to make their way back into positions of power in the early 1970s. Observers, Chinese and Western, could only guess whether the experience of May 7th schools and rectification had altered their outlooks and working styles; but the announcements of successful "rehabilitation" became significant in the explicit and the implicit content of Chinese news stories (Hinton, H., 1969, pp.40-4; JMJP, 14th, 17th March, 1973, *in* CNA No.458, 460; TKP, 13th April, 1973, *in* CNA No.463, 1973).

The optimistic programmes of judicial reform by political education and personal rehabilitation might well have worked some amazing human trans-formations. However, the economic system still depended upon some of the structures that nurtured the New Class elite which had so clashed with revol-utionary ideals and caused the tensions which produced the Cultural Revolution. In 1975 private plots and rural trade fairs still continued to threaten the collective economy of the countryside and the middle class peasant remained as a potential source of community disunity and class struggle. Though some govern-ment salaries had been reduced by 1975, the industrial wage scale was still rather steep and the unskilled labourers were much poorer than the senior workers or those with specialized skills. Professionalism and intellectual elitism continued, despite the enormous efforts made to democratize knowledge and eliminate the mystique of technology.

Observers in the early 1970s differed widely in their appraisals of the strength of these competing elites and their respective viewpoints. It was clear to all, however, that the problems of succession would be enormous in a nation where the cult of a single leader had so marked the political culture. The events which followed swiftly upon the Chairman's death in 1976 revealed that the tensions in China were now beyond the measures of compromise, rectification and reform adopted in the decade of recovery. Even the most astute of Western observers were shocked by the sudden force of conflict which so changed the situation in China after 1976. The country's system of justice would, in this latest series of events, once again be prominent as both an agent and a target of these larger struggles.

9   *Judicial Policy and Political Contest in Post-Mao China: Some Recapitulations and Conclusions*

The tumultuous struggles and reversals of the first 35 years of Chinese socialism still did not prepare us for the dramatic changes in the five years since the Chairman's death in 1976. These most recent times have surely been a "season of startling alliance".

The surprise legal developments of 1976 were almost routinely accepted amidst the excitement of impending ceremony and deepening alliance. China, long reluctant to create a regular "legal system" and often denounced as an "outlaw state" by first the Americans and then the Soviets, has at last, in 1979-80, adopted a new and remarkably conventional set of Westernized laws and judicial bureaucracies. American officials were reassured by this as yet another sign of "stability" and "maturity" among the Chinese "moderates" now ruling the country. China-bound corporate executives also appreciate these developments, as they note new legal guarantees for foreign investors and calculate the potential profits from the vast Chinese market. As David Rockefeller plans joint ventures with Communist officials in Peking and Teng Hsiao Peng bargains for "defensive" weapons at the Pentagon it is a time for rubbing eyes at these most amazing political and legal developments.

The growing alliance with the United States, like the new legal system, is possible at this time only because certain long-standing internal conflicts have been at least temporarily resolved. One cannot but notice that every new turn in foreign and domestic policy, each new legal code, each newly refurbished and expanded justice bureau is preceded by yet another shovel full of condemnation heaped upon the political grave of the now vilified "Gang of Four". These deposed members of the Communist Party Central Committee are much more than a clique of scapegoats. They are symbolic of a national political force (which they once led) that stands in clear opposition to current policies in almost all aspects of society, law and justice. In order to understand anything of the origins and implications of contemporary judicial practice it is necessary to consider the political ideas and social policies which distinguish the new dominant "moderate" leadership from the defeated "radicals", represented by the Gang of Four.

This chapter breaks with the prevailing mood of celebration to argue that the emerging legal system and the rise of the new "moderate" leadership are defeats for the Revolution and for the Chinese people as a whole. Current policies in Peking have systematically widened social inequalities in wages, power and prestige and have reversed the egalitarian spirit of the Cultural Revolution (1966-68). The new conservatism is reflected and reinforced in the new laws and judicial procedures which lend permanence to existing uneven property relations (including limited capitalism), outlaw key forms of political dissent developed during the Cultural Revolution, weaken the power of workers and citizens in government and production centres, and impose a heavy dominance of specialized professionals in law enforcement and adjudication.

This is more than just "leaning to one side" in a swing to the right of the dialectic process. China has taken the downhill path to modernization led by the new leadership down steep gradients of inequality and narrow bureaucratic defiles. There is nothing "moderate" about the new elite. The correct description of their ideas and their policies is *revisionism*. It is the defeated opposition who, despite their many mistakes, can be best described as the *revolutionary* alternative for Chinese development.

The revisionists are constrained, however, by 50 years of revolutionary Maoist traditions, by the centuries-old public mistrust of lawyers and formal legal procedures, by the need to maintain popular enthusiasm for labour-intensive production, and by the fiscal weakness of the state itself. China simply cannot afford to pay all or even most of those who handle crimes, conflicts, rehabilitation and other social services. The justice professionals must rely upon great numbers of volunteer activists, and thus dare not risk alienating the population by overcentralizing and formalizing justice.

The discussion will move through three main sections. First, an overview of the competing revolutionary and revisionist lines, the leadership, philosophy and policy over the past 30 years, and particularly in the decade since the Cultural Revolution. Second, a discussion of the 1978 Constitution, new criminal statutes, justice agencies and legal professionalism, with a contrasting view of revolutionary Maoist traditions which emphasize popular involvement through community organizations, informal procedures and the central importance of politics and class in defining crime and handling disputes. Finally, a discussion of future prospects, with attention to emerging patterns of crime and conflict and the social contradictions arising from China's startling new revisionist alliance.

Chinese Conflicts and Western Sympathies

Observers of China in the United States have long recognized the central importance of the Two Line Struggle. Indeed scholars have "taken sides" against one another in their relation to this conflict, just as earlier they were divided by their stand on the American genocidal adventure in South East Asia. Certainly, the sympathies of those who sit in council with corporate executives and State Department officials have always been clear. The following remarks have been offered recently by one of Henry Kissinger's top aides, Allen Whiting, and by Ross Terril of the established Harvard intelligentsia.

> The fall of Chiang Ching and her three Shanghai associates (who comprised the Gang of Four) removes the most poisonous elements in Peking affecting Sino-American relations.

> When the far leftist Gang of Four . . . were snuffed out in the tense darkness of one October night in 1976, the ten-year nightmare of Mao's Cultural Revolution was belatedly snuffed out with them (Whiting, 1976)

> . . . by 1977 a more pragmatic government headed by the modest Hua Kuo feng had begun to put a new stamp in China's affairs . . . Peking has at least defined the good society in refreshing terms (Terril, 1978, pp.9-10)

News editors have almost unanimously approved Peking's new "moderates" and condemned the radical opposition as "dogmatic purists" and "shrill-voiced ideologues". Unfortunately, such highly coloured accounts as they give tell us more about the interests of the dominant American elite than they do about the Two Line conflict in China.

What then are the origins and issues in this conflict which has so occupied the attention of Chinese leaders, people and overseas observers? When writing about this in the year before Mao's death, I stressed the philosophical nature of the dispute, arguing:

> This central struggle is fundamentally a conflict of competing ideas for economic development and political leadership, rather than a battle of personalities and clear political factions. The two Idea-Antagonists have been generally constant while the lists of their human supporters have changed (Brady, 1977a, p.128)

I am not at all sure that I would say the same today. The social and economic policies adopted by the dominant revisionists have so favoured certain sectors of the Chinese population as to build an increasingly solid *class base* for what had before been an ideological conservatism with overtones of economic interest. In considering this conflict anew it is even more important to understand historical and material developments as expressions of the deepening political antagonism. This will be of necessity a brief discussion, but there is a rich abundance of good sources on the subject.

The Two Line Struggle as History and Ideology

The Revolutionary Line and its adherents developed over three eras of sweeping social reforms and powerful mass movements: the Civil War (1927-49), the Great Leap Forward (1957-61) and the Cultural Revolution (1966-68). The Civil War formed the Communists into a shadow government and an instrument of class struggle, arousing the peasants against the landlords (Selden, 1969; Brady, 1974, pp.64-80). The Great Leap was focused especially on the rural areas, where collectivization was advanced and living standards and opportunities were expanded with the development of decentralized industry, technology and higher education (Dutt, 1967, pp.90-97; Salaff, 1975; Hsu, I. C., 1964). The Cultural Revolution was set chiefly in urban zones where the administration of schools, factories and government was challenged and reorganized along more egalitarian and participatory lines (Nee, 1973; Riskin, 1973; Gray, 1970).

The revolutionary ethic rests on three key principles: the "mass line" in political leadership, the "continuing revolution" in social development and "Red and expert" for the role of educated specialists. The mass line was created over the course of the Civil War. It has continued in the tradition of strong community organizations and popular mobilization as both an aide and a counterweight to the government bureaucracy (Mao Tse-tung, 1943; Selden, 1969; Schurmann, 1966a). The continuing revolution calls for ongoing reforms to eliminate the cultural influence of the old society and to close gaps in wages and prestige between city and rural zones, workers and farmers, white collar and blue collar workers, men and women. Those with higher education are expected to be both "Red and expert", developing specialized skills but seeking neither material privileges nor isolation from the labouring people (Mao Tse-tung, 1970; Mao Tse-tung, 1956; Schram, 1971b).

The competing Revisionist Line also traces back to three historic courses: post-war Reconstruction (1949-56), recovery from the failure of the Great Leap (1961-65), and the Thermidorean reaction to the Cultural Revolution (1976-present). During the Reconstruction era Soviet advisers were most influential, educating young Chinese specialists and pointing economic plans in the Soviet direction of sharp social and political stratification. In the mid-1960s, the excessive dislocations of the Great Leap prompted a reassessment and restoration of material incentives and centralized authority (Hoffman, 1963; Donnithone, 1966; Dutt and Dutt, 1970, pp.9-19). Since Mao's death the rightists have mounted a third and by far the most powerful offensive.

The ideas and policies advocated by the right have been fairly consistent throughout, though advanced with more boldness at each resurgence. Initially, conservatives such as Liu Shao chi (1957) justified their policies with selected excerpts from Mao's (generally radical) writings. In most recent years Teng Hsiao Peng and others have begun to cite what they call "the objective laws of socialist development" (Teng Hsiao Peng, 1978). These laws, being "objective", have no place for political contest or class struggle (Monthly Review Editors, 1979). The new conservatives are pledged to rapid modernization through the most expedient concentration of available capital and technology (JMJP, 2nd February, 1979). They would build industry up in the nation's strongest urban centres, and seek the co-operation of Western capitalist firms, though this means that the rural zones will lag behind and that China must abandon its tradition of "self reliance".

Modernization, say the conservatives, should be led by technological specialists and bureaucratic administrators working in stable hierarchies free of interference from "mass supervision" by community organizations and without the obligation to engage in political study/self-criticism or manual labour. Material incentives, bonuses and steep wage scales are required to spur individual effort and to distinguish clearly the contribution of essential specialists, administrators and skilled labour from the less crucial functions of ordinary workers and farmers (Hua Kuo Feng, 1979).

A summary of developments in the last decade will reveal the central importance of the Two Lines in the drawing of class and power relationships. The direction and velocity of change there should help in an understanding of current judicial practice and in comprehending future trends and events.

The stakes of struggle in the 1970s: class and power

As the upheavals of the Cultural Revolution ended with compromise and reform, one could detect important advances toward social equality. The "piece rate" system of payment had been abolished along with most individual bonuses and the 18-grade urban wage scale was collapsed somewhat in favour of the lower grades. In the countryside the 8-level wage scale, also based on occupation, was levelled off with rises for the poorer farmers and by the awarding of extra points to those judged by their fellow workers to be most co-operative and helpful in group projects. The "private plots" and "free markets" which had grown quite important in the rural economy were restricted, halting the deepening stratification of the rural population as a consequence of this limited capitalism (Whyte, 1974; Diao, 1970, pp.64-67; Tiewes, 1974, pp.337-39).

Educational policy is of central importance in a nation long ruled by an arrogant Mandarin scholar elite, and where gaps between the educated and the ordinary peasants are still enormous. The Cultural Revolution, of course, began in the schools with disputes over admission, curriculum and the relationship of students to teachers and administrators. By 1970 new reform policies specified that almost all middle school graduates should work for two or three years in the countryside, with their later admission to university determined not only by grades, but by the recommendations of their fellow workers (Hsia, A., 1972, pp.153-58, 177, 185). The "Red and expert" ideal was emphasized in courses of political study, criticism/self-criticism sessions, and in the insistence that students and teachers engage in some regular manual labour. The universities were directed to concentrate recruitment efforts among peasant and working youths, offsetting somewhat the advantages of those from more affluent cadre or intellectual backgrounds (Mao Tse-tung, 1970; Pfeffer, 1975; Cheng Shih yi, 1976).

The political system was profoundly changed with the formation of Revolutionary Committees which held power in urban production centres, municipal bureaucracies and schools. These committees included representatives of local mass organizations, along with Party officials, government officials, and military and technical specialists (Pfeffer, 1972; Townsend, 1974, pp.35-7). Grass roots associations of workers, women and students were strengthened and a new leadership was chosen often from among those most active as critics in the previous year's struggles. The Communist Party membership shifted, with many of the conservatives being demoted or transferred and a host of younger radicals added or advanced (Salaff, 1975, pp.3-19; Lee Hong Yung, 1978).

The "Gang of Four" itself reflected these changes, including three who had risen as rebel leaders of the Shanghai "power seizure". Chiang Ching, much more than "the wife of Mao", was promoter of new revolutionary art forms; and Wang Hung Wen was the fiery leader of the Shanghai textile workers. At 39 he was by far the youngest person ever to sit on the Central Committee of the Communist Party. Mao's own sympathies were obvious as he stood in Peking's Tien An Mien Square wearing a Red Guard arm band and he repeatedly appeared at the side of Wang Hung Wen (Lee Hong Yung, 1978, pp.146-49; Hinton, H., 1969, pp.40-44).

The radicals, understanding the determination of their conservative opponents, fought against revisionism to the very end. In 1976 they denounced efforts to turn back Cultural Revolution reforms in the Party's journal, *Red Flag* (19th February), as follows:

> The capitalist roaders energetically peddle the economic thinking of the bourgeoisie, saying that science and technology are more important

[than the mass line] . . . they advocate letting experts run factories . . .
support material incentives . . . oppose the activation of both central and
local initiatives and re-impose the practice of direct central control . . . lay
one-sided stress on things big and foreign and oppose self-reliance.

Within weeks of Mao's death the Four found themselves under house arrest,
stripped of power and isolated from their followers who were themselves the
object of a massive purge and a continuing campaign of vitriolic criticism.
Within a few months the new leadership had stabilized, now including Teng
Hsiao Peng and many others once bitterly attacked by the radicals as "rightists".
Reporters in Peking described streets full of rejoicing after the fall of the Gang;
and even people numbed by the sudden revelations of Watergate were surprised
by the sudden turn of events in China (Lieken, 1979; Onate, 1978).

It should be pointed out that not everyone cheered the fall of the Four in
China. There were protest riots and strikes in Shanghai, Fukien and Hopeh
provinces and elsewhere, though these received less coverage by foreign
reporters and were barely admitted to in the Chinese press. The official reason
given for the fall was that the Four had systematically wrecked the economy and
organized a coup against the government. Any serious examination of these
charges shows that the first is untrue (MacDougall, 1977) and the second is
simply ludicrous (Bettleheim, 1978b).

There were, however, serious weaknesses in the leadership and programmes
put forward by the revolutionaries and these deserve some mention. It may well
be that too much dependence upon the support of Mao led to the neglect of
organizing work among those who gained the most from radical policies: the less
skilled and temporary workers in the cities and the poorer farmers. That the
Four as individuals were often bombastic and dogmatic, and identified with
rampaging Red Guards whose behaviour verged on the anarchic may explain
why they alienated nearly all the bureaucracy and the intellectuals, some of
whom might otherwise have been expected to support the left. Their radical
supporters in the middle levels of power were probably not sufficiently
experienced or attentive to practical and scientific considerations. Finally, the
fall of Lin Piao in 1971, who overstepped his responsibilities as chief of the
army, seems to have seriously discredited the left with the PLA and given power
to officers of the right and centre (Hinton, 1972, pp.82-9; Bridgham, 1968).

The rise of Hua Kuo Feng and Teng Hsiao Peng in the new ruling centre-right
coalition has resulted in an almost total overturning of the Cultural Revolution.
They have mobilized the Chinese media not only to slander the Gang of Four
with absurd lies and innuendo, but also to attack radical ideology, intimidate the
remaining left opposition and fundamentally rewrite modern China's history.

Material incentives and individual bonuses have once again become the order
in China, with wage gaps widening, especially between ordinary workers and the
favoured intellectuals and officials. Piece work payment and the use of temporary

low paid rural labour in the cities is once more common, with the new leadership claiming that "efficiency has shot up" (Sun Yeh fang, 1979). In the countryside private plots and "free markets" are encouraged, leading to considerable inequality especially since smaller families receive proportionately more land. As farmers turn to concentrate on family plots and economic differences among them grow, collective work and unity can only decline. The class implications in all of this are clear and the leadership informs people that:

> The policy of more pay for more work reflects the objective law of socialist development. Any violation brings on retribution.

> Differences in skill and work should be reflected in the pay of the workers and those making outstanding contributions should be given extra material rewards (Li Hong Rin, 1979)

Education and the role of the intellectuals has been reversed even more drastically. A new system of standardized nationwide examinations is now administered to graduates of middle schools, with places for only 2-5% in the handful of universities. Since Chinese schools are financed entirely by local resources, children from poorer communes and industrial centres will be less well prepared for the exams than will those attending better urban schools attached to bureaux, universities and industrial plants. Those who fail the exams will be sent off to work in the countryside, with little chance of returning for higher education. Workers and farmers will no longer choose university candidates from among their co-workers (Pincus, 1979).

The intellectuals, both academic and technological, have been granted new prominence and are released from the ethical restraints of the "Red and expert" ideal (Hua Kuo Feng, 1979). Changes in the class composition of the student body are paralleled by increases in the wages of teachers, who were already one of the best paid group of workers in the country (Pepper, 1977). Teng Hsiao Peng recently declared:

> . . . teachers hold the key to a school's success. We must raise the political and social status of the people's teachers. We must seriously study teachers' wage scales. Proper steps should be taken to encourage people to devote their lives to education (Teng Hsiao Peng, 1978)

The new leadership has declared China's historic problem of intellectual arrogance suddenly resolved. The obligation of intellectuals to engage in political study/self-criticism and occasional manual labour has been abolished (Dittmar, 1973). That this runs counter to historic experience and Maoist traditions is rather openly acknowledged as, for example, in recent editorials from the Party's national press organ:

> In the wake of the emphasis of our Party's work being shifted to moderniz-
> ation, it has become increasingly important and urgent for a comprehensive
> and accurate understanding of the Party's policy toward intellectuals and for
> bringing their role into full play . . . some comrades, however, do not have a
> corresponding understanding . . . some ask if the Party's policy of uniting,
> educating, and remoulding the intellectuals still applies, now that the over-
> whelming majority are part of the working class. The intellectuals are no
> longer objects to be united with, educated and remoulded . . . leading
> comrades . . . must listen earnestly to the opinion of scientists and tech-
> nicians (JMJP, 2nd February, 1979)

Political authority has become increasingly bureaucratic and divorced from the
methods of the "mass line". Correspondingly, the political role of the populace
has been restricted and routinized. The Revolutionary Committees have been
replaced by professional administrators appointed by the state in almost all
production sites and municipalities. The mass organizations in the neighbourhoods, schools and workplaces have declined in terms of influence and mass
participation (Butterfield, 1978). Along with the purge of its younger and more
radical leaders, the Party has increasingly emphasized discipline within its ranks
(Lee Hong Yung, 1978, pp.81-7, 142-8; Yang yi, 1979). Young members from
the rebellious generation of the Cultural Revolution today face a dramatic
rightward shift and are advised that:

> We must consciously uphold Party rules and regulations and enforce strict
> party disciplines. Disciplinary measures must be taken against all violators . . .
>
> . . . of 36 million odd members of our Party, nearly one half joined the Party
> since the Cultural Revolution. They need to be educated in fundamental
> knowledge about the Party and in Party discipline (*Hung Ch'i*, 2nd February,
> 1979)

The ideological and class composition of the Party has changed considerably.
Thousands of cadres once denounced and demoted as "rightists" have been
"rehabilitated" and returned to posts of leadership. New members are
increasingly chosen from among the intellectuals and technologists or from
among the offspring of party or government cadres. In discussing the recent
selection of "representatives" to the National People's Congress, Party
commentators included both of these privileged elites together with the workers
and farmers when calculating the percentage of cadres chosen from "working-
class" origins. Save for the remnants of the old landlord and capitalist classes,
China today does not acknowledge any social contradictions based on economics.
As one of the leading official theoreticians noted:

> . . . there is no basic conflict of economic interests among the people,
> although there are partial contradictions . . . this kind of contradiction

can be resolved by self regulation of the socialist system (Shang Zhe, 1979)

The new revisionist ideology defines the state and Party in a bureaucratic role as the central co-ordinator and efficiency expert, rather than a catalyst for mass mobilization and egalitarian reform. The break with revolutionary tradition and the widening inequalities create potentially explosive tensions. To secure their position the new regime must neutralize the Maoist ideals and radical activists who comprise their real and potential opposition. The left must be branded as "anarchists" and contained by laws. This repressive threat is implicit along with promises for increased production in the mass media, official speeches and public rallies. The following recent excerpt from the Party's official daily is typical:

> A characteristic of anarchism is that it opposes centralization and authority, rejects leadership and discipline, and is interested in "absolute democracy" and "absolute freedom". To make personal gains some people take the promise of democracy as a pretext to neglect laws and make trouble, even going to the extent of violating normal social order and upsetting the highly favourable situation of stability and unity.

> What is the contradiction in the socialist mode of production? . . . contradictions commonly observed are . . . between social production on the one hand and the growing material and cultural needs of the members of society, along with the need for change and development on the other . . . the main thing is continually to increase labour productivity (JMJP, 12th August, 1979)

Political Contest and Judicial Policy

The Two Line Struggle and the recent triumph of revisionism is nowhere more evident than in the history of law and judicial policy. As I have noted elsewhere (Brady, 1974, 1977a), China has in fact developed two systems of justice reflecting the different ideas and social forces which lie behind the larger conflict in the national political economy. These I have described as the "popular" and "bureaucratic" models, and I need not repeat here the details of their philosophy, organization, history and practice, save to summarize the essential elements of difference which have remained since Mao's death.

The "bureaucratic" model is a natural consequence of the conservative notion that the Chinese revolution has been completed. Advocates argue that law is necessary to consolidate past gains, regulate future changes, ensure the steady development of production and protect state authority (Tung Pi Wu, 1956; Peng Zhen, 1979). A set of regular justice bureaucracies, including the courts, police and Procurate, share legal power in a check and balance arrangement designed to protect due process and maintain social order (Li, 1973; Lubman, 1969). The agencies are staffed by professionals and administered by specialists trained in the "Science of law and jurisprudence" (Liu Shao chi, 1957; Peng Zhen, 1979). Freedom for the citizenry is legally defined in terms of individual rights and prescribed judicial procedures. Crime is defined in terms of specific acts punishable by fixed penal sanctions (IPLR, 1958).

The popular model is tied to the radical ideals of continuing revolution, the mass line and self-reliance. Its adherents have resisted codification, arguing that China is yet in a transitional state and that current social arrangements should not be formalized in law while serious inequalities continue (Hsiang Shih, 1968; Stankhe, 1966). The mass organizations grouping workers, farmers, women and neighbourhood residents play a major role in both routine peace keeping and in the "mass supervision" of government and local authorities through "ongoing rectification" and periodic "mass campaigns" (Brady, 1977a, b). Justice professionals are expected to work closely with citizen activists and to maintain procedures which are informal and open to popular participation (IPLR, 1958; Lubman, 1967). Freedom is implicitly defined in social terms, as in the levelling of wage and status differences, the broadening of opportunities, and the responsiveness and democratic style of leadership. Crime is considered not so much in terms of a specific act as in the attitudes and motives of the offender, and political education is a central part of both crime control, investigation and rehabilitation (Li, 1973; Brady, 1977a).

The dialectic of co-operation and confrontation between these two systems of justice has continued through the decade of the 1970s. On the one hand there is fundamental agreement that certain forms of behaviour, such as robbery, assault, corruption and adultery, are criminal and intolerable. The justice professionals and the citizen volunteers co-operate quite effectively in handling such problems as in the combined efforts of volunteer security defence teams and the local police, or in the continuing role of lay People's Assessors in the People's Courts. Likewise, the mass organizations help with crime prevention through their efforts in the mediation of local disputes and in the process of criticism/self-criticism within small groups which seeks to overcome egoism and aggression (Lubman, 1967; Cohen, 1971).

On the other hand, conflict between the two justice models has been fairly continuous varying from quiet disputes over jurisdiction and procedure to sometimes violent struggles in the course of mass rectification campaigns (Leng, 1967). The Cultural Revolution shattered the judicial system perhaps more completely than any other institution of government, leaving the courts isolated, the lawyers' offices abandoned, the police weakened and insecure, and the Procurate almost moribund. All of these agencies were sharply criticized by radical activists for their elitism, overemphasis on formality, isolation from the masses and, most pointedly, for their repression of Red Guard students and Red

Rebel workers in the early months of the upheavals (Brady, 1974, pp.310-28). More than a few judges were dragged from their offices to be subjected to mass criticism at open "struggle meetings". Procurators, judges and some police officials were hustled off to May 7th Schools for ideological reform and manual labour in substantial numbers (Pfeffer, 1977; Casella, 1973). The National Police Chief was one of these national officials subjected to the most unrelenting criticism, and high officials in the Ministries of Justice and Public Security were sacked or transferred. Efforts to professionalize the legal system were dealt a serious blow with the closure of law schools and legal institutes (Cohen, 1973a,b, 1979; Lee Hong Yung, 1978, pp.117-19).

Some sort of compromise judicial system seemed to be in the offing at the time of Mao Tse-tung's death in 1976. The Constitution of 1975 emphasized the importance of the mass line in legal procedures, and the abolition of the highly specialized and bureaucratic Procurate continued the anti-professionalism of the Cultural Revolution (NPC, 1975, Wang Hsiao t'ing, 1978). Though the courts were restored to formal authority, the judiciary had been broadened to include great numbers of citizen activists who rose to prominence in the mass rectification movement. Judicial procedure in the reopened courts was considerably less formal, especially in the lower courts, with few prosecuting or defence lawyers present and representatives of mass organizations playing a prominent role in both the investigative and trial process (Edwards, 1977). In interviews with Western scholars Chinese judges and legal officials described procedures as follows:

> . . . our practice is to integrate the mass line and work specialized organiz-
> ations. When a case comes up, the judicial working personnel will go deep
> among the masses and carry out the investigation and research to identify the
> truth and . . . check out the evidence and ask the masses for their views. The
> court gives the final judgement when this work is done, when the facts are
> clear . . . When a case is influential or bears important educational signifi-
> cance, the materials of the case will be distributed to the public. . . . The
> masses can then hold a discussion on the case and put forward suggestions
> (Ruge, 1976)

The police were likewise enjoined to leave their offices and work more closely with representatives of the mass organizations in peace-keeping work. Police ranks were thinned by demotions or temporary removal of publicly criticized cadres to the May 7th Schools. The army was in the process of withdrawing from active peace-keeping, but still served important functions (Lambe, 1974). Indeed, it appears that many of the radicals intended that the militia (as a volunteer force drawn directly from the local community) might replace or at least complement the professional public security forces. In perhaps the most dramatic event to precede the fall of the four central committee radicals, it was the militia, and not the police which put down the Tien An Mien square riots in which the first organized opposition to the Four became visible (Ting Wang, 1978).

If the handling of ordinary "street" crime had been somewhat consolidated in a new working relationship between the courts, police and mass organizations, the handling of political conflicts was still very much undecided and at issue. The 1975 Constitution was in part an attempt to build mass line principles into bureaucratic procedures, but the whole previous history of the legal agencies indicates that "self-regulation" has not prevented the drift towards elitism and rigidity. The rather disappointing history of citizen–professional collaboration in the work of the People's supervisory committees would also point to the need for a continuing direct mass role in overviewing and guiding local officials and administrators. The Revolutionary Committees which controlled schools, factories and local government through the early 1970s provided this line of popular influence, through the "three-in-one" combination of PLA, Party and mass organizations in leadership triumvirates. Likewise, the infrastructure of committees, mass meetings and criticism/self-criticism sessions which compromised "ongoing rectification" helped to keep the egalitarian principles of the Cultural Revolution alive in the day to day operations of schools and work centres (Hinton, H., 1969). All of these measures, as well as the May 7th Schools, were designed to maintain revolutionary standards for government and social relations (Pfeffer, 1972).

The problem with these measures is that China has neither the fiscal nor personnel resources available to permit a thorough reorganization of leadership and must for its survival continue to rely on a considerable degree of centraliz- ation. The citizen activists in policy-making bodies were often unqualified by education or experience, and in a country like China the gaps between specialist and citizen are often enormous. To the extent that the demands of citizens in the rectification process of administrative councils were unrealistic, they served only to alienate intellectuals and officials. Finally, it is clear that the new reforms were gradually bureaucratized and removed from the effective influence of either the public or the revolutionary principles of the Cultural Revolution. Thus, for example, the May 7th Schools lost their cutting edge as a disruptive and challenging experience with semi-penal overtones to become a more relaxed and routine part of bureaucratic training by the mid-1970s (Tiewes, 1974).

Recognizing these difficulties and the continuing existence of wide social inequalities even after the Cultural Revolution, the radicals were reluctant to entrust the political and legal future of the country to even a reformed set of laws and bureaucracies. Despite the urgings of the resurgent conservatives in the early 1970s, the leftists continued to drag their feet on codification. The law schools were typically the last departments to reopen in the nation's universities after the Cultural Revolution. Legal officials lingered at May 7th Schools and anti-professionalism was still part of their language in official interviews (Cohen, 1973a; Hao Hsuang Lu, 1975; Lambe, 1974).

Most important and most controversial was the leftist insistence that mass campaigns remain as a part of the political vocabulary and an option for mass participation. While the campaigns were not recognized in the 1974 Constitution, few officials dared speak of China's history or its current situation without a compulsory bow to the advances brought about by the Cultural Revolution and earlier campaigns. The radicals also insisted upon the continuing rectification process through public challenge and demonstration. As one leftist advocate argued in a prominent legal journal:

> The masses, through the method of great blooming and contending, the writing of wall posters, the presentation of facts and the discussion of reasons, advance the People's democracy . . . the democratic debate on the part of the masses is not only the correct method for handling contradictions among the people, but it is also the method to solidify and educate the people to wage struggle against the enemy. It can thus be seen that the mass movement has tremendous vitality in the correct application of jurisdiction. The rightist fallacy that "mass movements undermine the legal system" is entirely baseless and a malicious slander. Such a fallacy only proves that they are afraid of the mass movement (Hsiang Shih, 1968).

Challenges such as these reasserted both the *theoretical* basis of popular justice, i.e. principles of "continuing revolution" and Mao's writings on the "correct handling of contradictions"; and the *practical* outlets for mass action beyond the limits of the legal bureaucracies. It is significant that the person chosen by the Central Committee to succeed Mao Tse-tung as Premier in 1976 was Hua Kuo Feng, a relatively unknown figure whose most important previous experience was as the national chief of the reformed police bureaucracy. Hua has been generally described as a "centrist" in the Two Line Struggle, who, like the police force he led, has tried to steer clear of the political battles continuing after the Cultural Revolution (Butterfield, 1977; Ting Wang, 1978). No such middle ground could be found in politics or in justice, however.

Attack from the Right and the New Legal Order as a Political Weapon

It was the uniformed professionals of police unit 4831 who burst into the homes of the Four radical leaders to arrest them soon after Mao's death. While defending the Four, Mao's nephew and the commander of the Peking workers militia were killed. The action of this most centrally controlled police unit indicated the formation of a new and repressive centre-right coalition. In planning a counter-attack that never materialized, the radicals counted heavily on the popularly recruited militia; but it remained inactive, neutralized by shock and bereft of leadership (Onate, 1978). Within a few months a national purge had removed or demoted hundreds of radicals at the middle levels of government and Party. A national campaign of vilification has continued against the Four, the Cultural Revolution, radical supporters and their ideas. The protest strikes and riots which followed in 1976-78 in Fukien, Kiangsi, and Shanghai were brought to heel by stern police action (Hua Kuo Feng, 1979).

Once again, justice has become both a central subject and object of political contest. Though the Four and their supporters were arrested without formal legal procedures, the government has moved quickly to fashion a new legal system along lines more thoroughly bureaucratic and professional than ever before. Indeed, the chief claims of the new regime to legitimacy are its commitment to economic modernization and legalization. In distinguishing itself from the radicals and the whole tradition of revolutionary politics, the new elite claim to act in the interests of the Chinese masses:

> Having had enough of a decade of turmoil caused by Lin Biao and the Gang of Four, the people want law and order more than anything else. Democratization and legalization which the Chinese people have long been yearning for, are now gradually becoming a reality. Political democracy protected by the legal system will certainly give a powerful impetus to the early realization of modernization (JMJP, 20th July, 1979)

The regime has claimed that the new laws and legal bureaus established or reorganized under their leadership offer new prospects for freedom and progress in China. They point to the new Constitution of 1978, new criminal and civil codes with pride and cite China as an outstanding example of "human rights" (Lung Yun, 1978).

Closer examination reveals that the new legal system is not an expression of social consensus but protracted conflict. The new codes are primarily designed to restrict dissent and to guarantee the increasingly unequal property relations. In many cases the penal codes are pointedly written to outlaw precisely those tactics which were used so successfully by the left during the Cultural Revolution. For example, the new criminal law enacted in January 1980 stipulates a term of detention or imprisonment of up to three years for anyone who:

1) uses threats or violence to obstruct a state functionary from carrying out his lawful duties;

2) disturbs public order by any means;

3) gathers a crowd which seriously disturbs public order at a railroad, bus station, airport, department store, or any public site;

4) flagrantly disrupts public order by gathering a crowd to engage in an affray;

5) commits acts of vandalism against cultural relics or historic sites protected by the state (PR, 17th August, 1979)

The Cultural Revolution, of course, began with student gatherings in public centres and attacks on religious shrines which they considered to be remnants of feudal superstition. The Red Guards later travelled by commandeered trains or buses to carry dissent to other towns, often ending with noisy demonstrations encircling local government or Party offices. Another important tactic has been the writing and posting of "big character posters" and "wall newspapers" critical of local authorities (*Hung Ch'i*, 30th March, 1967; JMJP, 16th June, 1968). These practices are also increasingly restricted and criminalized (*NY Times*, 15th, 22nd, 26th November, 1979). Following small protest demonstrations in March 1979 in Peking and Shanghai, the local authorities pronounced almost identical decrees against political dissent. These decrees virtually nullify the guarantees of free individual expression in the 1978 Constitution, as they proclaimed:

In order to strengthen the Socialist Legal System and protect the people's democratic rights, the Security Bureau with the approval of the municipal committee, issued a notice to the effect that participants in public assemblies and demonstrations must obey the direction of the People's police and that no one is allowed to intercept trains, create disturbances in government institutions or stir up troubles.

It is also stipulated that except in designated places, no one is allowed to put up slogans, posters, or wall newspapers on public buildings and the printing and selling of reactionary or pornographic books, journals and pictures are prohibited.

. . . owing to the pernicious influence of anarchism of the last ten years and more, some people mistake democracy for absolute individual freedom and they oppose all kinds of discipline and authority. While much of this influence is still in evidence today, many people are not accustomed to exercising their democratic rights or do not know how to use them in a correct way (JMJP, 6th April, 1979)

Of course, there were more than a few outrages and miscarriages of justice committed by Red Guards, police and courts in the heat of the Cultural Revolution (Fan, 1968, pp.130-40), and the new regime has cited this as reason for creating a new "socialist legality" (Munro, 1977; *Hung Ch'i*, 1st June, 1979; Butterfield, 1977). But the limited and precarious "freedom of expression" allowed by Peking's "Democracy Wall" must be compared with the larger policies of repression (Matthews, 1979; Butterfield, 1979; JMJP, 17th October, 1979). Most recently, too, another Cultural Revolution practice was marked out for elimination when the "National Conference on Judicial Work" convened by the Supreme Court resolved that:

> slander against a person's character . . . such as subjecting people to criticism at one public meeting after another and parading them on the streets as a form of public humiliation, must be abolished (PR, 16th August, 1979).

The judges' resolution was followed by the inclusion of new prohibitions in the criminal code. The new law is summarized by Peng Zhen, the Director of Legal Affairs for the National People's Congress, as follows:

> The Draft Criminal Law stipulates that, whoever insults another person by violent or other means, including the use of 'big character posters' or 'small character posters' or fabrication of facts to libel another person, to a serious degree, shall be sentenced to imprisonment for not more than three years or to detention.

> We must defend the right to criticism and counter-criticism, to refute opposing views in discussion . . . all of which must be strictly distinguished from libel and insults (Peng Zhen, 1979)

One needs little imagination to guess whom such new laws and proposals are designed to protect. Certainly it is not the ordinary citizens who are likely to be the focus of mass criticism at a public meeting or demonstrations, rallies and critical wall posters. The whole history of "mass campaigns" and "ongoing rectification" bears witness that these have been key forms of political dissent and popular justice action mounted against elitist or corrupt officials and intellectuals (Bennett, 1977; Brady, 1974).

Along with codification, the new regime has greatly expanded and professionalized the justice bureaucracies, with a corresponding decline in mass participation. It is highly significant that the government chose Chao Tse ang, Ching Hua and Huang hao ch'ing to be respectively, the new national chiefs of the courts, police and revitalized Procurate. All three men had been singled out for criticism and public censure during the Cultural Revolution and all three were removed from lower offices in the legal system. Their sudden "rehabilitation" and promotion is a clear indication of new rightist trends in the legal system (Wang Hsiao T'ing, 1978, pp.59-60). The legal profession was also sharply criticized for its arrogance and elitism in the past and as the Director of a leading legal research institute noted: "To this day many people in our profession have misgivings and are reluctant to return to practice" (Lin Heng Yuan, 1979).

Evidently their comeback is well underway, with a tremendous expansion of reopened law schools and training institutes enrolling thousands of new students (Lie Jie Gonng, 1979).

The legal process has become increasingly formal. Lawyers have replaced the representatives of mass organizations in presenting evidence and arguments at trials. Citizen participation is restricted to a secondary role as People's Assessors. Echoing the views of earlier bureaucrats, the current Minister of Justice believes legal decision-making to be beyond public capacity, as he argued that ". . . judicial work involves a high degree of thinking and is different from production work in a factory or mine" (PR, 10th August, 1979). Along with their elevated status and occupational prominence, justice professionals (along with other officials and intellectuals) have been receiving increased salaries and privileges. The previous insistence that judges, lawyers and law students engage in periodic manual labour and political education to combat elitist tendencies has been dropped along with the "Red and expert" ideals (PR, 17th August, 1979).

The regulation of government, like social order, is left increasingly to the professionals. The Procurate has been reconstituted and greatly expanded to meet its official role as the overseer of police and courts. While the Procurate is supposed to be responsible to both its own bureaucratic hierarchy and the various local People's Congress representatives, in fact the Congress is not and never has been sufficiently active to provide such regular guidance. The Procurate proudly announced (Gong Zeng, 1979) that in 1979 its various staff members had reviewed thousands of cases and reversed some 2000 instances of violation of the law by courts or police. The Procurate also received over 270,000 complaints from citizens (PR, 17th August, 1979), but the numbers are hardly impressive in comparison with the scale of complaints lodged during periods of mass rectification campaigns, and in the past the Procurate has never been sufficiently strong or committed to energetic supervision of the far more powerful police and court bureaucracies (Ginsberg and Stahnke, 1964). Finally, there is the inherent limitation in the nature of the Procurate's review and its available options for redress of grievances. The Procurate reviews other agencies only in terms of their conformity to specified legal procedures, not the broader and more ambitious dictates of revolutionary principles such as the mass line (NPC, 1978). Such a legalistic review leaves little place for citizen involvement, and the Procurate's action can extend no further than the reversal of individual decisions made by police courts or other bureaus. The Procurate is not empowered to consider or correct overall problems of citizen–professional relations or general failings of agencies such as bureaucratic isolation or elitism.

Revisionist Economics, International Capital
and the Role of Law

The new legal system serves not only to control dissent and centralize state power but also serves to extend and standardize the Peking regime's modernization strategies. The government has decisively broken with Maoist traditions by reducing worker participation in favour of "expert" management, by relying on increased material incentives, encouraging peasant capitalism, by regarding profitability as the central criterion for evaluation of production units, and by inviting large-scale foreign investment by capitalist firms and borrowing from capitalist nations. Each of these turns in policy has been confirmed in new legal statutes and contracts, and the new constitution guarantees against any further redistribution of property. The writing of economic strategies into the law helps to reassure both the emerging Chinese economic elite and Western investors and creditors. The contrasts between the current emphasis on legalism and the policies of the Maoist era is illuminating.

It should be remembered that the Chinese Maoists were always reluctant to adopt extensive or finalized legal codes precisely because they were still dissatisfied with continuing inequalities and vestiges of capitalism in Chinese society. Wu Tu peng argued during the Great Leap Forward that:

> A time of radical social change is not the time to codify laws . . . Law is the armour of the social system. If, for example, laws pertaining to property had been codified during the co-operative stage of agriculture they would now be quite out of date, since the commune movements have altered the whole basis of ownership (Greene, 1962a, p.187)

Today, in a time of renewed emphasis on material incentives, widened wage gaps and peasant capitalism, the government has undertaken to finalize property relations (Jiang Hua and Huang Huonging, 1979). The erosion of egalitarian commitments was already apparent in the language of the 1975 Constitution, and the Constitution of 1978 further legitimizes private production and brakes the process of collectivization in favour of individual incentive (Cohen, 1979, pp.806-9; NPC, 1975, 1978). The new Penal Code was introduced in 1979 by Peng Zhen with the forthright assertion that:

> One of the major purposes of the criminal law was to defend socialist property owned by the whole people and by the collective and the legitimate property of individuals, including income savings, houses and other means of livelihood, and means of production such as plots of land, animals and trees owned or used by an individual or family according to law.

The discipline of labour is a central concern of the new legal order. While radicals have tended to rely on political education and mobilization of energies through mass organizations, the new regime has followed the bureaucratic tradition of creating new regulatory laws and agencies. The new Constitution of 1978 specifies that one of the "duties" of Chinese citizens is "to maintain labour discipline"; and accompanying reports by national officials stress the need for "unity and iron discipline" among workers. This contrasts with the 1975 Constitution which contained no such language and which included, for the first time, the right to strike (NPC, 1978). Mao Tse-tung had earlier remarked that "Strikes and boycotts are means of struggle against bureaucracy . . . When the use of struggle by criticism cannot solve the problem, we must allow the strike to be used" (Cohen, 1979, p.833).

The formal legal contract has become the new basis of relationships between the central government and local units of production. The individual plant or commune manager is recognized as the sole authority in these contracts which exclude the increasingly passive mass organizations from decision-making. The highly paid professional managers are evaluated almost entirely on the basis of profits earned by their enterprises, with little concern for such Maoist goals as egalitarian wage levelling or democratic participation. New laws have also established "work standards" to be enforced by the newly created "Economic Divisions" of intermediate courts. These courts are empowered both to settle labour management disputes through mediation and to punish those guilty of "seriously defective or shoddy work, neglect of duty, embezzlement" or other offences involving heavy economic losses or breaches of authority (PR, 10th August, 1979). The tone of these policies and the direction for the future is unmistakeable in the official announcement of labour legislation in 1977:

> Rules and regulations ought never to be eliminated. Moreover, with the developmnt of production and technology, rules and regulations must become stricter and people must follow them more precisely. This is the law of nature (PR, *in* Bettleheim, 1978b)

China's growing alliance with capitalist nations and her blooming partnerships with multi-national corporations have also been formalized. The legal contract has become the new standard of measurement for production and new laws guarantee foreign investors sizeable advantages and only limited controls by the Chinese government. A corporation need only invest a minimum capital share of 25% to qualify for two years' initial tax exemption and partial tax refunds for later reinvestment. The lack of any limits above 25% means that a multi-national company could legally take 100% of the profits produced from the use of Chinese labour and materials. Legal guarantees against nationalization imply that multi-national exploitation of the country could become a permanent feature. The economic plans developed by the new leadership lay heavy stress on the importation of Western technology and capital investment; yet there is no mention of potential social and political contradictions. We are thus confronted with the astonishing prospects of a socialist government committed to enforcement of increasingly strict labour regulations to ensure the profits and production of foreign-controlled capitalist firms.

In summarizing the politics and motivations of the new legal order it would be unfair to ignore China's imperative need for stability and central direction of what is still a backward and precarious economy. Likewise, it is certain that the intellectuals and professionals need some reassurance and encouragement after the shock of criticism and sanction in the Cultural Revolution. There is nothing inherently repressive about disciplinary regulations or necessarily exploitive about limited foreign investment. Certainly, too, the "cult of Mao" contributed to immaturity and adventurism among many of the radical young cadres and activists. The excesses of the Cultural Revolution and China's historic xenophobia did require constructive criticism and correction, perhaps in the form of new codes and a stabilized legal system.

What has occurred, however, is far more than that. The most important principles of Maoist thought and the most progressive reform policies have been overturned. The elimination of revolutionary committees and the weakening of mass organizations leaves the bureaucracy without an effective popular counterweight. The rewriting of history and the practical rejection of revolutionary ideologies such as mass line and the continuing revolution has weakened the theoretical base of popular activism and reform even as its organizational means have been eliminated. The intimidation and purge of radical cadres from the national to the local level further releases the established elite from the constraints of challenge and criticism. All of the political and legal changes are paralleled by increased inequality resulting from the emphasis on material incentives, hierarchical rigidity and limited rural capitalism. China is not merely facing a problem of ideological conservatism, but the threatened emergence of a new and exploitive ruling class. While this is not yet an accomplished fact, it cannot be reversed by the moderate means of criticism/self-criticism and elite re-education.

Legitimizing the New State and the Promise of "Individual Rights"

The revisionist leadership hopes that the new legal system will both strengthen their popular legitimacy and their effective powers. They have organized a national "mass campaign" of their own design which features public readings of the new laws and lectures by legal professionals (Ye Jian Ying, 1979). The laws and accompanying lectures have for months dominated the newspaper columns, broadcasts and public speeches (Hua Kuo Feng, 1979; *Hung Ch'i*, 4th May, 1979). Yet there is much in these laws which contradicts public needs. Not only do the new laws cement existing social inequalities and power relations, but they strengthen new alliances, especially those which conservative officials would make with the intellectual class and the capitalist nations. The laws and the re-established justice agencies have undertaken to repress political dissent and to enforce labour discipline. Yet the new economic policies can only lead to greater domestic dissatisfaction. The current emphasis on professionalism and formality in justice agencies and procedures is paralleled by the increased centralization of decision-making and the decline of citizen participation in both peace-keeping and political expression.

The change from revolutionary to revisionist policies is perhaps crystallized in the new concept of freedom advanced in the 1978 Constitution and the regime's official statements. The notion of freedom implicit in popular justice and the Maoist tradition is a clearly social one, measured by the velocity of egalitarian change and the responsiveness of government to the public community. This rebellious and restless definition of freedom has been carried on the banners of the Long March, the Great Leap Forward and the Cultural Revolution. It was still present even in the compromise Constitution of 1975 which contained the following passage:

> Article 13: Speaking out frankly, airing views fully, holding great debates and writing big character posters are new forms of carrying on socialist revolution created by the masses of the people. The state shall ensure to the masses the right to use these forms to create a political situation in which there are both centralism and democracy, both discipline and freedom, both unity of will and personal ease of mind and liveliness, and so help consolidate the leadership of the Communist Party of China over the state and consolidate the dictatorship of the proletariat (NPC, 1975, p.17)

The new leadership has promised the people "individual rights" protected with new guarantees for free expression and due process under the law (Li Bo yon, 1979). Thus far, the record indicates that these guarantees are hardly binding in the case of serious dissent. However, even in its idealized form this kind of freedom is bourgeois in theory, and sterile in practice. It fragments liberty into pieces of personal rights and privilege and makes government answerable only to its own laws and regulatory bodies rather than to mass action and revolutionary principles. This notion of freedom is borrowed directly from the class societies of capitalism or revisionist socialism (as in the USSR).

The alternative revolutionary conception measures freedom in social terms by the extent of the "community control" which the people exercise over social institutions and by the movement toward equality in social relations and material conditions. The limits of liberty are not set in law, but in the dialectical interface of community organizations, Party and state. This more ambitious dimension of freedom is increasingly circumscribed by the present Hua Kuo Feng regime. The abolition of Revolutionary Committees and "ongoing rectification" has reduced public influence and led to a decline in mass participation. The widening of wage gaps, tightening of school admissions and rigidification of hierarchies in government and production means a lowering of horizons for most workers and peasants. The favoured intellectuals and the conservative bureaucrats have buried the radical opposition at the national level and seem now determined to bury Maoist principles with the Chairman himself. The Constitution of 1978 is intended as the tombstone of the continuing revolution and the invigorated justice bureaucracies are its pallbearers; but social contradictions are not as easily laid away as even the greatest of heroes.

Reflection on the Role of Law and Implications for China's Future

While I have argued that China is now on the road to revisionism and a new kind of ruling-class dominion, the present situation is still subject to change. For one thing, the conservative officials have not yet fully integrated the intellectual class into political leadership and class alliance. For another, there is yet a simmering of dissent and leftist sentiments remaining especially from the Great Leap and the Cultural Revolution. The revisionist leadership has promised to raise living standards substantially in the next few years, and failure to do this could lead to a drop in popular support expressed either in lower productivity from resentful workers or a renewed mobilization of criticism and rectification from the left.

Given the entrenched position of the new regime and the confirmation of present policies and power relations in statutes, it would doubtless take a massive upheaval on the scale of the Cultural Revolution to reverse present trends. The problem, from the left's view, is that such events have always been initiated and co-ordinated from the national level, to be then energized and implemented by the local cadres and activists. No such left leadership now exists at the national level. There are, however, certainly lines of division between the centrists (such as Hua Kuo Feng) and rightists (such as Teng Hsiao Peng). The police, PLA and some of the middle-level party cadres are generally counted today as aligned with the centre, while the intellectual class and large parts of the bureaucracy (including the courts and Procurate) could be expected to support the more conservative policies led by Teng. Should the revisionist policies fail to bear fruit in terms of domestic production and living standards, it is possible that the centre elite might lead the lower-level leftist cadres in a renewal of rectification.

The sudden reversals in China's "Season of Startling Alliance" have shocked many friends and foes of Maoist China alike, but only those first "illusioned" by political caricatures can easily be "dis-illusioned" by subsequent political events. The seeds of conflict have long been present in the contradictions of the Chinese political economy. There, recent events have underscored the volatile and complex nature of the transformation to socialism. Certainly the final outcome of a revolution is not determined by the initial seizure of power. Milovan Djilas (1957) has well described the evolution of revisionism and the "New Class" in the Soviet Union; and Mao Tse-tung (1956) warned of this possibility in China even before the Great Leap Forward. As Sweezy and Bettleheim so correctly observed:

> Without revolutionary enthusiasm and mass participation, centralized planning becomes increasingly authoritarian and rigid with resulting multiplication of economic difficulties and failures. In an attempt to solve these increasingly serious problems the rulers turn to capitalist techniques, vesting increasing power within the economic enterprises in managements and relying for their guidance and control more and more on the impersonal pressures of the market. Under these circumstances, the juridical form of state property becomes increasingly empty and the real power over the means of production, which is the essence of the ownership concept, gravitates into the hands of the managerial elite (Sweezy and Bettleheim, 1971, p.29)

The new Peking leaders and their appreciative supporters in the West now hope that the "anarchic" era of mass mobilization, political conflict and social experiment is past. The Chinese state now pursues "modernization" with single-minded zeal and by almost any means necessary. One can appreciate their impatience to reach industrial parity after China's long history of humiliation and threat at the hands of the West and, most recently, the USSR. However, the reformulation of national purposes ignores the social and moral aspect of socialist transformation and measures development only in steel tonnage and transport mileage. The dangers of this type of narrowness and expediency have been well recognized and described, not only by the defeated Maoist radicals, but also by other socialist nations emerging in the Third World. Che Guevara, in particular, pointedly rejected this falsely "practical" path to modernization for Cuba, insisting:

> There is still a long stretch to be covered in the construction of an economic base, and the temptation to take the beaten path of material interest as the lever of accelerated development is very great. There is the danger of not seeing the forest because of the trees. Pursuing the wild idea of trying to realize socialism with the worn-out weapons left by capitalism (the market place as the basic economic cell, profit making, individual material incentives, and so forth), one can arrive at a dead end. And one arrives there after having travelled a long distance with so many forked roads where it is difficult to receive the moment when the wrong path was taken. Meanwhile the adapted

economic base has undermined the development of consciousness. To construct communism simultaneously with the material base of our society, we must create a new man (Guevara, trans. in Bonachea and Valdes, 1969, p.256)

The Peking leadership has deliberately disregarded such observations and the weight of China's own revolutionary traditions in choosing the downhill path to modernization. Nothing so clearly expresses their determination as their haste in writing new political and economic principles into law.

The new legal order has been erected as both girder and facade for the revisionist state, its stratified social relations and expedient development strategies. New prohibitions against political dissent loom behind the official propaganda attack on radical Maoist ideas, the Gang of Four and followers, even Mao himself. State bureaucracies have been invested with sole regulatory power over administration and peace-keeping, while citizens organizations are disbanded or reduced to auxilliary roles. The managerial elite is freed from obligation to Maoist ethics and granted increased power under legal contract arrangements which equate success only with profitability. The increasingly uneven division of wealth is guaranteed against redistribution by new statutes, just as foreign investments and the exploitation of Chinese labour and resources are protected by new laws and judicial bodies.

In formulating a critique of the present Chinese legal order one returns to Marxist critiques of capitalist law and finds much that is sadly relevant. The layering of law as a protective and regulating armour upon an increasingly unequal and undemocratic social order has been described as a central feature of developed capitalism. Marx's own commentary was brief but cogent:

> It is furthermore clear that here as always it is in the interests of the ruling section of society to sanction the existing order as law and legally to establish its limits through usage and tradition . . . and such regulation and order are themselves indispensable elements of any mode of production, if it is to assume social stability and independence from mere chaos and arbitrariness (Marx, 1972, p.793)

The Soviet theorist Pashukanis (1978) described the capitalist state's reliance on formal law as an expression of social alienation born of class conflict. The state serves as the (falsely) neutral arbiter of conflict and laws define the obligation and duties of citizens whose sense of shared community is too weak to support social order on a more informal or organic basis. Pashukanis demonstrated that increasing reliance on law and formal administration was a feature of developing capitalism; but he recognized that law would continue as a diminishing part of the political vocabulary during the period of socialist transition as long as social isolation and fragmented consciousness remained.

Clearly the experience of the Soviet Union and recent events in China indicate that social isolation can not only continue, but even deepen if expedience sets the course of socialist transition and if "New Class" elites form to undermine egalitarian reform and democratic participation in decision-making. The state and its legal apparatus do not wither; but rather it is the revolutionary forms and organs of popular participation which become hollow and ultimately bureaucratic. Such has been the recent fate of the Revolutionary Committees, the rural communes and the various student, worker and urban community organizations in China. The Peking leadership's increasing reliance on law is necessary, then, not only to suppress radical dissent, regulate the domestic market economy, protect property relations and win public acceptance. Law must also provide some sort of framework of social obligation to replace the universals of Maoist ethics and the self-correcting dynamics of voluntary "self reliant" mass associations.

The closing argument here should not be construed as a condemnation of all law or as blanket praise for popular spontaneity and community autonomy. Such an anarchist position would be totally neglectful of China's pressing need to coordinate closely her meagre technical and capital resource. Moreover, law can serve revolutionary ends even as it now sets the course of revisionism; and China has provided an excellent example of the former. The early land reform statutes and marriage laws of the 1940s and 1950s were instruments of radical social change. The relations of property and marriage specified in those laws were far in advance of existing conditions and the laws both legitimized and accelerated the collectivization of land, reduction of class inequality and improvement of women's rights. The state threw its full weight behind these laws, but the mass organizations of peasants and women were also mobilized and strengthened through their direct role in the enforcement of the laws (see Meijer, 1971, pp.85–157 and Hinton, W., 1967). The new legal order now under construction in China owes nothing to these revolutionary legal traditions. It remains to be seen what it owes to the masses of Chinese working people as opposed to the looming power of an elitist "New Class".

References

I. Lists of Abbreviations cited in the Text

A. Organizations

CC-CCP Central Committee, Chinese Communist Party
CCP Chinese Communist Party
KMT Kuomintang (Chinese Nationalist) Party
NPC National People's Congress
PLA People's Liberation Army
PRC People's Republic of China

B. Translation services and serial publications

CB *China Broadcasts* (Summary of important radio and television media broadcasts, weekly).
CLG *Chinese Law and Government* (translations of selected legal and political writings from Chinese professional journals, speeches by major policy makers, selected press articles, quarterly).

CNA *China News Analysis*
CNIP *China News Internal Publications*
CNS *China News Service*
CSocAnth *Chinese Sociology and Anthropology*
All of the above are weekly summaries which provide translations of important articles from the national and regional newspapers, as well as some selected magazines.

FLP Foreign Language Press, Peking (official publishing house for People's Republic of China, provides translations of most important works by leading political figures, as well as legal documents, such as Constitutions or criminal codes).
NCNA New China News Agency, Peking (also HH, or "Hsin Hua" News Agency) (official national press service for overseas release).
JPRS Joint Publications Research Service (translations of important newspaper articles, magazines, and political, legal, social and cultural documents and literature).
SCMM *Survey of China Mainland Magazines* (translations from a variety of national magazines, often in excerpted form, weekly, published by US Consulate, Hong Kong).

SCMP *Survey of China Mainland Press* (translations of national and regional newspapers, weekly, published by US Consulate, Hong Kong).

URI Union Research Institute, Hong Kong (publishes a wide range of documentary collections and scholarly commentaries, in both occasional form, and in annual and quarterly journals or volumes, such as *Communist China* (annual) and *Communist China Problems of Research Series* (occasional)).

C. Chinese national and regional daily newspapers

CCJP Ch'eng chiang Jih Pao, Hankow
CFJP Chieh Fang Jih Pao, Shanghai
JFJP Jieh Fang Jih Pao, Peking
JMJP Jen Min Jih Pao, Peking (official Communist Party organ)
KMJP Kuang Ming Jih Pao
NFJP Nan Fang Jih Pao, Northeast
SHJP Shun hsi Jih Pao
STJP Sing Tao, Jih Pao, Hong Kong
SWJP Sin Win Jih Pao, Shanghai
SYJP Shen Yang Jih Pao
TCP Ta Chun Pao, Canton
TKP Ta kung Pao
WHP Wen Hai pao
WLP Wen Lui Pao, Shanghai

D. Chinese national and regional magazines

CKCN Chung kuo Ch'ing nien
CT Chang T'se (China Youth)
HH Hsueh Hsi (Study)
HHYP Hsin Hua Yueh Pao
JMCPS Jen Min Chiu Pen She, Peking
JMFC Jen Min fa Chih
PC *People's China* (English publication, also other foreign language)
PCKS Pei Chung Kung She
PR *Peking Review* (English and other foreign language weekly review)
SSST Shih-Shih Shou ts'e (Current Scene)
TF Tse fan
TKCK Tzu' kuo Cho-k'en

E. Professional journals and theoretical reviews

CFYC Cheng fa yen Chiu (Political-Legal Studies)
CHCC Chi Hua Ching Chi (Planned Economy)
FH Fa Hsueh (Study of Law)
FJC Feng Jo Ch'uan (Political-Legal Research)
HH Hsueh Hsi (Study)
Hung Ch'i (Red Flag) — official theoretical organ of Communist Party

JMCY Jen Min Chaio Yu (People's Education)
TCYC T'ung Chi Yen Chiu (Statistical Research)

F. Cultural Revolution era publications (Red Guard and revolutionary organizations)

CCK Chian ch'un Kuang (Shanghai Red Guards)
CKSJP Ching kanng shang Jih Pao (newspaper of Peking University Red Guard, perhaps the most famous and rebellious of all the Red Guard units)
CPY Chi' Pen Yen (Peking Red Guards)
FPLHH Fan P'eng Lo Hei hsien
HCNT Hsi chiang Nu t'ao (Wuchow Red Guards)
HHWP Hsueh Hung wei pao
HKK Hsin Kuang Kung (Canton Red Guards)
HPT Hsin Pei ta (Peking University Red Guards)
HWPP Hung wei Ping Pao
IEWCP I erh wu chun Pao (Canton Red Guards)
KCKKL Kung chiao Kung ko lien (Canton Red Guards)
KYCLCCTWTLCC Kuan yi ch'ing li chieh chi Tui-wu Tzu liao chuan chi (Wuhan Red Guards)
PHHP Pi Hsueh Huang po (Canton Red Guards)
SCLWCP San chun Lien Wei Chan pao (Canton Red Guards)
TFH Tung fa hung (Peking University Red Guards)
THPP Tung hsien peng Pao (Shanghai Red Guards)
WKTH Wen Ko T'ung hsin (Shanghai Red Guards)
WLWCFYC Wang Kuei wu Cheng fa yen chiu

II. Chinese and Western Reference Sources

The transliteration of Chinese names in the text follows the practices adopted by the official translation services in China. Therefore, the "Wade" system is employed throughout most of the book and for all Chinese names which initially appear before 1976, while the "Pin Yin" system is used for translating those names which appear for the first time after that date. While this sacrifices something in the way of neatness, those readers who do not speak Chinese will doubtless find it easier to identify Chinese persons and their writings if the names appear here just as they do in the published primary sources.

Adler, S. (1957). *The Chinese Economy*. Monthly Review Press, New York.
Ahn Byung-joon (1971). Adjustment to the Great Leap Forward. Conference on Ideology and Politics in Contemporary China, Santa Fe, New Mexico (unpub.).
Alley, R. (1968). Some Fighting communes of Chunghua. *Eastern Horizons* **2**, No. 3.
Anonymous Magistrate (1920). Letters from a Chinese Magistrate: collected from Pleing and Tientsin Press. Unpublished papers in collection of the Hoover Institution, Stanford University, Palo Alto, California.
Ashbrook, A. (1968). *An Economic Profile of Mainland China*. Praeger Publishers, New York.
Balkan, S., Berger, R. and Schmidt, J. (1980). *Crime and Deviance in America*. Wadsworth, Belmont, California.
Barcata, L. (1968). *China: in the Throes of the Cultural Revolution*. Hart, New York.

Barnett, A. D. (1962). *Communist China in Perspective.* Praeger Publishers, New York.

Barnett, A. D. (1964). *Communist China: The Early Years.* Praeger Publishers, New York.

Barnett, A. D. (1966). Cadres, bureaucracy, and power in Communist China. Seminar on Modern East Asia: China, Columbia University, New York (unpub.).

Baum, R. (1970). Elite Behaviour under Conditions of Stress: the Lessons of the 'tang ch tian p'ai' in the Cultural Revolution. Conference on Modern China, Banff, Canada (unpub.).

Baum, R. and Tiewes, F. (1968). *Ssu-Ch'ing: the Socialist Education Movement.* China Research Monograph No. 2, Centre for Chinese Studies, University of California Press, Berkeley.

Bennett, G. (1970). China's continuing revolution: will it be permanent? *Asian Survey*, **X**, No. 1.

Bennett, G. (1972). Elites and explanations. In *Elites in the People's Republic of China.* (R. Scatapino, ed.) University of Washington Press, Seattle.

Bennett, G. (1977). Mass campaigns and social control. In *Deviance and Social Control in Chinese Society.* (A. Wilson *et al.*, eds) Praeger Publishers, New York.

Bennett, L. (1972). *China in Ferment.* University of California, Berkeley.

Berman, H. (1970). Soviet perspective on Chinese law. In *Contemporary Chinese Law.* (J. Cohen, ed.). Harvard University Press, Cambridge, Massachusetts.

Bernstein, T. (1967). Leadership and mass mobilization in the Soviet and Chinese collectivization campaigns. *China Quarterly*, **31**.

Bettleheim, C. (1978a). Letter of resignation. In *China since Mao.* Monthly Review Press, New York.

Bettleheim, C. (1978b). The Great Leap Backward. In *China since Mao.* Monthly Review Press, New York.

Bierne, P. (1979). Beyond instrumental Marxist criminology. *Social Problems*, **43**.

Blaustein, A. (ed.) (1962). *Fundamental Legal Documents of Communist China.* F. B. Rothman Publ., South Hackensack, New Jersey.

Bodde, D. (1964). Basic concepts in Chinese law: genesis and evolution. Seminar on Modern East Asia, Columbia University, New York (unpub.).

Bodde, D. and Morris, C. (1968). *Law in Imperial China.* Harvard University Press, Cambridge, Massachusetts.

Bonachea, R. and Valdes, N. (1969). *Chei Selected Works.* M.I.T. Press, Cambridge, Massachusetts.

Bonachea, R. and Valdes, N. (1968). *Law in Imperial China.* Harvard University Press, Cambridge, Massachusetts.

Boorman, H. L. (1965). Political struggle and economic growth. *China Quarterly*, **21**.

Brady, J. (1974). *Conflict and Community in the Chinese Legal System.* Doctoral dissertation, University of California, Berkeley (unpub.).

Brady, J. (1975). The Talking Stone: evolution and action of people's criminology. *Insurgent Sociologist*, **IV**, No. 4.

Brady, J. (1977a). Political contradictions and justice policy in People's China. *Contemporary Crisis*, **1**.

Brady, J. (1977b). Political economy and justice policy in the United States and China. *Journal of Political Repression*, **4**.

Brady, J. (1981a). Sorting out the exiles' confusion: dialogue on popular justice. *Contemporary Crisis*, **9**.

Brady, J. (1981b). Towards a popular justice in the United States. *Contemporary Crisis*, **9**.

Brady, J. (1982). Fair and impartial railroad: the jury, the media and political trials. *Journal of Criminal Justice*, **16**.

Brady, J. (in press). Criminology, crime and justice in the People's Republic of China.

In *International Handbook of Contemporary Developments in Criminology* (E. Johnson, ed.). Greenwood Press, New York.

Bridgham, P. (1968). Mao's Cultural Revolution in 1967. *China Quarterly,* **34**.

Bridgham, P. (1971). The Lin Piao Affair. *China Quarterly,* **49**.

Buchholz, E. (1972). *Socialist Criminology.* Lexington Books, Lexington, Massachusetts.

Burgess, J. (1966). *The Guilds of Peking.* Ch'eng wen Publ., Taipei.

Burlatsky, I. (1968). China at the crossroads. *Mirovania ekonomika.* Translated *in* CLG, Vol. I, No. 3.

Butterfield, F. (1976). Peking publishers abuses of rights. *New York Times,* Feb 28.

Butterfield, F. (1977). Behind the scenes power figure. *New York Times,* Sept 23.

Butterfield, F. (1978). China to drop revolutionary units. *New York Times,* Mar 6.

Butterfield, F. (1979). Another dissident on trial in Peking. *New York Times,* Oct 13.

Caplan, G. (1976). Criminology, criminal justice and the war on crime. *Criminology,* **14**.

Casella, A. (1973). Naniwan May 7th School. *China Quarterly,* **53**.

CC-CCP (1958a). Resolution on the establishment of People's Communes in the rural areas, August 29. In *Communist China, 1955-1959. Documents with Analysis* (1971, CFIA). Harvard University Press, Cambridge, Massachusetts.

CC-CCP (1958b). Resolution on some questions concerning the People's Communes (urban areas), December 10. In *Communist China, 1955-1959. Documents with Analysis* (1971, CFIA). Harvard University Press, Cambridge, Massachusetts.

CC-CCP (1959). Resolution concerning the anti-Party clique headed by P'eng Teh huai, August. In *The Essential Works of Chinese Communism* (1969, W. Chai, ed.). Bantam Press, New York.

CC-CCP (1967). Decision on public security, March 1. In *The Chinese Cultural Revolution* (1968, K. H. Fan, ed.). Grove Press, New York.

CCP-Fukien Province (1962). Vigorously launch the Socialist Education Campaign. In *Ssu-Ch'ing: the Socialist Education Movement* (1968, R. Baum and F. Tiewes). University of California Press, Berkeley, California.

Central Intelligence Agency (CIA) (1962). *The Economy of Communist China 1958-62.* Washington, D.C.

CFIA-EARC Center for International Affairs/East Asia Research Center (1971). *Communist China, 1955-1959. Documents with Analysis.* Harvard University Press, Cambridge, Massachusetts.

CFIA-EARC Center for International Affairs/East Asian Research Center (1972). *Cultural Revolution in the Provinces.* Harvard University Press, Cambridge, Massachusetts.

Chai, W. (ed.) (1969). *The Essential Works of Chinese Communism.* Bantam Press, New York.

Chan Wing-tsit (Trans.) (1953). *Instruction for Practical Living and other Neo-Confucian Writings by Wang Yang-ming.* Columbia University Press, New York.

Chand, G. (1958). *The New Economy of China.* Vora and Co., Bombay.

Chang, P. (1973). Political rehabilitation of cadres in China: a traveller's view. *China Quarterly,* **54**.

Charles, D. (1961). The dismissal of Marshall P'eng Teh-huai. *China Quarterly,* **8**.

Chen, C. S. (1967). *Rural People's Communes in Lieu-chiang.* (C. P. Ridley, Trans.). Hoover Institute, Stanford University, Palo Alto, California.

Chen, J. T. (1970). The May Fourth Movement. *Modern Asia Studies,* **IV**, No. 1.

Chen, J. (1974). China's new leadership and its foreign policy. *Pacific Community,* **5**, No. 2.

Chen, P. (1973). *Law and Justice: The Legal System in China.* Dunellen Publishers, New York.

Chen Shih hsiang (1973). *Artificial Flowers during a Natural Thaw.* Centre for Chinese Studies, University of California, Berkeley (unpub.).

Chen, T. (1960). *Thought Reform of the Chinese Intellectuals.* Hong Kong University Press, Hong Kong.

Chen, T. (1967). *The Chinese Communist Regime.* Praeger Publishers, New York.

Chen, W. C. (1955). *Wartime Mass Campaigns in Communist China.* Human Resources Research Institute, Maxwell A.F.B., Alabama.

Ch'eng-chih Shih (1956). *People's Resistance in Mainland China.* Union Research Institute, Hong Kong.

Ch'eng-chih Shih (1962). *Urban Commune Experiments in Communist China.* Communist China Problems of Research Series, Union Research Institute, Hong Kong.

Cheng li Chang (1955). *The Chinese Gentry.* University of Washington Press, Seattle.

Cheng P'u (1951). Thoroughly destroy the old legal system. *In* CLG, Vol. I, No. 3.

Cheng Shih yi (1976). Open door education. *Peking Review,* Jan 2.

Cheng Wejan (1969). The Traditional Chinese Form of Litigation. Conference on Chinese Law, Lake Como, Italy (unpub.).

Chesneaux, J. (1972). *Popular Movements and Secret Societies in China 1848-1950.* Stanford University Press, Palo Alto, California.

Chi, Barrie (1979). Crime and punishment in China. *New York Times,* Oct 7.

Ch'i Pen Yu (1967). Speech before public security policemen of Peking and the Red Guards, February 1. *In* JPRS, 1967b, Vol. II.

Chi shien Li (1951). Opening address at the third plenum of the second Central Committee of the KMT Revolutionary Committee, June 24. In *Chinese Communism in Action* Vol. II (1953, A. Steiner, ed.). University of California Press, Los Angeles.

Chiang Ching (1966). Forum on work in literature and art in the PLA. February 6, Shanghai. In *The Chinese Cultural Revolution* (1968, K. H. Fan, ed.). Grove Press, New York.

Chiang Kai Shek (1947). *China's Destiny.* Dennis Dobson, London.

Chin, Hungdah (1977). Criminal punishment in China. *Journal of Criminal Law and Criminology,* **68**.

China Viewpoints (1958). *Contradictions.* PACL, Hong Kong.

Chou en Lai (1951). Political report to the Third Session of the NPC, October 23. In *Chinese Communism in Action* Vol. II (1953, A. Steiner, ed.). University of California Press, Los Angeles.

Chou en Lai (1956). Report on Work of Government to 4th session of the 1st National People's Congress, June 26. In *Communist China, 1955-1959. Documents with Analysis* (1971, CFIA). Harvard University Press, Cambridge, Massachusetts.

Chou en Lai (1957). Address to the Eighth Party Congress. In *Proceedings of Eighth Party Congress.* Foreign Language Press, Peking.

Chou Ming Li (1964). China's Industrial Development. *China Quarterly,* **17**.

Chow Ching-Wen (1960). *Ten Years of Storm.* Holt, Rinehart & Winston, New York.

Christiansen, S. A. (1968). Letters from a People's Commune. *Eastern Horizon,* **VII**, No. 3.

Chuan, T. (1968). The Mo Liao System. In *Chinese Bureaucracy and Government; Selected Essays.* (J. Jiang, ed.). Harvard University Press, Cambridge, Massachusetts.

Chung li, C. (1955). *The Chinese Gentry.* University of Washington Press, Seattle.

Cohen, J. (1965). The criminal process in China. Conference on Soviet and Chinese Communism, Lake Tahoe, California (unpub.).

Cohen, J. (1966). Chinese mediation on the eve of modernization. *California Law Review,* **54**, No. 2.

Cohen, J. (1968a). The Chinese Communist Party and judicial independence. *Harvard Law Review,* **82**, No. 2, 1968-69.

Cohen, J. (1968b). *The Criminal Process in the People's Republic of China.* Harvard University Press, Cambridge, Massachusetts.

Cohen, J. (ed.) (1970). *Contemporary Chinese Law: Research Problems and Perspectives.* Harvard University Press, Cambridge, Massachusetts.

Cohen, J. (1971). *Drafting Mediation Rules for Chinese Cities.* Studies in Chinese Law No. 13, Harvard East Asian Research Series. Harvard University Law School, Cambridge, Massachusetts.

Cohen, J. (1973a). Chinese law at the crossroads. *China Quarterly,* **53**.

Cohen, J. (1973b). Notes on legal education in China. *Harvard Law School Alumnii Bulletin,* Feb.

Cohen, J. (1979). China's changing constitution. *China Quarterly,* **17**.

Committee for Concerned Asia Scholars (CCAS) (1971). *China: Inside the People's Republic.* Bantam Books, New York.

Cowen, Z. (1962). Legal and cultural changes in China. Symposium on Economic and Social Problems of the Far East, Hong Kong (unpub.).

CRCJ-Center for Research on Criminal Justice (1977). *The Iron Fist and the Velvet Glove.* CRCJ, Berkeley, California.

Crook, I. and Crook, D. (1959). *Revolution in a Chinese Village: Ten Mile Inn.* Routledge & Kegan Paul Ltd., London.

Crook, I. and Crook, D. (1966). *The First Years of Yangyi Commune.* Routledge & Kegan Paul Ltd., London.

Crozier, M., Huntington, S. and Watanuki, J. (1975). *The Crisis of Democracy: Report to The Trilateral Commission.* New York University Press, New York.

Dernberger, R. (1970). Economic realities and China's political economies. In *China After the Cultural Revolution.* (Atomic Scientists, eds) Random House, New York.

Diao, R. (1970). The impact of the Cultural Revolution on the Chinese economic elite. *China Quarterly,* **42**.

Dinucci, M. (1967). Articles appearing as foreign correspondent's reports from China on July 1, 18, 22, 29. In *Nuova Unita* (NU), Rome, Italy; in JPRS No. 42525.

Dittmar, L. (1973). The structural evolution of criticism-self criticism. *China Quarterly,* **56**.

Djilas, M. (1957). *The New Class.* Praeger Publishers, New York.

Donnithorne, A. (1966). Centralized Economic Control in China. Unpublished conference proceedings, Chicago, Illinois.

Donnithorne, A. (1972). China's cellular economy: some economic trends since the Cultural Revolution. *China Quarterly,* **52**.

Doolin, D. and Golas, P. (1964). On contradiction in the light of Mao. *China Quarterly,* **19**.

Dunlap, A. M. (1956). *Behind the Bamboo Curtain.* Public Affairs Press, Washington, D.C.

Dutt, G. (1963). Some problems of China's rural communes. *China Quarterly,* **16**.

Dutt, G. (1967). *Rural Communes of China.* Asia Publ. House, New York.

Dutt, V. P. and Dutt, G. (1970). *China's Cultural Revolution.* Asia Publ. House, New York.

Eastman, L. (1971). Social traits and political behaviour in Kuomintang China. Seminar on Modern East Asia: China, Columbia University, New York (unpub.).

Eckstein, A. (1973). Economic growth and change in China: a twenty year perspective. *China Quarterly,* **54**.

Edwards, R. (1977). Reflections on crime and punishment in China. *Columbia Journal of Transnational Law,* **16**.

Escarra, J. (1961). *Chinese Law: Conception and Evolution.* (R. Browne, Trans.). University of Washington Press, Seattle.

Esmein, J. (1973). *The Chinese Cultural Revolution.* Anchor, Garden City, New Jersey.

Fan, F. H. (ed.) (1968). *The Chinese Cultural Revolution.* Monthly Review Press, New York.

Fisher, A. (1972). *Preliminary Findings From the 1971 Department of Defense Survey of Drug Users.* Department of Defense, Alexandria, Virginia.

Foreign Language Press (1957). *Proceedings of Eighth Party Congress*, Vols I-IV. FLP, Peking.

Foreign Language Press (1964). Constitution of the PRC adopted by National People's Congress. FLP, Peking.

Foreign Language Press (1967). *Selected Works of Mao tse Tung*, Vols I-V. FLP, Peking.

Foreign Language Press (1974). Constitution of the PRC (1st revision). FLP, Peking.

Foreign Language Press (1978). Constitution of the PRC (2nd revision). FLP, Peking.

Frankenberg, R. (1971). Education in China. *Eastern Horizon,* **X**, No. 6.

Gao Ji (1981). Madness reigned in last days. *Peking Review,* Jan 2.

Ganat, C. (1960). China's economic crises. *Far Eastern Economic Review,* **2.**

Garrett, S. S. (1970). *Social Reformers in Urban China.* Harvard East Asian Research Series. Harvard University Law School, Cambridge, Massachusetts.

Ghosh, S. K. (1973). Who commands the law . . . Party or Army? *China Report* **VIII.**

Gillin, D. (1970). Some Reasons for the KMT Defeat in 1949. Seminar on Modern East Asia: China, Columbia University, New York (unpub.).

Ginsberg, G. (1965). The People's Procuratorate in Communist China: the period of maturation. *China Quarterly,* **24.**

Ginsbergs, G. and Stahnke, A. (1964). The genesis of the People's Procurate 1949-55. *China Quarterly,* **20.**

Ginsbergs, G. and Stahnke, A. (1968). The People's Procurate in China: the Institution in the Ascendant 1954-7. *China Quarterly,* **34.**

Golas, P. (1968). Early Ch'ing guilds. Conference on Urban Society in Traditional China, Wentworth, New Hampshire (unpub.).

Goldman, M. (1969). The unique blooming and contending of 1956-62. *China Quarterly,* **37.**

Goldman, R. (1961). Peking University Today. *China Quarterly,* **7.**

Goldman, R. (1962). The Rectification Campaign at Peking University. *China Quarterly,* **12.**

Gong Zhen (1979). People's new democratic legal system. *Hung Ch'i,* Feb 2.

Gray, J. (1970). The economics of Maoism. In *China After the Cultural Revolution.* (Atomic Scientists, eds). Vintage Press, New York.

Greenblatt, S. (1977). Campaigns and the manufacture of deviance in Chinese society. In *Deviance and Social Control in Chinese Society.* (A. Wilson, R. Wilson and S. M. Greenblatt, eds) Praeger Publishers, New York.

Greene, F. (1962a). *China.* Ballantine Books, New York.

Greene, F. (1962b). *The Wall Has Two Sides.* Jonathan Cape, London.

Greene, F. (1964). *A Curtain of Ignorance.* Doubleday and Co., New York.

Grey, A. (1970). *Hostage in Peking.* Michael Joseph, London.

Gudoshnikov, L. M. (1957). *Legal Organs of the People's Republic of China,* Moscow. Trans. JPRS, 1959.

Guillain, R., Lindsay, M. and Van der Sprenkel, S. (1951). *New China: Three Views.* John Day Publishers, New York.

Gunawardhana, T. (1967). *China's Cultural Revolution.* Colombo Apothecaries, Colombo, Ceylon.

Hao Hsuang Lu (1975). Interview. *New York Times,* Aug. 13.

Hansen, J., Novack, G., Peng Shu-tse and Frank, P. (1972). *Behind China's Great Cultural Revolution.* Pathfinder Press, New York.

Harper, P. (1969). The Party and the unions in Communist China. *China Quarterly*, **37**.

Hinton, H. (1969). *Communist China's Domestic Political Scope*. Institute for Defense Analysis, Arlington, Virginia.

Hinton, W. (1967). *Fanshen*. Monthly Review Press, New York.

Hinton, W. (1972a). *Hundred Day War: the Cultural Revolution at Tsinghua University*. Monthly Review Press, New York.

Hinton, W. (1972b). *Turning Point in China*. Monthly Review Press, New York.

Hipkin, B. (1981). Law and modernization in China. In *Law and Social Research* (S. Spitzer, ed.). Jai Press, New York.

Hirst, P. (1972). Marx and Engels on law, crime and morality. *Economy and Society*, **1**.

Hoffman, C. (1963). A Survey of Work Incentives in Communist China. First Research Conference on the Economy of China, Berkeley, California (unpub.).

Hoffman, C. (1969). Work incentive policy in Communist China. *China Quarterly*, **17**.

Hsia, A. (1972). *The Chinese Cultural Revolution*. Seabury Press, New York.

Hsia Tao-Tai (1967). *Guide to Selected Legal Sources of Mainland China*. Library of Congress, Washington, D.C.

Hsiang Shih (1968). New problems in the realm of legal studies. CFYC *in* CLG, 1969, Vol. I, No. 2.

Hsiao, G. (1965). *Basic Legal Institutions in Communist China; Comparative Studies of Communist Societies Project*. University of California Press, Berkeley.

Hsiao, K.-C. (1961). *Rural China: Imperial Control in the 19th Century*. University of Washington Press, Seattle.

Hsieh Fei (1958). We must overcome rightist ideology on the political-legal front. *In* SCMM No. 135, 1958.

Hsieh Fu chih (1967). Speech before the Peking Public Security Bureau and the Red Guards. *In* JPRS, 1968, Vol. II.

Hsu, F. L. K. (1963). *Clan, Caste, and Club*. D. Van Nostrand, Princeton, New Jersey.

Hsu, I. C. (1964). The reorganization of higher education. *China Quarterly*, **19**.

Hua Kuo Feng (1979). Report to the Eleventh Party Congress. *Hung Chi*, June 1.

Hucker, C. (1975). *China's Imperial Past*. Stanford University Press, Palo Alto, California.

Hughes, T. J. and Luard, D. E. T. (1959). *The Economic Development of Communist China*. Oxford University Press, Oxford.

Hung, W. (1934). *Outlines of Modern Chinese Law*. Shanghai.

Institute of Criminal Law Research (1962). Lectures on general principles of criminal law in the PRC. *In* JPRS No. 13331, Mar 20.

IPLR — Institute for Political-Legal Research at Central People's Law School (1958). *Lectures on General Principles of Criminal Law in the People's Republic of China*. Trans. in JPRS No. 23244.

Jacobs, D. and Baerwald, H. (1963). *Chinese Communism: Selected Documents*. Columbia University Press, New York.

Jiang Hua and Huang Honging (1979). Reports on the People's democratic legal system. *Hung Ch'i*, Mar 6.

Jiang, J. (ed.) (1968). *Chinese Bureaucracy and Government: Selected Essays*. University of Washington Press, Seattle.

Jernigan, T. R: (1905). *China in Law and Commerce*. Macmillan & Co., London.

Johnson, C. (1959). *Communist Policies Toward the Intellectual Class*. Communist China Problem Research Series, URI, Hong Kong.

Johnson, C. (1969). The changing nature and locus of authority in Communist China. Conference on Government in China, August, 1969, Guernavaca, Mexico (unpub.).

Kahn, E. J. (1975). *The China Hands*. Penguin Books, New York.

Kashin, A. (1968). Cultural Revolution: victors and vanquished. *China Report*, **IV**, No.2.

Kau King-mau (1969). Patterns of recruitment and mobility of urban cadremen. Conference on Urban Society and Political Development in Modern China, St. Croix, Virgin Islands (unpub.).

Khan, A. Z. M. (1972). Class struggle in Yellow Sandhill Commune. *China Quarterly*, **51**.

Kiang Wen Han (1952). Land reform in Shanghai suburbs. *China Monthly Review*, **8**, No. 1.

King, H. H. (1968). *A Concise Economic History of Modern China*. Praeger Publishers, New York.

King James Version (1973). *The Holy Bible*. Regency Publications, Nashville, Tennessee.

King, V. (1966). *Propaganda Campaigns in Communist China*. Research Programme on Problems of International Communication and Security, Centre for International Studies, M.I.T. Press, Cambridge, Massachusetts.

Klatt, W. (1970). A review of China's economy in 1970. *China Quarterly*, **43**.

Klockars, K. (1979). *Criminology*, **16**.

Kojima, R. (1971). Development of the ideas of the Great Leap Forward after the Cultural Revolution. *The Developing Economies*, **IX**, No. 4.

Kraus, R. (1977). Class conflict and the vocabulary of social analysis in China. *China Quarterly*, **69**.

Kuangming Province Revolutionary Committee (KPRC) (1968). Proclamation of the Revolutionary Committee. *In* SCMP No. 4243, 1968.

Lamb, F. (1976). Interview with Chinese legal officials. *China Quarterly*, **66**.

Lambe, W. (1974). Interview with Chinese legal officials. *China Quarterly*, **54**.

Lee, L. T. C. (1967). Towards an understanding of law in Communist China. Symposium on Economic and Social Problems of the Far East, Hong Kong (unpub.).

Lee Hong Yung (1978). *The Politics of the Chinese Cultural Revolution*. University of California Press, Berkeley.

Legge, J. (Trans.) (1960). *The Chinese Classics, Tu Hio: The Great Learning*. Hong Kong University Press, Hong Kong.

Leng, Shao-chuan (1967). *Justice in Communist China*. Oceana Publications, New York.

Lewis, J. W. (1966). *Leadership in Communist China*. Cornell University Press, Ithaca, New York.

Li, V. (1969a). The evolution and development of the Chinese legal system. Conference on Government in China, Cuernavaca, Mexico (unpub.).

Li, V. (1969b). The public security bureau and political-legal work in Hui-Yang Hsien. Conference on Urban Society and Political Development in Modern China, St. Croix, Virgin Islands (unpub.).

Li, V. (1970). The operation of a public security station. Seminar on Modern East Asia: China, Columbia University, New York (unpub.).

Li, V. (1973). Law and penology: systems of reform and correction. *Annals of the Academy of Political Science*, **402**.

Li, V. (1975). The role of law in Communist China. *China Quarterly*, **44**.

Li, V. (1977). *Law without Lawyers*. Westview Press, Boulder, Colorado.

Li, V. (1979). Human rights in a Chinese context. In *The China Difference* (R. Terrill, ed.). Harper & Row, New York.

Li Bo yon (1979). Report on organic law of People's Court and the new socialist legal system. *Hung Ch'i*, Mar 6.

Li Hong Rin (1979). What sort of socialism should we uphold? *Peking Review*, June 5.

Lie Jie Gonng (1979). Report on the criminal code. *Peking Review*, July 20.

Lieberthal, L. (1973). Post liberation suppression of secret societies in Tientsin. *China Quarterly*, **54**.

Lieberthal, K. (1974). Post liberation suppression of secret societies in Tientsin. Seminar on Modern East Asia, Columbia University, New York (unpub.).

Lieken, R. (1979). Comments on China since Mao. *Monthly Review,* **3**.

Lifton, R. (1963). *Thought Reform and the Psychology of Totalism.* W. W. Norton, New York.

Lifton, R. (1973). *Home from the War: Vietnam Veterans.* Simon and Schuster, New York.

Lin Heng Yuan (1941). On the intra-Party struggle. In *The Essential Works of Chinese Communism* (1969, W. Chai, ed.). Bantam Press, New York.

Lin Heng Yuan (1957). Report to Eighth Party Congress. In *Proceedings of Eighth Party Congress* Vol. I. Foreign Language Press, Peking.

Lin Heng Yuan (1979). Advance the People's new democratic legal system. *Peking Review,* July 20.

Liu Shao Chi (1939). How to be a Good Communist. In *Essential Works of Chinese Communism.* (W. Chai, ed.) Bantam Press, New York.

Liu Shao Chi (1957). Report to Eighth Party Congress. In *Proceedings of Eighth Party Congress* Vol. I. Foreign Language Press, Peking.

Liu Shao teng (1979). Education of political legal workers. *Democracy and the People's Legal System.* Peking, Trans. JPRS No. 626421.

Lo Jui Ching (1957). Report to Eighth Party Congress. In *Proceedings of Eighth Party Congress* Vol. II. Foreign Language Press, Peking.

Lo Jui Ching (1958). Be relentless toward the enemy, be gentle with our own people, June 18. *In* SCMM No. 139.

Lo Jui lung (1951). Report to the third plenary session of the East China Committee on political and military affairs. HHYP *in* SCMM No. 104.

Lowe, Chuan-Hua (1933). *Facing Labour Issues in China.* China Institute of Pacific Relations, Shanghai.

Lu Ting Yu (1958). Education must be combined with productive labour, July 1. In *Communist China, 1955-1959. Documents with Analysis* (1971, CFIA). Harvard University Press, Cambridge, Massachusetts.

Lubenski, G. (1970). *Drug Abuse in the 23rd Infantry Division.* US Department of Defense, Washington, D.C.

Lubman, S. (1967). Mao and mediation. *California Law Review,* **55**.

Lubman, S. (1969). Form and function in the Chinese criminal process. *Columbia Law Review,* **69**.

Lubman, S. (1970). Chinese political-legal elites. Conference on Political Elite in Communist China, Banff, Canada (unpub.).

Lung Yun (1978). On counter-revolutionary offenses and capital punishment. *Peking Review,* July 13.

Macciochi, M. (1972). *Daily Life in Revolutionary China.* Monthly Review Press, New York.

MacDougall, C. (1977). Chinese economy in 1976. *China Quarterly,* **60**.

MacFarquhar, R. (1960). *The Hundred Flowers Campaign and the Chinese Intelligentsia.* Praeger Publishers, New York.

MacFarquhar, R. (ed.) (1966). *China Under Mao: Politics Takes Command.* M.I.T. Press, Cambridge, Massachusetts.

MacFarquhar, R. (1968). Totalitarianism via industrialization? *Problems of Communism,* **5**.

MacFarquhar, R. (1974). *The Origins of the Cultural Revolution.* Columbia University Press, New York.

Malden, W. (1965). A new structure emerging in China? *China Quarterly,* **22**.

Mao tse Tung (1927). Report on investigation of the Peasant Movement in Hunan. In *Selected Works of Mao tse Tung* Vol. I. (1967). Foreign Languages Press, Peking.

Mao tse Tung (1928). The struggle in the Chingkang Mountains. In *Selected Works of Mao tse Tung* Vol. I (1967). Foreign Language Press, Peking.

Mao tse Tung (1943). Some questions concerning methods of Leadership. In *Selected Works of Mao tse Tung* (1967). Foreign Language Press, Peking.

Mao tse Tung (1949). On the People's democratic dictatorship. In *The Essential Works of Chinese Communism* (1969, W. Chai, ed.) Bantam Press, New York.

Mao tse Tung (1950). Report to the CC-CCP, June 6. In *Chinese Communism in Action* Vol. II (1953, A. Steiner, ed.). University of California, Los Angeles.

Mao tse Tung (1956). On the correct handling of contradictions among the People. In *Selected Works of Mao tse Tung* Vol. III (1967). Foreign Language Press, Peking.

Mao tse Tung (1957). Speech at CCP National Conference on propaganda work. In *Selected Works of Mao tse Tung* Vol. III (1967). Foreign Language Press, Peking.

Mao tse Tung (1970). Red and expert. In *Mao Papers* (J. Chen, ed.). Oxford University Press, New York.

Martin, R. (1976). The Massachusetts correctional system. *Crime and Social Justice*, **6**.

Marx, K. (1970). In *A Contribution to the Critique of Political Economy*. (M. Dobb, ed.). International Publishers, New York.

Marx, K. (1972). *Capital*. Vol. III. Lawrence and Wishart, London.

Marzotto, M., Platt, T. and Snäre, A. (1975). A Reply to Turk. *Crime and Social Justice*, **4**.

Matthews, J. (1979). Chinese dissident gets 5-year term. *Boston Globe*, Oct 7.

Meijer, M. J. (1949). *The Introduction of Modern Criminal Law in China*. Konninkijke Drukkerij de Unie, Batavia.

Meijer, M. J. (1971). *Marriage Law and Policy in the People's Republic of China*. Hong Kong University Press, Hong Kong.

Miller, A. (1974). Political issues and trust in government. *American Political Science Review*, **66**.

Monthly Review Editors (1979). New theories for old. *Monthly Review*, **31**.

Moore, B. Jr. (1966). *Social Origins of Dictatorship and Democracy*. Beacon Press, Boston.

Munro, D. (1964). Chinese Communist treatment of the 100 Schools period. Conference on Communist Historiography, Oxfordshire, Great Britain (unpub.).

Munro, D. (1977). *The Concept of Man in Contemporary China*. University of Michigan Press, Michigan.

Munro, R. (1977). China, for want of a formal legal code. *New York Times*, Oct 12.

Mu Fu-Sheng (1962). *The Wilting of the Hundred Flowers*. Praeger Publishers, New York.

Myrdal, J. (1965). *Report from a Chinese Village*. Random House, New York.

Nee, V. (1973). Revolution and bureaucracy: Shanghai. In *China's Uninterrupted Revolution* (J. Peck and V. Nee, eds). Pantheon, New York.

Nelson, H. (1972). Military forces in the Cultural Revolution. *China Quarterly*, **51**.

Newton, W. (1959). Communist China after Wuhan. *Far Eastern Economic Review*, **1**.

Onate, A. (1978). Hua Kuo feng and the arrest of the Gang of Four. *China Quarterly*, **75**.

Ong, S. (1955). *Labour Problems in Communist China*. Human Resources Research Institute, Lackland A.F.B., Texas.

PACL — People's Anti-Communist League (1960). *Urban Communes*. PACL, Taipei.

Pan, S. and de Jueghar, R. (1968). *Peking's Red Guards*. Twin Circle, New York.

Pashukanis, E. B. (1978). *Law and Marxism*. Ink Links, London.

P'eng Chen (1951). Report on political and legal work in the General Administrative Council, May. In *Chinese Communism in Action* Vol. I (1953, A. Steiner, ed.). University of California Press, Los Angeles.

Peng Zhen (1979). Report on the draft criminal code. *Peking Review*, July 13.

Pepinsky, H. (1973). The People vs. the principle of legality in the PRC. *Journal of Criminal Justice*, **1**.

Pepinsky, H. (1975). Reliance on formal written law and freedom and social control in the US and the PRC. *British Journal of Sociology*, **26**.

Pepinsky, H. (1976). *Crime and Conflict: A Study of Law and Society.* Academic Press, New York and London.

Pepper, S. (1971). Socialism, democracy, and Chinese Communism: a problem of choice for the intelligentsia. Conference on Ideology and Politics in Contemporary China, Santa Fe, New Mexico (unpub.).

Pepper, S. (1977). Education and changes after the fall of the Gang of Four. *China Quarterly*, **72**.

Pfeffer, R. (1968). Crime and punishment: China and the United States. *World Politics*, **21**, No. 1.

Pfeffer, R. (1970). Crime and punishment: China and the United States. In *Contemporary Chinese Law: Research Problems and Perspectives* (J. Cohen, ed.). Harvard University Press, Boston, Massachussets.

Pfeffer, R. (1972). Serving the People and Continuing the Revolution. *China Quarterly*, **52**.

Pfeffer, R. (1975). Leaders and Masses. *Academy of Political Science Proceedings*, **34**.

Pincus, F. (1979). Higher education and socialist transformation in China since 1970. *Review of Radical Political Economics*, **IX**.

Platt, A. (1974). Prospects for a radical criminology in the United States. *Crime and Social Justice*, **1**.

Platt, A. (1978). Street crime: a view for the Left. *Crime and Social Justice*, **9**.

Pound, R. (1947). The Chinese Constitution. *New York University Law Review*, **22**.

Pound, R. (1948a). *Some Problems of the Administration of Justice in China.* National Chengchi University, Nanking.

Pound, R. (1948b). Progress of the law in China. *Washington Law Review*, **23**.

Powell, R. (1968). The increasing power of Lin Piao and the Party soldiers (1959-66). *China Quarterly*, **34**.

Pye, L. (1968). *The Spirit of Chinese Politics.* M.I.T. Press, Cambridge, Massachusetts.

Pye, L. (1969). Mass participation in Communist China: its limitations and the continuity of culture. Conference on Government in China, Cuernavaca, Mexico (unpub.).

Quinney, R. (1977). *Class State and Crime.* Longman, New York.

Radvanyi, J. (1970). The Hungarian Revolution and the 100 Flowers Campaign. *China Quarterly*, **43**.

Rickett, A. and Rickett, A. (1964). Professionalism and the Chinese Communist Judiciary. Seminar on Modern East Asia: China, Columbia University, New York (unpub.).

Riskin, C. (1973). Maoism and motivation. In *China's Uninterrupted Revolution* (J. Peck and V. Nee, eds). Pantheon, New York.

Robinson, T. W. (1971). The Wuhan Incident. *China Quarterly*, **47**.

Ruge, G. (1976). An interview with Chinese legal officials. *China Quarterly*, **32**.

Salaff, J. (1967). The urban communes in Communist China. *China Quarterly*, **29**.

Salaff, J. (1975). Urban social structure in the wake of the Cultural Revolution. *China Quarterly*, **29**.

Schram, S. (1963). Urban-rural income differences in Communist China—1952-53. *China Quarterly*, **36**.

Schram, S. (1977a). Mao tse-Tung and the theory of permanent revolution. *China Quarterly*, **216**.

Schram, S. (1971b). *Mao tse-Tung and Liu Shao Chi.* Centre for Chinese Studies. Berkeley, California.

Schurmann, F. (1961). Peking's recognition of crises. *Problems of Communism*, **5**.

Schurmann, F. (1961). China's new economic policy. *China Quarterly*, **17**.

Schurmann, F. (1966a). *Human Volition and Organizational Demand: the Problem of Re-socialization.* (Unpublished MS).

Schurmann, F. (1966b). *Ideology and Organization in Communist China.* University of California Press, Berkeley, California (unpub.).

Schwartz, B. (1965). Fifteen years of Communist China. *China Quarterly*, **12**.

Selden, M. (1967). The Yenan legacy: the mass line. Conference on Micro-societal Study of the Chinese Political System, Wentworth, New Hampshire (unpub.).

Selden, M. (1969). *The Yenan Way.* Doubleday, New York.

Shang Zhe (1979). Persistently carry forward socialist democracy. *Hung Ch'i*, June 1.

Sharan, P. (1968). *Political Systems of China.* Meent Publishers, Delhi.

Sheeks, R. (1967). Science, technology and the Cultural Revolution in China. Seminar on Modern East Asia: China, Columbia University (unpub.).

Shih Liang (1952). Report on the reform and reorganization of the People's Courts, August 13. In *Chinese Communism in Action* Vol. II (1953, A. Steiner, ed.). University of California, Los Angeles.

Siamonds, J. D. (1969). P'eng Te-hua. *China Quarterly*, **37**.

Simirenko, A. (ed.) (1966). *Soviet Sociology.* Quadrangle Books, Chicago.

Snow, E. (1964). *Other Side of the River.* Hutchinson, New York.

Snow, E. (1971). *The Long Revolution.* Hutchinson, New York.

Solomon, P. (1978). *Soviet Criminologists and Criminal Policy.* Columbia University Press, New York.

Spitzer, S. (1975). Toward a Marxian theory of deviance. *Social Problems*, **22**.

S. S. (pseudonym) (1967). Recent events in China. *China Report*, **4**, No. 2.

Stahnke, A. (1966). The background and evolution of Party policy in the drafting of legal codes. *American Journal of Comparative Law*, **15**.

Stalin, J. (1970). *The Foundations of Leninism.* Foreign Language Press, Peking.

Steiner, A. (1953). *Chinese Communism in Action*, Vols I, II. University of California Press, Los Angeles.

Sun Yeh fang (1979). Report on modernization in agriculture. *Peking Review*, Sept. 4.

Sweezy, P. and Bettleheim, C. (1971). *On the Transition to Socialism.* Monthly Review Press, New York.

Tai Sung an (1972). *Mao Tse Tung's Cultural Revolution.* Bobbs-Merrill, New York.

Tan, C. (1963). Political Thought of Sun Yat Sen. Seminar on Modern East Asia: China, Columbia University, New York (unpub.).

Tang, P. S. (1955). Power struggle in the Chinese Communist Party. *Problems of Communism*, **6**.

Tang, P. S. and Maloney, J. (1970). *Communist China in 1967.* Union Research Institute, Hong Kong.

Teng Tyu Hui (1950). The political significance of agrarian reform, December 27. In *Chinese Communism in Action* Vol. II (1953, A. Steiner, ed.). University of California Press, Los Angeles.

Teng Hsiao Peng (1957). Report on Rectification Campaign, Third Plenum of Eighth Party Congress. In *Communist China, 1955-1959. Documents with Analysis* (1971, CFIA). Harvard University Press, Cambridge, Massachusetts.

Teng Hsiao Peng (1978). Speech at National Education Conference. *Peking Review*, May 5.

Terrill, R. (1978). *The Future of China After Mao.* Dell, Philadelphia.

Thornton, R. (1973). *China: The Struggle for Power.* Indiana University Press, Bloomington.

Tiewes, F. (1974). China before and after the Cultural Revolution. *China Quarterly*, **58**.

Tigar, M. (ed.) (1971). Socialist law and legal institutions. In *Law Against the People*. Anchor, New York.

Ting Wang (1978). A concise biography of Hua Kuo feng. *Chinese Law and Government*, **1**.

Topping, S. (1971). Revolutionary committees instill discipline. *Report from China*. New York Times Publ., New York.

Townsend, J. (1963). Democratic management in the rural communes. *China Quarterly*, **16**.

Townsend, J. (1968). Intra-party conflict in China: disintegration in an established one-party system. Conference on Established One-Party Systems, Jenner, California (unpub.).

Townsend, J. (1969). *Political Participation in Communist China*. University of California Press, Berkeley.

Townsend, J. (1974). *Politics in China*. University of California Press, Berkeley.

Tsao-Wen-yen (ed.) (1953a). *The Law in China as Seen by Roscoe Pound*. China Culture Publication Foundation, Taipei.

Tsao-Wen-yen (1953b). *Development of Chinese Law*. China Culture Publication Foundation, Taipei.

Ts'as Tsu Tan (1964). On the relationship between crime and class struggle. *Cheng fa Yen Chiu*. Trans. in *Chinese Law and Government*. Vol. 1, No. 1 (1968).

Tung Pi Wu (1957). Report to Eighth Party Congress. In *Proceedings of Eighth Party Congress* Vol. II. Foreign Language Press, Peking.

Union Research Institute (URI) (1953-75). *Communist China: Problems Research Series*. Union Research Institute, Hong Kong.

Union Research Institute (URI) (1962). *Urban Commune Experiments in Communist China. Communist China: Problems Research Series*. Union Research Institute, Hong Kong.

Van der Sprenkel, O., Guillain, M. and Lindsay, M. (1951). *New China: Three Views*. John Day Publishers, New York.

Van der Sprenkel, S. (1962). *Legal Institutions in Manchu China*. Athlone Press, London.

Van der Sprenkel, S. (1968). Conflict resolution, social control and the law: urban practice. Conference on Urban Society in Transitional China, Wentworth, New Hampshire (unpub.).

Vogel, E. (1967a). Preserving order in the cities: the Chinese Communist approach. Conference on Urban Society and Political Development in Modern China, St. Croix, Virgin Islands (unpub.).

Vogel, E. (1967b). *Cadres, Bureaucracy and Political Power in Communist China*. Columbia University Press, New York.

Vogel, E. (1969). *Canton under Communism*. (1st edn) Harvard University Press, Cambridge, Massachusetts.

Vogel, E. (1971). *Canton under Communism*. (2nd edn) Harvard University Press, Cambridge, Massachusetts.

Wakeman, F., Jr. (1975). *The Fall of Imperial China*. Free Press, New York.

Walker, R. L. (1955). *China under Communism*. Yale University Press, New Haven, Connecticut.

Waller, D. J. (1971). *The Government and Politics of Communist China*. Doubleday, New York.

Waller, D. (1973). *The Kiangsi Soviet Republic: Mao and the National Congresses of 1931 and 1934*. China Research Monograph No. 10, Center for Chinese Studies, Berkeley, California.

Wang Chao-tien (1967). *Red Guard Tells His Own Story.* People's Anti-Communist League, Taipei.

Wang Cui wu (1979). Procurate system and People's Democracy. JMJP, Apr 13 (Trans JPRS No. 73781).

Wang Hsiao t'ing (1978). An evaluation and analysis of China's revised constitution. *Chinese Law and Government,* **9.**

Watt, J. (1972). *The District Magistrate in Late Imperial China.* Columbia University Press, New York.

Wei, H. (1955). *Courts and Police in Communist China to 1952.* Human Resources Research Institute, Maxwell A.F.B., Alabama.

Wertherin, R. (1971). Prospects for China. *Eastern Horizons,* **6,** No. 4.

Wheelwright, E. L. and MacFarlane, B. (1970). *The Chinese Road to Socialism.* Monthly Review Press, New York.

White, L. (1973). Corruption re-defined in liberated Shanghai. Regional Seminar of the Centre for Chinese Studies, Berkeley, California (unpub.).

Whitehead, R. (1971). A revolution in education: Peking University today. *Eastern Horizon,* **X,** No. 6.

Whiting, A. (1976). As quoted *in New York Times,* Oct 17.

Whyte, L. (1974). Inequality and stratification in China. *China Quarterly,* **64.**

W.K. (1966). China's third Five Year Plan. *China Quarterly,* **25.**

Wou, O. Y. K. (1971). The district magistrate professional in the early Republican period. Seminar on Modern East Asia: China, Columbia University, New York (unpub.).

Yang, C. K. (1959). *A Chinese Village in Early Communist Transition.* Massachusetts Institute of Technology, Cambridge, Massachusetts.

Yang yi (1979). Observe and safeguard Party rules. *Hung Ch'i,* Apr 13.

Ye Jian Ying (1979). Report to National People's Congress. *Peking Review,* July 20.

Yomiuri Shimbum Staff (1968). *This is Communist China.* David McKay Co., New York.

Yu, F. T. C. (1955). *The Strategy and Tactics of Chinese Communist Propaganda as of 1952.* Human Resources Research Institute, Maxwell A.F.B., Alabama.

Yu, F. T. C. (1964). *Mass persuasion in Communist China.* Praeger Publishers, New York.

Yu, P. C. (1951). Devils into men. *People's China,* **IV,** No. 9.

Yuan Li-Wu (1965). *The Economy of Communist China.* Praeger Publishers, New York.

Index

L3